WITHDRAWN

THE POLITICS
OF
OPPOSITION

KTO STUDIES
IN
AMERICAN HISTORY

Consulting Editor: Harold M. Hyman
William P. Hobby Professor of History
Rice University

THE POLITICS
OF
OPPOSITION

Antifederalists and the

Acceptance of the

Constitution

Steven R. Boyd

kto press

A U.S. Division of Kraus-Thomson Organization Limited
Millwood, New York

Maps of New York State and North Carolina
by Laurel Ann Casazza

First printing

Printed in the United States of America

Library of Congress Cataloging in Publication Data

Boyd, Steven R
   The politics of opposition: antifederalists and the
acceptance of the Constitution.

   (KTO studies in American history)
   Bibliography: p.
   Includes index.
   1. United States—Constitutional history.
   2. United States—Politics and government—1783–1789.
   I. Title.   II. Series.
JK116.B65   342'.73'029   79-14640
ISBN 0-527-10465-5

To the memory of
Douglass G. Adair
and
Martin Diamond

CONTENTS

LIST OF
MAPS AND TABLES

PREFACE

In 1776 representatives of thirteen of the English colonies in North America declared themselves free and independent states. In the next five years eleven of those states replaced their colonial charters with new state constitutions (Connecticut and Rhode Island modified their colonial charters). During the decades of the 1780s and 1790s five of these original state constitutions were replaced with new frames of government. This pattern of frequent constitutional change initially appeared on the national level as well. In 1776 the colonists overthrew the British constitution and replaced it with the Articles of Confederation. Six years after their adoption, the Articles were replaced with a new constitution. But, unlike the states, which continued to replace their constitutions well into the nineteenth century, the federal Constitution endured.

One key to the long-term success of the Constitution lies in its initial acceptance by both Federalists and Antifederalists. Historians, seeking to explain this success, attribute it to the economic upswing that occurred simultaneously with the adoption of the Constitution, the ratification of the Bill of Rights, the crucial role of a venerated head of state, and an ideological conservatism that resisted constitutional change. These considerations, however, all came into play primarily after the first Congress assembled in the spring of 1789. They cannot explain why the people, a majority of whom opposed the Constitution in 1787, accepted the new government even before it was set into motion. Yet such acceptance did take place and provided the opportunity for the economic, political, and ideological factors noted above to take effect. To explain this historians have stressed the lack of organization among the opponents of the Constitution, which contributed to their defeat in the state conventions and handicapped them sufficiently after ratification to give the Federalists time to set the new government into motion and to win the people's support.

My research, however, indicates a hitherto unsuspected degree of organization among the Antifederalists. Rather than being unorganized, inept, and ineffectual, the Antifederalists proved to be an able, national political party. They had a concrete program and leaders to promote it; they campaigned effectively for seats in the state conventions; following ratification they persisted in their opposition in petition campaigns to repeal ratification and in state legislative elections; and through the conclusion of the first federal elections found support for their program and ideology. Ironically, it was because of this party activity that the American people came to accept the new Constitution. Precisely how and why that acceptance occurred is the focus of the following pages.

This study began as a doctoral dissertation with Professor Merrill Jensen at the University of Wisconsin. My debt to Professor Jensen is overwhelming: not only did he listen patiently to my ideas, and encourage me to revise with an eye to publication, but he also allowed me complete access to the files of the Documentary History of the Ratification of the Constitution and the Documentary History of the First Federal Elections projects while I was employed by the latter.

I am also indebted to two scholars whose work on the Antifederalists antedates my own. While our conclusions differ, my ideas are grounded in the work of Jackson Turner Main and Robert Rutland. In addition, several past members of the Jensen seminar have been particularly helpful. Robert A. Becker, Kenneth R. Bowling, John P. Kaminski, Richard Kohn, and James K. Martin read all or part of the manuscript, shared ideas and information, and assisted in every way.

Several colleagues at the University of Texas at San Antonio have also contributed to this work. Richard A. Gambitta and R. Michael Stevens have listened to my ideas as I have worked them out over the last three years, while David R. Johnson offered timely advice as well. The Adams Manuscript Trust and the director of the Yale University Library have kindly granted special permission to quote from the Adams Family Papers and the Baldwin Collection respectively. Professor Harold Hyman, the editor of this series of American history monographs, has offered encouragement while Marion Sader and

Janice Tully at Kraus-Thomson Organization have saved me from errors of clarity and style. Finally, I wish to thank Sandi, who has read
the manuscript and discussed it with me at length over the past years.
The dedication is to the two men who first introduced me to the study
of early American politics.

STEVEN R. BOYD
San Antonio, Texas

June 1978

ABBREVIATIONS
USED IN NOTES

I utilize the following symbols in footnote references to manuscript repositories in accordance with the Library of Congress, *Symbols of American Libraries*.

CtHi	Connecticut Historical Society	NhHi	New Hampshire Historical Society
CtY	Yale University	NHpR	Roosevelt Library
De-Ar	Delaware Hall of Records	NjHi	New Jersey Historical Society
DLC	Library of Congress		
G-Ar	Georgia State Archives	NKiS	Senate House Museum, Kingston
ICarbS	Southern Illinois University		
ICU	University of Chicago	NN	New York Public Library
M-Ar	Massachusetts Archives	NNC	Columbia University
MB	Boston Public Library	NUtHI	Oneida Historical Society
MBevHi	Beverley Historical Society	PHarH	Pennsylvania Historical and Museum Commission
MdHi	Maryland Historical Society		
MeHi	Maine Historical Society	PHi	Pennsylvania Historical Society
MHi	Massachusetts Historical Society		
		PPAmP	American Philosophical Society
MiU-C	Clements Library, University of Michigan		
		PPL	Library Company of Philadelphia
MNF	Forbes Library		
N	New York State Library	RI-Ar	Rhode Island Archives
Nc-Ar	North Carolina Department of Archives and History	Sc-Ar	South Carolina Archives
		Vi	Virginia State Library
NcD	Duke University	ViU	University of Virginia
NcU	University of North Carolina	ViW	College of William and Mary
Nh	New Hampshire State Library	WHi	State Historical Society of Wisconsin
Nh-Ar	New Hampshire Archives		
NHi	New York Historical Society		

THE POLITICS
OF
OPPOSITION

Chapter 1

PROLOGUE TO REVOLUTION

Proposals to revise the Articles of Confederation were as old as the document itself. From the time the Articles were submitted to the states in 1777, through their ratification in 1781, and until the meeting of the Federal Convention in 1787, there were repeated attempts to revise or replace them. For ten years, however, these efforts were unsuccessful. Preoccupation with the war effort, ideological opposition to centralized political authority, and sectional antagonisms prevented the proponents of reform from achieving their goals.[1]

By the fall of 1786, however, the situation was materially different. A majority of the members of Congress, including many former opponents of reform, conceded the need for a revision of the Articles. Thus a proposed amendment to grant to Congress the power to regulate trade met with widespread support. So did efforts to persuade New York, the last state necessary, to accept the impost amendment first submitted to the states in 1783, but New York could not be persuaded. Also, a more comprehensive proposal by a committee of Congress to revise and expand the powers of the Confederation government was not adopted by Congress. The refusal of New York to ratify the impost amendment and the failure of Congress to refer the report of their own Grand Committee to the states lent credence to the contention that extraordinary measures were necessary to secure required reforms.[2]

One such extraordinary measure was already underway. In January 1786, the Virginia legislature appointed commissioners to meet with representatives of various states "for the purpose of framing such regulations of trade as may be judged necessary to promote the general interest."[3] The report of the Annapolis Convention instead called for a second meeting in Philadelphia in May 1787, "to devise such further provisions as shall appear to them necessary to render the Constitution of the Federal government adequate to the exigencies of the Union. . . ."[4] Despite the widespread sentiment in Congress and among the states for reform, this recommendation of the Annapolis Convention encountered considerable opposition. The dubious constitutionality of such a proposal led Rufus King and Nathan Dane, congressional delegates from Massachusetts, to speak out against it in Congress and before the Massachusetts House of Representatives.[5] King and Dane did not oppose reform, but both men argued that under the Articles of Confederation all amendments must originate with Congress. A convention was therefore an extra-legal and unconstitutional forum. James Sullivan, a prominent Boston lawyer, and Samuel Adams, president of the Massachusetts Senate, shared this attitude.[6] Massachusetts was not alone. Stephen Mix Mitchell and William Samuel Johnson, congressional delegates from Connecticut, shared King's views concerning the legality of a convention as did Secretary for Foreign Affairs John Jay.[7] Henry Lee, a delegate from Virginia, aptly summarized the opinions of the opponents of a convention: They "consider Congress not only the constitutional but the most eligible body to originate and propose necessary amendments to the Confederation. . . ."[8]

Aside from the legal question, critics of a convention were reluctant to grant unlimited powers to a single body whose sole purpose was to propose reforms sufficient to "render the Constitution adequate to the exigencies of the union." Mercy Warren, the wife of James Warren, the speaker of the Massachusetts House, and Nathan Dane and Samuel Adams all saw hazards in such a convention. So did members of the Connecticut and Rhode Island legislatures who warned that a convention would be dangerous to the liberties of the people.[9] New York legislator Abraham Yates, one of the most outspoken critics of a stronger central government, opposed the appointment of delegates on these grounds and George Read of Delaware, a former member of the Confederation Congress, also had reservations.[10]

Objections, both legal and political, were overcome by a combination of factors. First was the widespread support for some reform of the Articles. By the fall of 1786 no substantive group in Congress or in the state legislatures denied the need for reform. Thus, when Virginia seized the initiative by appointing delegates to a convention on December 4, 1786, New Jersey and Pennsylvania followed suit as did

North Carolina and Delaware. By February, when the question of congressional sanction of the convention was brought to the floor, seven states had already appointed delegates. This had some impact on New Englanders who feared their region would not be represented at Philadelphia and that their interests would suffer accordingly.[11] Second, neither Rhode Island nor New Hampshire, states that opposed a convention, was present in Congress. The ranks of the opponents of a convention were further depleted when the New York delegates, under new instructions from their legislature, moved for a convention.[12] Shays' Rebellion, an agrarian protest movement centered in but not limited to Massachusetts, also induced some former opponents of a convention to support it, for they feared that the rebellion "posed an imminent and possibly fatal threat to the nation, and that the cure, presuming there was one, could only be found in radical surgery performed on the existing Constitution."[13] Finally, delegates in Congress realized that they could not agree among themselves on amendments and that the convention presented an opportunity to resolve what they perceived to be a political crisis of major magnitude. George Washington aptly described the position of those with reservations about a convention: "In a fire the best method must be found . . . and Congress is not that mode."[14]

While acquiescing in the proposal for a convention, many members of the legislatures sought to appoint only "safe" men and to limit the powers of the delegates through specific instructions. In January 1787, for example, George Read suggested that the Delaware legislature, in its act of appointment, "so far restrain the powers of the commissioners . . as that they may not extend to any alteration in that part of the fifth article of the present Confederation which gives each state one vote in determining questions in Congress." The legislature did just that a month later.[15]

Samuel Adams and Abraham Yates were also cautious. Thus a committee chaired by Adams recommended that the state's delegates be instructed "by no means to interfere with the fifth of the articles of the Confederation which provides for the annual election of delegates to Congress, with a power reserved to each state to recall its delegates or any of them." The delegates were also not to agree to any alteration in the provision restricting a person from serving in Congress "for more than three years in any term of six."[16] In New York, Yates proposed similar restrictive instructions. In neither case were the proposed instructions adopted. Instead, both states appointed delegates to a convention whose "sole and express purpose" was to revise the Articles of Confederation.[17]

Instructions were only one precautionary measure. As Rufus King put it, "If Massachusetts should send deputies for God's sake be careful who are the men."[18] King had little to fear on that ground for he was one of four selected to represent the state. Connecticut also appointed two critics of the convention mode of reform out of a delegation of four. Two of New York's three delegates were selected because of their opposition to any fundamental reform of the Articles, and Virginia included in its delegation Richard Henry Lee and Patrick Henry. Both men were outspoken opponents of centralized political power.[19]

Eventually twelve of the thirteen states appointed delegates to the Philadelphia Convention. This was a major victory for the proponents of reform for, as Nathan Dane pointed out, the appointment of delegates "fairly committed" the legislature to carrying out the convention's proposals. Hosea Humphrey, a Connecticut legislator, made the same point when he argued against the appointment of such delegates. Rhode Island, by refusing to appoint delegates, and those prominent political leaders who declined their appointments—e.g. Erastus Wolcott of Connecticut, Abraham Clark of New Jersey, Patrick Henry and Richard Henry Lee of Virginia, and Willie Jones of North Carolina—were keeping their options open.

In the spring of 1787, nonetheless, the Federalists had clearly seized the initiative while the men who would eventually lead the opposition to the Constitution—Lee, Henry, and Jones—were neutralized. They did not become Antifederalists—opponents of the Constitution—during the spring or summer of 1787 because of their own uncertainty, which was shared by members of the convention, Congress, and the state legislatures, as to what the results of the summer's work would or even should be. During May, for example, Henry Knox declared that he hoped the convention would have the hardihood to propose a national government.[20] Virginia delegate George Mason acknowledged that the "most prevalent idea I think at present is a total change of the federal system and instituting a great national council."[21] James Madison and Charles Pinckney both arrived at Philadelphia with resolutions providing for a national as opposed to federal government.[22] The men who knew of these proposals for a national government and later became Antifederalists did not believe they would be adopted. Therefore, they did not move to a position of hostility toward the convention. William Shippen, for example, alluding to Henry Knox's plan for a national government remarked that "Ye know the General has very big ideas. . . ."[23] To Arthur Lee "amendments by some additional powers and the altera-

tion of others . . . was the object of the appointment [of delegates]"
and all that the state legislatures would approve.[24] Accordingly, he
drafted his own set of amendments to the Articles of Confederation
which he forwarded to George Mason as a model of the kinds of reform
Lee believed both desirable and acceptable to the thirteen states.[25]

A number of others also proposed plans. Richard Henry Lee outlined his ideas to George Mason;[26] "Lycurgus" and "Amicus Patriae"
laid theirs before the public.[27] Arthur Lee accurately observed that
"many and various" were the "plans of the different members."[28] Because of this diversity, men like Elbridge Gerry, George Mason, John
Francis Mercer, and Richard Henry Lee—all later Antifederalists—
looked to the convention as a potential source from which "we may
derive some good."[29] These, and men like them, began to differ with
the convention at different times during the summer, and in response
to the extent and degree of reform proposed there.

At the outset of the convention then, in May 1787, both Gerry
and Mason agreed to debate the Virginia plan, with its provisions for a
national government with sovereign powers over foreign affairs and
finances, a two-house legislature, and an independent executive and
judiciary.[30] Gerry and Mason spent two weeks debating this plan
because of their commitment to the formation of a stronger central
government. Important too was the fact that the Virginia plan was
only an interim report. The rules adopted by the convention allowed
unlimited debate on any subject and reconsideration of any issue on
motion of any one delegate. The Virginia plan therefore was indicative
of the sentiments, goals, and aspirations of only some members of the
convention.

Since the Virginia plan was only one alternative, the convention
adjourned on June 13 so other plans could be introduced. One such
plan, presented on June 15, was the work of delegates from New
Jersey, New York, Connecticut, Delaware, and Maryland. As such the
New Jersey plan was not solely the work of future Antifederalists, but
it was indicative of their views. The Articles of Confederation were to
remain the constitutional basis of government with specified additional powers. In addition a federal executive and judiciary would
be created and all acts of Congress "made by virtue and in pursuance of
the powers hereby vested in them" would by the Articles of Confederation be the supreme law of the states and the nation.[31] The New
Jersey plan was the subject of debate for the ensuing week. On June 19
it was defeated by a vote of seven states to three with Maryland divided.

June 19 was a critical day. The rejection of the New Jersey plan clearly indicated that the proponents of a national rather than federal government were in control of the convention. The fundamental issue of where sovereignty should reside was decided in favor of the central government instead of the states. At this point the proponents of a federal government like the one provided for in the Articles of Confederation could have withdrawn, condemned the convention for exceeding the bounds of its appointment, and effectively disrupted the drive for constitutional reform. They did not in part because of the rule of the convention which allowed reconsideration of any decision at a later date. As late as July 27 William Paterson believed the New Jersey plan could become the order of the day, and proponents of limited change caucused twice in August to consider how to redirect the course of the convention.[32]

While the rule allowing reconsideration retarded the formation of an opposition among members of the convention, the secrecy rule checked the emergence of one out of doors. New York delegate Robert Yates, for example, although dissatisfied with the course the convention was taking, declared that "while I remain a setting member [of the convention] these rules must be obligatory."[33] Even William Shippen, a brother-in-law of Richard Henry and Arthur Lee, and certainly one of the best informed of those not in the nationalist coterie, on the very day the convention rejected the New Jersey plan told his son only that the convention was "very busy and very secret." He knew that Hamilton had spoken three hours the day before and that the members planned to remain in Philadelphia two or three months longer. Beyond that he could say only, "You wish to know everything, and I tell you almost everything."[34]

Abraham Yates reacted very critically to this secrecy. Viewing it as a means to "palm the report upon the legislatures before they have time to consider or consult with their constituency," he warned that he would be prepared.[35] There was little, however, that he could do. As the Philadelphia *Independent Gazetteer* commented, "The mere idle reports of busybodies and the absurd foolish suggestions of trifling pretenders are not to be viewed and considered as the real and regular proceedings of the Convention."[36] In June, Yates had nothing more concrete than those idle reports on which to base any attack.

Secrecy was only one factor retarding the emergence of an opposition. The men who eventually became Antifederalists during the summer were divided over the need for reform. On June 30, for example, Richard Henry and Arthur Lee spent the evening "comparing notes with G[eorge] Mason."[37] While Arthur Lee's own proposals for constitutional reform varied markedly from those being considered by the convention, he remained persuadable. Richard Henry Lee was also receptive. Two weeks after talking to Mason he informed Francis Lightfoot Lee that the government being outlined in Convention would be "not unlike the B[ritish] Constitution, that is, an executive with two branches composing a federal legislature and possessing adequate tone. . . ."[38]

Others proved less receptive to the reports emanating from Philadelphia. In New York, Alexander Hamilton charged that Governor George Clinton declared "in public company" that the "present Articles of Confederation were adequate to the exigencies of the Union, that the appointment of a Convention was calculated to impress the people with the idea of evils that did not exist," and that whatever the reform proposed, it "would serve only to throw the community into confusion."[39] Such a statement, if indeed made, may have been based on information Clinton obtained from Robert Yates and John Lansing, two New York delegates who withdrew from the convention on July 10. No longer bound by the injunction of secrecy, they could have advised Clinton of the convention's decision to abandon the Articles, a decision Lansing saw no prospect of reversing. That decision would certainly have been opposed by Clinton, a most zealous proponent of preserving "all the rights of sovereignty for his state."[40]

Hamilton's attack on Clinton appeared in the *New York Daily Advertiser* on July 21. Five days later, an alleged "Admirer of Antifederal Men" also criticized those who questioned the work of the convention, while a week after that a "gentleman from New York" informed the printer of the *Pennsylvania Packet* that the "Antifederal disposition of a great officer of that state seriously" alarmed the citizens of New York.[41] Outside of the city people were informed of Clinton's opposition through newspaper reprintings of Hamilton's attack and the remarks of the "Admirer of Antifederal Men." One Boston poet responded with an "Impromptu on Reading . . . of Governor Clinton's Insurgency and Antifederalism":

> Since late events his schemes disclose
> That Clinton should Dan Shays oppose
> To save one state—what was the reason
> But this—he hoped tho' unseen
> HIMSELF to wreck the whole THIRTEEN
> Without a partner in the treason.[42]

"An Old Soldier" in Lansingburgh, New York, however, commented that it was the "height of ingratitude to villify a character which ought to be esteemed, and even revered for his services" to his country in both a military and civilian capacity. If these charges are true, "An Old Soldier" added, evidence should be made available to substantiate them. Until that evidence is offered "for God's sake let us not traduce a character so valuable to us, but by every means in our power support him in all measures tending to the general good of our country."[43]

Although upstate Clintonians were prompt to rise to Clinton's defense, in the city, where access to the press was greater, Clinton's supporters did not act. One reason was a rumor in Congress that in discussing the report of the committee of detail "a misunderstanding" took place. As a result the convention was "so far from agreeing that it would be a doubt whether they would agree in time so as that this Congress can take up the matter."[44]

Furthermore, even if the convention did agree on a specific proposal it would not have the approval of New York because Robert Yates and John Lansing, two of the state's three delegates, had decided not to return to Philadelphia. On July 27, the day after the convention adjourned to allow the committee of detail time to prepare its report, William Paterson of New Jersey wrote to Lansing urging him to return to Philadelphia "so that . . . all the states, except Rhode Island will be on the floor."[45] Some time later Alexander Hamilton also attempted to persuade one of the two delegates to return with him to Philadelphia.[46] But on August 26 Lansing's brother advised Abraham Yates that he found "little inclination in either of them [Robert Yates or John Lansing] to repair again to Philadelphia" and he doubted if either would return.[47]

After the committee of detail presented a draft constitution, others followed the lead of Yates and Lansing. Thus on the afternoon of August 6 James McHenry, Daniel Carroll, Daniel St. Thomas Jenifer, John Francis Mercer, and Luther Martin—the entire Maryland delegation—met at Daniel Carroll's lodgings. The meeting was held at the request of McHenry in order to unite the Maryland delegation behind a motion to postpone the report of the committee of detail in order "to try the affections of the house to an amendment of the confederation without altering the sovereignty of the suffrage."[48] To his chagrin McHenry discovered that the delegation was hopelessly split. Daniel Carroll argued that the Articles of Confederation could not be amended "to answer its intentions," while Martin and Mercer maintained the contrary.[49]

The next day McHenry, Mercer, Carroll, and Jenifer did agree that amendments should be added to the report of the committee of detail relating to the right of the Senate to originate money bills, and a requirement that "no navigation act shall be passed without the assent of two thirds of the representation from each state."[50] Mercer was still dissatisfied with the report and proposed to "produce a better one since the Convention had undertaken to go radically to work."[51] Instead, with his own delegation divided, Mercer followed the lead of Yates and Lansing and withdrew. McHenry, although wavering, remained.

Other men who were dissatisfied with the report also remained. On August 20 Mason, Martin, and Elbridge Gerry met with delegates from Connecticut, New Jersey, Delaware, and South Carolina in order to agree upon a "plan of conventional opposition" to the system as proposed. These delegates, chiefly representatives of small states, were concerned about the danger the Constitution would pose to "the existence of essential rights of all the states," as well as to the "liberty and freedom of their citizens."[52] The former objection was ameliorated in part by the compromises in the convention between August 24 and September 4. For Luther Martin these were not enough. When he realized a motion to append a bill of rights to the draft constitution "would be in vain," he took his leave.[53]

Elbridge Gerry was also on the verge of departing. On August 21 he wrote that had he known what was going to occur throughout the course of the convention nothing would "have induced him to come."[54] Two days later he added that he had been a spectator for some time, and three days before Martin's departure, he explained "I would not remain here two hours was I not under the necessity of staying to prevent my colleagues from saying that I broke up the representation."[55]

During August dissatisfaction within the convention grew. Only two men, however—John Francis Mercer and Luther Martin —withdrew, and their departure did not stimulate an immediate attack on the Constitution in Maryland. During July and August, only in New York and Pennsylvania, in the latter among state Constitutionalist party leaders, were the suspicions of the spring and early summer converted into an open and active opposition.

In Pennsylvania, as in New York, the convention's secrecy rule retarded the conversion of suspicious Constitutionalists—a label applied to proponents of the state constitution—into active Antifederalists. But once there was agreement on the fundamentals, and once state leaders outside the convention learned of the outlines of the new Constitution, antifederalism did emerge.[56] The activities of these Antifederalists, i.e., critics of the Constitution in draft form, are most clearly delineated in the Federalist newspaper attacks on them. From those attacks it appears that George Bryan, a principal author of the "democratic" state constitution, or some other constitutional leader, either obtained a copy of, or at least learned in some detail the outlines of the proposed constitution reported to the convention on August 6. Subsequently meetings were held, a Federalist newspaper correspondent charged, at the home of Bryan and his brother-in-law, Jonathan Bayard Smith, from which pamphlets "designed to excite prejudices against the new federal government and thereby prevent its adoption by this state" were prepared for circulation throughout the state.[57]

No such pamphlets have been found, but Federalists' charges that Bryan, Smith, and the Constitutionalists in general were preparing to attack the convention's results seem plausible. John Kean of Harrisburg learned from a "gentleman of office," while the convention was in session, that "the members of the Convention aimed only to make a form of government which would tend to aggrandize themselves." When the Constitution was made public Kean was prepared to "view it with a scrutinizing eye" and opposed its adoption.[58] In Carlisle, Richard Butler warned that "our [state] Constitutional people" were readying themselves while in Philadelphia Anthony Wayne declared there were "turbulent spirits now in this city preparing to attack it [the Constitution] in whatever form it may appear."[59]

One of those turbulent spirits was David Redick, a member of the Supreme Executive Council from Washington County. Redick arrived in Philadelphia on August 17 to attend the council. Alarmed by rumors of the convention's work, he wrote to Pennsylvania's congressional delegate, William Irvine, attacking both Pennsylvania's delegates to the convention and the anticipated changes. His wording was almost identical to that used in an essay which appeared in the *Freeman's Journal* on August 22 signed "Z."[60] "Z" had been writing to newspapers as early as April when he favored limited changes in the central government, preferably through the addition of specified commercial powers to Congress. On August 22 "Z" warned of a junto in Pennsylvania with "principles inimical to the rights of freemen," principles which had led them to oppose the state constitution. This junto, according to "Z," was governed by the private interests of a few selfish and ambitious individuals who restricted the choice of delegates to the Federal Convention "almost exclusively to their own narrow party in the city—for even the venerable Franklin was excluded on their first choice." Playing upon sectional animosities within the state "Z" noted satirically that western Pennsylvanians could take solace in the appointment of Gouverneur Morris to the delegation, a man who, although not a citizen of Pennsylvania, had "the sublime merit of being the ready tool of the great Head of the Junto," Robert Morris.[61]

This attack on the Pennsylvania delegation prompted a bitter response from a "Northern Liberties" correspondent in the *Independent Gazetteer*. Addressing himself to those who were "trying to lay a foundation for a formal opposition to the new federal government in Pennsylvania," he warned that "if they persevere in abusing our worthy and most useful characters, and treasonably oppose the only thing that can save our country . . . and if a coat of tar and feathers will not deter them from this seditious practice, they very possibly may meet with a HALTER."[62]

Despite this threat of a halter Antifederalists in Pennsylvania and New York, during September, continued their attack on the convention in both public and private. On September 1, a correspondent in the *Pennsylvania Packet* suggested that the present constitution, the Articles of Confederation, was not the source of the nation's difficulty and, therefore, that the convention was not going to the real source of the problem. Three days later in New York "Rough Carver" (an obvious play on the "Rough Hewer" pseudonym utilized by Abraham Yates in 1783 during debate on the impost amendment) warned that "we have men among us who are assiduously striving to form a party against federal attachments," in this instance against the reforms to be proposed by the Philadelphia Convention.[63]

One member of that party openly attacked the "aristocratic junto" in New York who were seeking to silence those who did not "subscribe to their political creed." "Rusticus" insisted that it was the right and responsibility of every citizen to express his "approbation or disapprobation of public measures," including the work of the convention.[64] As "Antidefamationist" expressed it, "the free citizens of this continent will never consent to have a Constitution crammed down their throats. They have an undoubted right to examine before they accede, and to deny if they do not approve."[65]

Members of the convention had a similar option, and by the end of August some members raised the possibility of not approving. On August 31 Elbridge Gerry first suggested what Antifederalists out of doors had already hinted: the need for amendments to the report of the convention prior to final adoption. George Mason in turn declared that if some of the questions yet to be settled were done so "improperly" he too wished to "bring the whole subject before another general convention."[66] Edmund Randolph, presaging a major theme in the ensuing campaign over ratification, endorsed Mason's suggestion declaring that if "the final form of the Constitution should not permit him to accede to it, that the state conventions should be at liberty to propose amendments to be submitted to another general convention."[67]

Not yet ready to speak out publicly against the Constitution, all three placed their hope in the decisions yet to be made by the committee on unfinished business and the convention as a whole. Ten days later Randolph moved that the ratification process "close with another general convention with full power to adopt or reject the alterations proposed by the state conventions," but was urged by George Mason to postpone the motion in order to see "what steps might be taken with regard to the parts of the system objected to."[68] Only on September 15, the next to last day of the convention, did Mason, Randolph, and Gerry emphatically declare their unwillingness to sign the Constitution and agree that the most desirable alternative was a second general convention.

In one sense, the willingness of the "dissenting trio"—Gerry, Randolph, and Mason—to remain and participate in the work of the convention until the very end is striking, for the extent of the proposed constitutional reforms was clear well before September. The changes in structure alone—to a bicameral legislature, independent executive, and permanent judiciary—which were accepted from the outset of the convention, were momentous when measured against the Articles of Confederation. The proposed expansion of federal power to include not only the power to regulate trade and levy taxes (changes recommended under the Articles), but also to provide for the common defense and promote the general welfare, was equally significant. Furthermore, while this expansion of federal power only potentially diminished that of the states, there were express prohibitions on powers hitherto exercised by the states. Thus under the new Constitution the states could neither issue paper money nor impair the obligation of contracts. Finally, there was no reservation to the states of those powers not expressly granted to the central government. The cumulative effect of these changes, when measured against the Articles of Confederation, was revolutionary and recognized as such by the members of the convention. Why then did Gerry, Mason, and Randolph remain? Because all three men conceded the need for an extensive reform of the Articles of Confederation. Indeed they accepted the abolition of the

Articles as a necessary first step. Beyond that there were different emphases. Gerry was particularly distressed over the absence of a Bill of Rights while Mason believed southern interests were dangerously unprotected. Randolph offered a long list of objections concerning the size of the House, the presidential veto, and the vagueness of the powers of the state and central governments. All three, though, agreed that a second constitutional convention was necessary so that the proposed Constitution "may be adapted to the exigencies of government and [the] preservation of liberty."[69]

In proposing a second constitutional convention, Gerry, Mason, and Randolph embraced the revolutionary decision of the convention to bypass the amendment procedures of the Articles of Confederation. The convention delegates merely asked the members of the Confederation Congress to forward the Constitution to the states with a recommendation that the state legislatures call special conventions to assent to and ratify the Constitution. As soon as nine states had ratified the Constitution it would become operable among those states. Gerry, Mason, and Randolph accepted the basic outlines of that plan but wanted to allow the states to propose amendments to "be submitted to and finally decided on by another general convention" before the Constitution would become the law of the land.[70]

Under both proposals the Confederation Congress was being asked to act as an agent in its own destruction and the state legislatures, hitherto bastions of hostility to centralized power, to vest state conventions with the authority to adopt a new form of government that materially restricted their own powers. Despite the enormity of these requests there was a considerable likelihood they would be approved, at least to the point of Congress forwarding the Constitution to the states and the states in turn calling the conventions. There were several reasons for that. In the first place, as the critics of a convention had pointed out the previous spring, the Congress and state legislatures were "fairly committed" by their earlier action sanctioning the convention. In addition, the membership of the convention and Congress overlapped significantly. Richard Henry Lee complained that this overlap was so great that "it is easy to see that Congress could have little opinion [of its own] upon the subject."[71] The widespread recognition of the need for some reform was also likely to encourage legislators to approve state convention resolutions. Finally, the Federalists, as the proponents of the new Constitution chose to call themselves, seized the initiative. They had a concrete proposal and a clear-cut plan of action. The revolution of 1787 was well underway.

NOTES TO
CHAPTER 1

1. See Merrill Jensen, *The American Revolution Within America* (New York, 1974) and his introduction to Merrill Jensen, ed., *The Documentary History of the Ratification of the Constitution* (Madison, 1976–); H. James Henderson, *Party Politics in the Continental Congress* (New York, 1974); Joseph P. Davis, *Sectionalism in American Politics: 1774–1787* (Madison, 1977).

2. Edmund Cody Burnett, *The Continental Congress* (New York, 1941), pp. 659–65.

3. Governor Patrick Henry to the Executive of the States, 23 February 1786, Jensen, *Ratification*, 1: 181.

4. Proceedings and Reports of the Commissioners at Annapolis, Maryland, 11–14 September 1786, *ibid.*, p. 184.

5. Edmund Cody Burnett, ed., *Letters of Members of the Continental Congress*, 8 vols. (Washington, 1921–1936), 8: 478–81, 500–505.

6. Nathaniel Gorham commented to Henry Knox regarding Samuel Adams's "doubts and difficulties," 18 February 1787, Knox Papers, MHi. See also James Sullivan to Rufus King, 25 February 1787, Charles R. King, *Life and Correspondence of Rufus King*, 6 vols. (New York 1894–1900), 1: 213–15.

7. On Mitchell's opposition see Mitchell to Johnson, 18 September 1786, Burnett, *Letters*, 8: 645–46; and Jeremiah Wadsworth to Rufus King, 16 December 1787, King, *Life*, 1: 264. Benjamin Gale declared to William Samuel Johnson: "Your opposition to the Convention has won you great honor among republicans," 19 April 1786, George Bancroft, *History of the Formation of the Constitution of the United States of America*, 2 vols. (New York, 1882), 1: 418. Jay wrote Washington that "the policy of such a Convention appears questionable," 7 January 1787, *Documentary History of the Constitution of the United States of America, 1786–1870*, 5 vols. (Washington, 1894–1900), 4: 54.

8. To St. George Tucker, 20 October 1786, Burnett, *Letters*, 8: 490.

9. Nathaniel Gorham to Henry Knox, 18 February 1787, and Mercy Warren to Henry Knox, 2 May 1787, Knox Papers, MHi; Report of Debates, *Hartford Connecticut Courant*, 21 May 1787.

10. Philip Schuyler to Henry Van Schaack, 13 March 1787, Henry C. Van Schaack, *Memoirs of the Life of Henry Van Schaack* (Chicago, 1892), pp. 149–155; George Read to John Dickinson, 17 January 1787, W. T. Read, *Life and Correspondence of George Read* (Philadelphia, 1870), pp. 438–39.

11. Rufus King to Elbridge Gerry, 18 February 1787, Burnett, *Letters*, 8: 541.

12. Worthington C. Ford, et. al., eds., *Journals of the Continental Congress, 1774–1789*, 34 vols. (Washington, 1904–37), 32: 72–74.

13. Robert A. Becker, "Combustibles in Every State: A Frame of Reference for Shays' Rebellion," unpublished manuscript in possession of the author.

14. To Henry Knox, 1 February 1787, John C. Fitzpatrick, ed., *The Writings of George Washington from the Original Manuscript Sources, 1745–1799*, 39 vols. (Washington, 1931–44), 32: 151–53.

15. To John Dickinson, 17 January 1787, Read, *Life*, pp. 438–39; Max Farrand, ed., *The Records of the Federal Convention of 1787*, 4 vols. (New Haven, 1911–37), 3: 563–65.

16. "Resolve Relative to the Appointment of Commissioners," 22 February 1787, Misc. Resolves, Chapter 43A, M-Ar.

17. Philip Schuyler to Henry Van Schaack, 13 March 1787, Van Schaack, *Life*, pp. 149–55. The credentials of the states' delegates are in Farrand, *Records*, 3: 559–86.

18. To Elbridge Gerry, 7 January 1787, Burnett, *Letters*, 8: 527.

19. Philip Schuyler to Henry Van Schaack, 13 March 1787, Van Schaack, *Life*, pp. 149–55; James Madison to George Washington, 18 March 1787, *Documentary History of the Constitution*, 4: 94–95.

20. To Mercy Warren, 31 May 1787, Warren Letters, MHi.

21. To Arthur Lee, 21 May 1787, Robert A. Rutland, ed., *The Papers of George Mason, 1725–1792*, 3 vols. (Chapel Hill, 1970), 3: 882.

22. Madison and Pinckney's proposals are in Farrand, *Records*, 3: 493–609. Although the terms federal and national government are used interchangeably now, they had distinct meanings in the eighteenth century. Thus, when Madison, Pinckney, and Knox spoke of a federal government they meant a central government strictly controlled by the states. A national government was itself sovereign, and therefore independent of such control. For a further discussion see Merrill Jensen, *The Making of the American Constitution* (New York, 1964), chap. 5.

23. To Thomas Lee Shippen, 12 May 1787, Shippen Papers, DLC.

24. *Ibid.*, 29 May 1787.

25. See Mason to Lee, 21 May 1787, which enclosed Lee's proposed amendments, Rutland, *Mason*, 3: 882–83.

26. Sherman's plan is in Farrand, *Records*, 3: 615–16; Lee to Mason, 15 May 1787, Rutland, *Mason*, 3: 876–79.

27. *Philadelphia Independent Gazetteer*, 11 April 1787; *New Haven Connecticut Journal*, 31 May 1787.

28. Arthur Lee to Thomas Lee Shippen, 29 May 1787, Shippen Papers, DLC.

29. Richard Henry Lee to Thomas Lee Shippen, 17 April 1787, Shippen Papers, DLC.

30. Farrand, *Records*, 1: 20–23.

31. *Ibid.*, pp. 235–45.

32. To John Lansing, 27 July 1787, Lansing Misc., NHi.

33. To Abraham Yates, 5 June 1787, Yates Papers, NN.

34. To Thomas Lee Shippen, 19 June 1787, Shippen Papers, DLC.

35. To Robert Yates, 9 June 1787, Yates Papers, NHi.

36. 22 June 1787.

37. William Shippen to Thomas Lee Shippen, 30 June 1787, Shippen Papers, DLC.

38. To Francis Lightfoot Lee, 14 July 1787, Lee Family Papers, ViU.

39. *New York Daily Advertiser*, 21 July 1787. This report was reprinted in the *Philadelphia Pennsylvania Packet*, 26 July; *New Haven Gazette*, 1 August; *Hudson Weekly Gazette*, 2 August; *Baltimore Maryland Gazette*, 10 August; *Boston Massachusetts Gazette*, 10 August; *Boston Massachusetts Centinel*, 11 August; *Boston Gazette*, 13 August; *Newberryport Essex Journal*, 15 August; *New Haven Gazette*, 16 August; *Springfield Hampshire Chronicle*, 21 August; *Charleston Columbian Herald*, 23 August; *Portland Cumberland Gazette*, 23 August; *Providence Gazette*, 25 August; *Lansingburgh Northern Centinel*, 27 August; *Northhampton Hampshire Gazette*, 29 August; *Bennington Vermont Gazette*, 3 September; *Pittsburgh Gazette*, 8 September; *Keene New Hampshire Recorder*, 11 September 1787.

40. Louis Otto to Comte de Montmorin, 25 July 1787, Farrand, *Records*, 3: 63.

41. *New York Daily Advertiser*, 26 July 1787; *Philadelphia Pennsylvania Packet*, 3 August 1787.

42. *Boston Massachusetts Centinel*, 18 August 1787.

43. *Lansingburgh Northern Centinel*, 10 September 1787.

44. Abraham Yates to Jeremiah Van Rensselaer, 29 August 1787, Burnett, *Letters*, 8: 641–42.

45. 27 July 1787, Lansing Misc., NHi.

46. Alexander Hamilton to Rufus King, 20 August 1787, Harold C. Syrett, ed., *The Papers of Alexander Hamilton* (New York, 1961–), 4: 235.

47. Abraham Lansing to Yates, 26 August 1787, Yates Papers, NHi.

48. Farrand, *Records*, 2: 190.

49. *Ibid.*, pp. 190–91

50. *Ibid.*

51. *Ibid.*, p. 212.

52. *Ibid.*, 3: 282.

53. *Ibid.*, p. 291.

54. Elbridge Gerry to Ann Gerry, 2 August 1787, Sang Autograph Collection, ICarbS.

55. *Ibid.*, 23 August and 1 September 1787.

56. There is no evidence that Constitutionalists learned the precise details of the plan emerging in the convention. But, the rumors of an entirely new form of government filled the Philadelphia press throughout the summer and were seemingly confirmed by "coffee shop" gossip. For one example of that gossip see William Shippen to Thomas Lee Shippen, 30 June 1787, Shippen Papers, DLC.

57. *Philadelphia Independent Gazetteer*, 8 August 1787.

58. A. Boyd Hamilton, ed., "An Autobiography: Extracts Taken From the Life of John Kean of Harrisburg," *Notes and Queries*, 3 vols. (Harrisburg, 1895–96), 3: 94.

59. Butler to William Irvine, 26 August 1787, Irvine Papers, PHi; Wayne to General Jackson, 18 August, Wayne Papers, PHi.

60. See Redick's letters to Irvine, 29 August and 10 and 14 September 1787, Irvine Papers, PHi.

61. *Philadelphia Freeman's Journal*, 22 August 1787.

62. *Philadelphia Independent Gazetteer*, 30 August 1787.

63. *New York Daily Advertiser*, 4 September 1787.

64. "Rusticus," *New York Journal*, 13 September 1787.

65. *Ibid.*, 20 September 1787.

66. Farrand, *Records*, 2: 479.

67. *Ibid.*

68. *Ibid.*, p. 564.

69. Elbridge Gerry to president of Senate and Speaker of House of Representatives of Massachusetts, 18 October 1787, *ibid.*, 3: 129.

70. Farrand, *Records*, 2: 631.

71. Richard Henry Lee to Edmund Randolph, 16 October 1787, Burnett, *Letters*, 8: 658.

Chapter 2

OFFICIAL ACTION AND ANTIFEDERALIST REACTION

Decisions of far-reaching significance were made during September and October 1787. On September 27 the Confederation Congress unanimously approved transmitting the proposed Constitution to the states. This "neutral" transmission was the result of compromise. Pro-Constitution delegates waived an explicit recommendation in support of the Constitution in exchange for Antifederalist delegates abandoning their demand that the Constitution be forwarded with proposed amendments. That unanimity was one factor that induced state legislatures to comply with the recommendation of the Federal Convention to call state conventions to consider the Constitution.

Antifederalist acquiescence in the resolution of transmittal was important too because it implied that men like Richard Henry Lee and Abraham Yates, although opposed to the Constitution, were willing to operate within the framework of the Constitution, Article V, which provided for ratification by state conventions. Indeed, following congressional action, Lee, according to a pseudonymous newspaper essayist, "New England," met with Abraham Yates, Melancton Smith, and the remainder of the New York congressional delegation, and Governor Clinton. Lee also consulted with Elbridge Gerry, then in New York en route from Philadelphia to Massachusetts.[1] During these early October meetings Lee, Gerry, and the New Yorkers decided that the best plan would be for the state legislatures to delay action on the report of the Federal Convention until the spring sessions, and when they adopted resolutions calling for conventions that they schedule those conventions to meet simultaneously. The

Antifederalist leadership in New York also decided to embark on an extensive propaganda campaign to convince the public of the need for amendments to the Constitution, which could best be secured through a second constitutional convention. Finally, they agreed that once the state conventions did meet, Antifederalist delegates should communicate with their counterparts in the other conventions, agree on a specific set of amendments, and unite in their demand for a second constitutional convention to incorporate those amendments into the Constitution before its adoption by the states.[2]

With their strategy set, Lee set out to communicate the plans to political allies in the various states. During October Lee wrote to Samuel Adams in Massachusetts, William Shippen in Pennsylvania, and Edmund Randolph and George Mason in Virginia, outlining this plan of action.[3] In each case Lee also stressed the need for the recipients of his letters to convey his objections to former allies of Lee's in the Confederation Congress: Dr. Samuel Holten and James Lovell in Massachusetts and Dr. James Hutchinson in Pennsylvania.[4] Lee urged Mason not only to solicit the support of Virginia's chancellor, Edmund Pendleton, but also that of his brother, Henry Pendleton of South Carolina as well as "Thomas Stone and others of influence in Maryland."[5]

Finally, Lee wrote and arranged for the publication of his pamphlet, *Observations Leading to a Fair Examination of the System of Government Proposed by the Late Convention . . . In a Number of Letters from the Federal Farmer.*[6] In the *Federal Farmer Letters,* as in his personal letters to Adams, Shippen, Edmund Randolph, Mason, and George Washington, Lee reiterated the objections he first raised on the floor of Congress. The Constitution, while it "abound[ed] with useful regulations," was defective in its structure.[7] It created an improper blending of executive and legislative responsibilities in the presidency and Senate and a lack of "power and responsibility" in the democratic branch, the House of Representatives. Furthermore, the scope of powers to be exercised by the new government, extending to the "general welfare," was too great, particularly since the fundamental rights of the people were not explicitly secured in a Bill of Rights.[8]

Despite these objections, Richard Henry Lee did not call for rejection of the Constitution. Instead, he urged that Antifederalists in the various states propose amendments in their state conventions, which were to meet simultaneously in April or May, and submit those proposed amendments to the Confederation Congress "so that a new general convention may weave them into the proffered system."[9] In a

second convention the structural errors could be remedied, the powers
to be exercised restricted, and the fundamental rights of the people
properly secured.

For Antifederalists like Yates, who had previously opposed increasing federal powers within the structure of the Articles of Confederation, and Clinton, who in July had suggested that there was no
need for a revision of the Articles of Confederation, Lee's strategy was
acceptable. Yates and Clinton too wanted to point out the defects in
the proposed Constitution, alert the populace to the dangers it posed,
and have the opportunity to amend the proposed Constitution in a
second constitutional convention. Amend, though, as Yates and Clinton well knew, had a range of meanings and the proposal for a second
constitutional convention held out the possibility that, mimicking
the Federal Convention that was called for the "sole and express" purpose of revising the Articles of Confederation, the Constitution could
be abandoned altogether in favor of a revision of the Articles of Confederation.

Antifederalists of various persuasions then repeated Lee's and
Clinton's criticisms concerning both the nature and structure of the
proposed Constitution. The heart of their objections was that the proposed Constitution removed sovereignty from the thirteen states and
vested it in one national government. That meant that powers previously exercised by the state governments, if used at all, would hence-
forth be exercised by the central government.[10] The most significant
of those was the virtually unlimited one to tax. Alarming too was the
new government's mandate to legislate for the "general welfare" and
to adopt whatever measures were "necessary and proper" to achieve
that end. With such legislation the "supreme law of the land" and
enforceable in national courts, the end result would be the total destruction of the state governments.

Antifederalists also charged that the new government would not
exercise these powers in a manner responsive to the wishes of the
majority of the people. The Senate, they claimed, was an aristocratic
body, the president an elective king. Even the House of Representatives, the one democratic element in the new government, was too
small to mirror effectively and act in accordance with the interests of
the small farmers, mechanics, and artisans spread across the land. The
Antifederalists contended that not only would the government operate independent of, or even in opposition to, the wishes of the majority of the people, it would also silence all its critics, for there were no
guarantees of the rights of free assembly, speech, and petition for a

redress of grievances. The agreed-upon mechanism to resolve these problems: a second constitutional convention.

This then was the Antifederalist counterplan communicated to state leaders by direct meetings in New York and Philadelphia; through Richard Henry Lee's correspondence with Antifederalists in Massachusetts, Pennsylvania, and Virginia; and in Antifederalist essays and pamphlets like the *Federal Farmer Letters*, which were distributed during October and November by the Federal Republican Committee of New York, and a host of lesser known Antifederalists in Massachusetts, New Hampshire, Pennsylvania, and Virginia. The advantage of such a plan was readily apparent. Differences among Antifederalists could be submerged in a general agreement to support the demand for amendments through a second convention. The tactical disadvantage of the plan quickly became apparent, for even as Lee was taking the lead in the formation of a national Antifederalist alliance, the state legislatures were undercutting one key portion of his plan: the proposal for simultaneous conventions.

Pennsylvania, the first state to act, called a state convention on September 29, 1787. This prompt action was possible because the legislature was in session in Philadelphia when the Federal Convention adjourned. More important, leaders of one of the state's two political parties pressed for rapid action.

The Republicans were the opponents of the state constitution and supporters of the proposed federal one. Most Republicans resided east of the Susquehanna River with the party's strongest support in the city and county of Philadelphia and its immediate environs. The party included a large number of farmers, but a significant portion of its members was engaged either in trade or the professions. The leaders of the Republican party reflected these differences. Robert Morris, George Clymer, and James Wilson were prominent because of their extensive accumulated wealth and their speculations in land, commerce, and government currency. All three men had been members of the Federal Convention, and Wilson was to serve in the state convention as well. Clymer and Wilson were also part of the Republican majority in the current Assembly.[11]

Constitutionalists, in contrast, were predominantly small farmers residing west of the Susquehanna River, or urban artisans and shopkeepers. They supported the state constitution and the bulk of the Constitutionalists became Antifederalists. The leaders of the Constitutionalists, who became the leaders of the Antifederalists in Pennsylvania, included an urban elite and western legislators. The former consisted of George Bryan—in 1787 the fourth judge of the Pennsylvania Supreme Court—his son Samuel, and Bryan's brother-in-law Jonathan Bayard Smith. Blair M'Clenachan, a prominent Philadelphia merchant and Jonathan Dickinson Sargeant were also part of this leadership group, as were three members of the College of Philadelphia faculty—Dr. John Ewing, Dr. James Hutchinson, and Dr. William Shippen. David Redick, James McLene, and John Smiley, in 1787 members of the Supreme Executive Council, represented the western wing of the party, as did Robert Whitehill and William Findley, in 1787 members of the Assembly.[12]

The Republicans, enjoying a temporary majority in the Assembly, pressed for immediate action. They wanted to implement the recommendation of the Federal Convention before adjournment because they were uncertain of the outcome of the state legislative elections scheduled for October 13. Naturally the Constitutionalists took the opposite tack and sought to postpone action until the next session of the legislature when they might have a majority. On September 28, the day before the scheduled adjournment of the Assembly, George Clymer moved that the legislature adopt a set of convention resolves. Antifederalists objected that Congress had not transmitted the Constitution to the legislatures and that the Assembly could not therefore legally consider it. Robert Whitehill argued the people should be allowed time to consider the proposed Constitution and through the forthcoming elections instruct their representatives accordingly. William Findley supported Whitehill. Both contended that the legislature could take no action until Congress, which had sanctioned the Philadelphia meeting, recommended the calling of a state convention.[13]

In a Republican dominated house these arguments went unheeded. Six Constitutionalists broke ranks to join the Republican majority in a 43 to 19 roll call vote in favor of calling a convention. Outnumbered, eighteen of the nineteen opponents boycotted the afternoon session, which was to set the date for the elections and the date and place of meeting of the convention.[14] Lacking a quorum, the members present sent the sergeant at arms to request the attendance of the missing members. Seven of them were located at "the house [of] a great constitutional partisan Major [Alexander] Boyd with two constitutional members of the [Supreme Executive] Council. . . ."[15] The seven, acting with the advice of councillors McLene and Smiley and Judge George Bryan, refused to attend. The House, informed of their refusal by the sergeant, then adjourned until 9:00 the next morning.

In the early hours of the morning news reached Philadelphia that

Congress had recommended that the states call conventions in compliance with the recommendation of the Federal Convention. When the Assembly convened the sergeant at arms was again sent to bring back the seceders. When two members were located but still refused to attend, a "number of volunteer gentlemen" forcibly carried them to the Assembly chamber.[16] James McCalmont, one of the two, protested in vain and a quorum was declared present. McCalmont then attempted to change the site of the convention from Philadelphia to Lancaster or Reading, but his efforts were easily defeated. The Assembly approved a resolution calling for elections for delegates on the first Tuesday in November, with the convention to assemble in Philadelphia on the third Tuesday in November.[17]

By prompt action the Pennsylvania Federalists established the legal framework for ratification before any state legislature officially received the report of the convention. Connecticut Federalists were not far behind. There opponents failed to block prompt approval of a convention resolve which provided for a December convention. The lower house did include a number of Antifederalists, including Amos Granger of Suffield and Elisha Fitch of Salisbury, both of whom had opposed the appointment of Federal Convention delegates the preceding May, but Granger, Fitch, and the men like them were a small minority. The House approved a convention resolve "almost unanimously," on October 16, the same day it was introduced.[18]

In the twelve-member council the proportion of Antifederalists was greater, and included James Wadsworth who, in addition to his seat on the council, was comptroller general of the state and an outspoken critic of congressional reform. Erastus Wolcott, also a councillor, had declined appointment to the Philadelphia Convention in May while he, Wadsworth, and William Williams were all attacked in the Federalist dominated press because of their antifederalist views.[19] Stephen Mix Mitchell, like Wadsworth a dual officeholder, had opposed congressional approval of a convention in February 1787, and refused to return to Congress in September to vote on passage of the Constitution to the states. Joseph Platte Cooke, like Mitchell a member of the state's congressional delegation, was in New York when Congress approved forwarding the Constitution to the states. There is no record of Cooke's voicing any objection to transmitting the Constitution to the states, but New York Antifederalist Hugh Hughes, himself a member of the New York inner circle of Antifederalists, later reported Cooke "much opposed to the new form" of government. Their presence notwithstanding, the council also promptly approved a convention resolve.[20]

That Connecticut Antifederalists agreed to a state convention is understandable. Most Antifederalist leaders did not oppose the calling of conventions. But that the Connecticut leaders apparently made no effort to delay the meeting of the convention suggests a breakdown in communication between the leadership meeting in New York and Connecticut Antifederalists. Such an explanation seems even more plausible given the lack of awareness of local conditions in Connecticut demonstrated by John Lamb and New York Antifederalists in the following months.[21]

A similar breakdown in communication momentarily handicapped Antifederalists in the Massachusetts legislature. The legislature that considered the report of the Federal Convention had been elected the preceding May. Those elections, held in the aftermath of Shays' Rebellion, saw a significant turnover in the lower house, with sixty or more incumbents replaced by "new men." In June this change was accentuated even further by a marked increase in attendance by representatives of numerous small, rural, and usually unrepresented towns.[22] This electoral revolution, while it alarmed political conservatives, did not cause a drastic change in the direction of the commonwealth's economic policies. During June the lower house blocked continued repression of Daniel Shays and his followers. The house did not significantly reform the commonwealth's tax structure, however, or comply with Shaysites' demands regarding the courts, economic policy, or the place of meeting of the general court.[23]

The importance of the last issue was dramatically underscored in October when the legislature reconvened. In the Senate neither Hampshire nor Berkshire county was represented while in the House the same two counties, although entitled to seventy-three representatives, had only nine present. Worcester County, a Shaysite and later Antifederalist stronghold, was equally underrepresented with only twelve of fifty-two representatives present.[24] The Antifederalists present were further handicapped by the absence of clearly defined goals. A letter from Elbridge Gerry recommending that the legislature delay action on the Constitution until the next session was still en route from New York to Speaker of the House James Warren, and President of the Senate, Samuel Adams.[25] Subsequently the Senate approved a convention resolve on October 22. Samuel Adams, who in February 1787, was wary of the reforms a general convention might propose, concurred.[26] In the House, the Antifederalists present worked at cross purposes. Dr. Daniel Kilham of Newburyport objected that the Federal Convention exceeded its authority in drafting an entirely new Constitution and argued that the Confederation could not be dis-

solved "unless in the way stated in the Articles [of Confederation]."
On the other hand, William Widgery, a representative from Maine,
and later an Antifederalist leader in the state convention, did not
oppose transmitting the Constitution to the people, but argued that it
should be adopted or rejected by direct vote of the people as had been
the case with the state constitution. The division among opponents
also surfaced when motions were made for the convention to meet in
York, district of Maine, and Worcester, in the central part of the state.
The opposition could not agree on an alternative site to Boston, the
place fixed on in the Senate resolve, and lost the vote.[27] Lacking news
from Gerry in New York, Warren, Widgery, and their allies agreed to
a resolution which provided for the election of delegates in November,
with the convention to assemble in Boston on January 9.

Georgia, whose legislature assembled in special session at Augusta on October 16, was the fourth state to approve a convention
resolve. The call for a special session was the result of the threat of
Indian warfare on the Georgia frontier. When presented with the report of the Federal Convention the legislature unanimously approved
a state convention in the hope of getting "more and better help against
the Creeks from a strengthened central government."[28] The convention resolve provided for elections on December 4 and 5, the same day
as state elections for the unicameral legislature. Each county was to be
represented by up to three delegates who were to assemble at Augusta
on the fourth Tuesday in December, consider the Constitution, and
"adopt any part or the whole thereof."[29]

Unanimity also characterized the action of the New Jersey
House, which approved a convention resolve on October 26. The
prospect of the elimination of state import duties like those which
New York collected on all goods shipped into the state was a major
factor in the widespread support for the Constitution in New Jersey.
In an attempt to undercut this economic motive, it was later alleged
that Abraham Clark, a prominent East Jersey political leader and one
of New Jersey's congressional delegates, in collaboration with New
York's Governor Clinton, advised various members of the New Jersey
legislature that New York state was willing to make "large concessions" to New Jersey, including giving up the impost and refunding
duties previously collected if the state would refuse or at least delay
recommending a convention. Even if true, and that cannot be ascer-
tained, Clark did not reach Trenton, where the legislature was in
session, until after it had already passed a convention resolve and adjourned.[30]

Among those states which early approved a state convention resolve, only in Virginia was the opposition as intense as in Pennsylvania. Led by Patrick Henry, representatives in the House repeatedly sought to avoid complying with the resolve of the Federal Convention and Confederation Congress by providing a "constitutional door" for previous amendments. The opposition of Southside representatives —i.e., men representing counties south and west of the James River—was anticipated well before the legislature assembled in Richmond in October. In preceding sessions Patrick Henry and Southside representatives, whose constituents were chiefly small farmers saddled with considerable private debts, had opposed legislation complying with the treaty of peace, granting the impost to Congress, or establishing federal regulation of trade.[31] The motives, both economic and ideological, which had induced those men to oppose these measures previously, were equally applicable to a Constitution which made treaties the supreme law of the land, and granted to the central government the virtually unrestricted power to tax and otherwise regulate interstate trade and foreign commerce.

The Constitution, the convention's letter of transmittal, and the resolution of the Confederation Congress were laid before the Virginia House of Delegates on the opening day of the session, and made the order of the day for Thursday, October 25.[32] When debate opened on the subject, Frances Corbin introduced a series of resolutions which proposed that a convention "be called according to the recommendation of the Congress." Patrick Henry opposed the measure because there were errors and defects in the Constitution. He agreed that a convention should be called, but wanted to revise the Corbin resolution to make explicit the convention's authority to amend the Constitution.[33]

Henry's remarks prompted an immediate response from George Nicholas and Corbin. Nicholas "reprobated" Henry's amendment which would have empowered the convention to ratify, reject, or amend the Constitution. He maintained that Henry's amendment would "convey to the people of this state and the continent that the legislature of Virginia thought amendments should be made to the new government." George Mason in turn defended the amendment because the Constitution as presented, Mason contended, was "repugnant" to the interests of Virginia. The differences were finally resolved by John Marshall, later chief justice of the United States Supreme Court. Marshall proposed that the House agree to call a convention and "that the Constitution be laid before them for their free and ample discussion." The House, after some further discussion, "came into Mr. Marshall's opinion," and the resolution was adopted unanimously.[34]

As agreed to by the committee of the whole, and passed by the House the same day, Virginia provided for a convention which could fully and freely discuss the Constitution. The delegates were to be elected in the same manner as members of the House on the first day in March in each city, county, and corporation. The qualifications for electors and delegates were the same as for members of the House with the exception that delegates did not have to reside in the county they represented. Two thousand copies of the resolutions were also ordered printed for distribution by members of the House. The executive was to transmit the act to the legislature and executive of each state.[35]

Federalists were pleased with this decision. The Assembly not only provided for a state convention but did so with no mark of disapprobation. In contrast to the states where Federalist majorities eagerly pressed forward, Virginia Federalists willingly accepted spring elections and a summer convention in order to have an opportunity to augment their own numbers and "see what other states would do" regarding the Constitution. Federalists approved the provision to forward the resolutions to the executives of the other states because it demonstrated Virginia's neutral compliance with the recommendations of Congress.[36] Antifederalists won concessions as well. The convention was set for June, and the elections in March, thus providing ample time to conduct a campaign for convention delegates within the state, and to coordinate their efforts with Antifederalists throughout the South and the nation.

The "neutral" resolution was, however, less the result of compromise than of divisions within the Antifederalists' ranks. In the initial debate over the Corbin resolution and the Henry amendment Henry had expected the support of George Mason. Mason did second the amendment, but he "disappointed" the Henryites "in their expectations" because of his declaration that "notwithstanding his objections, so federal was he, that he would adopt it [the Constitution] if nothing better could be obtained."[37] Thus the apparent unanimity of the House for the Marshall compromise. It attracted the support of Federalists as well as moderate Antifederalists like Mason, who had been in contact with Richard Henry Lee, and Governor Edmund Randolph, who had his own following in the House. Henry, while less satisfied with the resolution, temporarily acquiesced in the measure.

Henry, however, renewed his attack through Samuel Hopkins, a representative from Muhlenberg County, on November 30 when Hopkins introduced resolutions to provide funds to defray the expenses of delegates to the June convention. Although nothing further was required, Hopkins's resolution also proposed to defray the expenses of any deputy or deputies to "confer with the convention or conventions of any other state or states in the union," if the state convention deemed such interstate cooperation necessary.[38] Henry and Mason seconded the resolutions. Henry declared that "if this idea was not held forth our southern neighbors might be driven to despair seeing no door open to safety should they disapprove the new Constitution."[39] Henry's support of the resolution was expected, but Mason's seconding of the resolutions "was [a] matter of astonishment" because he had previously agreed that the House should not take a position either for or against the Constitution.[40]

Much to the chagrin of Federalists, the resolutions were passed by the Henry-Mason coalition and sent to committee. Four days later the committee reported out a draft bill embodying the essence of Hopkins's resolutions of the 30th. The delegates to the June convention were vested with "all and every the privileges which are had, possessed and enjoyed by members elected to and attending on the General Assembly." Provision was also made for payment to deputies "appointed to a second general convention if the same shall be deemed necessary" or "to confer with the convention or conventions of any other state or states" on the subject of the proposed plan of federal government.[41]

On December 7 and 8, in the committee of the whole, these resolutions were diluted. Instead of a specific provision for the payment of travel expenses for deputies to a second convention, the final bill provided for the "payment of such reasonable expenses as may be incurred in case the convention . . . deem it necessary to hold any communications with any of the sister states or the conventions thereof."[42] Read a third time on December 11, the amended bill was forwarded to the Senate where it was approved the next day. A final attempt to declare "the sense of the house on the subject" of the Constitution was made on December 26.[43] Antifederalist Meriwether Smith moved that a circular letter be sent to the state legislatures 'intimating the likelihood of amendments here."[44] This motion, like the draft bill of November 30, was amended so that the governor was simply instructed to forward the act of December 11 to the other states.

Despite these modifications the actions of the House underscored its hostility to the Constitution in an unamended form. On October 25 the House adopted a neutral convention resolve that was compatible with both the recommendation of the Federal Convention and the plans of Antifederalist leaders. Five weeks later Henry engineered House approval of resolutions providing for a second constitutional convention and a circular letter to the states informing them of that action. Both measures left open a "constitutional door" for amendments and demonstrated the antifederalism of the majority of the members of the house. Henry was not able to strike a fatal blow against the Constitution as Federalists feared he might. It was, however, certain that he would be a member of the convention. More important, even discounting the potential of Henry's oratory on the convention, if the question of ratification hinged on ratification with or without amendments, the Virginia House of Delegates, and presumably the state at large, was Antifederalist.

By the time the Virginia legislature completed action, Delaware had unanimously ratified the Constitution. This prompt action accurately reflected the widespread popularity of the Constitution in Delaware, a state where every prominent political leader was for the Constitution except Dr. James Tilton, who, according to Henry Knox, "was not in the Philadelphia Convention and therefore is mainly against it."[45] Tilton's opposition was not strong enough for him, as a member of the legislative council, to oppose calling a state convention, and Delaware's unanimous ratification of the Constitution in December 1787 accurately reflected the wishes of the people of that state.[46]

In contrast to the relative political quiet in Delaware, the Constitution sparked an extended debate in neighboring Maryland where Baltimore Federalists initiated a discussion of the Constitution in September as part of a local campaign to unseat incumbent assemblyman Samuel Chase. Chase had been an active leader in the Revolution, and more recently a major figure in the drive for an issue of state paper money. The preceding spring he declined an appointment to the Federal Convention in order to remain in Maryland where he continued to press for a paper emission.[47] During the summer, Chase did not speak out against the Constitution, but his opposition was anticipated. By mid-September the issue of the Constitution was embroiled in the fall elections for the state house. In the campaign Chase initially did not mention the Constitution. When publicly asked whether he supported it, Chase stated that he had not made up his mind and praised the state constitution "under which" the people of Maryland "had lived happily for more than ten years."[48] In a later speech he "was not quite so violent" against the Constitution and pledged that "he would, if elected [to the General Assembly] use his endeavors to call a convention."[49] Chase also circulated a handbill designed to "satisfy every voter of his being a perfect federal man," but Federalists charged that he was "in principle, inclination and interest against the new Constitution."[50]

Following his reelection, Chase and his supporters circulated a petition with "Antifederalist" instructions to the town's assembly-men. These instructions proposed that when the legislature adopted resolutions providing for the election of convention delegates, the delegates be left "at liberty to approve or reject [the Constitution] as they may think proper."[51] Federalists, of course, recognized the potential of such instructions. Chase was personally popular in Balti-more, despite his antifederalism, and instructions allowing him to think for himself would provide him with the opportunity to work against the wishes of his predominantly Federalist constituents. In response, one Federalist declared that the convention delegates were "not to think for the people but merely declare their will," an attitude not previously held by Maryland Federalists or by Federalists in states where they were a minority.[52]

This early focus on the Constitution had little immediate im-pact. Chase was reelected and the legislature did not meet until its regular session began on November 23, 1787. At that time the House took up Governor Randolph's letter enclosing the resolutions of the Virginia legislature respecting the Federal Constitution, a letter from Secretary Charles Thomson enclosing the resolutions of Congress of September 28, and the report of the Federal Convention. The House's initial action was to request from the state's delegates to the Federal Convention a report on the proceedings of the convention. The mo-tion, Daniel Carroll believed, originated from an "Antifederal dispos-ition," but had the support of many "from the purest motives," and passed 28 to 22. The House then agreed unanimously that the pro-ceedings of the Federal Convention be submitted to a convention of the people "for their full and free investigation," the exact phraseol-ogy of the Virginia resolutions. On November 24 the Senate and House both considered the Constitution in separate actions. The House drafted resolutions providing that electors qualified to vote for members of the House be eligible to vote for delegates to a convention to be held at Annapolis. Two days later they set the date of election of delegates for "the first Monday in April" and stipulated that the delegates were to be residents of the state for three years and residents for twelve months of the country from which they were elected. The convention was also empowered to adjourn from "day to day" and a majority was declared sufficient to ratify the Constitution.[53]

The Senate meanwhile adopted resolves which differed from those of the House on three key points. The Senate proposed submitting the Constitution to a convention of delegates "for their assent and ratification"; holding the elections for delegates on the third Wednesday in January, with the convention to meet at Annapolis on the first Monday in March; and requiring a £500 property qualification of delegates. The House, when presented with the Senate resolutions, refused to yield, and on December 1 the Senate concurred in the House measure to avoid prolonging the session.[54]

Antifederalists in the House thus scored several victories. They defeated the Senate proposal for a £500 property qualification; made the eligibility requirements for voters and delegates the same as for elections to the lower house; won out in their demand that the elections be held on the first Monday in April with the convention to assemble at Annapolis on April 21; and secured provisions stipulating that the convention could adjourn from day to day. Antifederalist strength in the legislature, however, was more apparent than real. The motion to call the state's delegates to the Federal Convention to report passed with the support of Federalist legislators, while the stipulation regarding adjournment from day to day appears to have been an alternative forced on the Antifederalists by their inability to persuade the legislature to schedule the convention even later in the spring, when cooperation with the Virginia convention could occur. Maryland, like the other middle states, was solid in its support for the Constitution.

The pattern of political activity in Maryland was duplicated in North Carolina. There early discussion of the Constitution took place during the state legislative election, but the issue was not fully considered until the regularly scheduled fall session of the legislature. On November 21, 1787, Governor Samuel Johnston laid the report of the Federal Convention before the House and Senate but not until December 5 did the two houses meet in conference on the issue. The Constitution was then read and several resolutions agreed to. These resolutions provided that all inhabitants qualified to vote for representatives to the House were to meet on the last Friday and Saturday in March to elect five persons to serve as delegates from "each county and one person from each borough town" to a state convention for the purpose of "deliberating and determining on the said Constitution."

All freeholders were eligible to a seat in the convention, which was to meet on the third Monday in July at a place to be determined. The next day both houses balloted independently on a place for the convention to meet (a potentially divisive issue) and Hillsborough was chosen. Final action was taken on December 22 when provisions for the payment of delegates were approved.[55]

The tenth state to act, New Hampshire, did so in a special session of the legislature which assembled in Portsmouth on December 11. New Hampshire's legislature had been in session during September but for purely partisan reasons the state's Federalist president, John Sullivan, allowed the regular session to adjourn on September 28. He later stated that he preferred a special winter session when a number of prominent Federalist leaders, absent from the September session, would be able to attend.[56] Not until November 11 did Sullivan call a special session of the legislature to meet in December. A quorum assembled on December 11 and two days later approved a convention resolve which provided that the election of delegates be held on January 14, with the convention to meet at Exeter on the second Wednesday in February.[57]

The convention resolve reflected the success of Federalist strategy. The time prior to the elections was brief, thereby limiting Antifederalist opportunities to mobilize public opinion in the interior towns. Federalists also defeated an attempt to double the number of delegates, a measure which would have "reduced the effectiveness of the group of vocal and influential Federalists who expected to dominate discussion of the Constitution . . ." in the convention, and exempted convention delegates from the state constitutional provision prohibiting dual officeholding, thereby allowing Federalist state executive and judicial officers like President Sullivan, Superior Court justices Samuel Livermore and Josiah Bartlett, and state treasurer John Taylor Gilman to serve.[58]

Partisan political maneuvering, like that employed by President Sullivan, was duplicated in New York where Governor George Clinton waited until December 3 to summon the legislature into session for its scheduled January session, despite appeals for an earlier meeting. By his inaction Clinton confirmed his hostility toward the Constitution and set himself at the head of the Antifederalist, hitherto the Clintonian, party in New York. This party, in 1787, included former convention delegates John Lansing and Robert Yates, congressional delegates Abraham Yates and Melancton Smith, General John Lamb, who had just returned from a diplomatic mission to the Mediterranean and was collector of the state impost, and Lamb's son-in-law, Charles Tillinghast. Jeremiah Van Rensselaer, a former Albany son of liberty and future congressional candidate, was also allied with Clinton, as were Dutchess County politicians John DeWitt and Gilbert Livingston, and Queens legislator Samuel Jones.[59] These men, and Clintonian legislators as well, were of a conspicuously lower social and economic class than their political rivals. In this the leaders reflected their constituents who, like their counterparts in Massachusetts, Pennsylvania, and Virginia, were predominantly small farmers or artisans. Furthermore, Clintonians, like Henryites, Shaysites, and Constitutionalists, shared a common hostility to a significant expansion of congressional powers.[60]

During the months between the congressional transmittal of the Constitution and the assembling of the legislature, the New York papers printed many Antifederalist essays. "Cato," "Brutus," "A Countryman," "Cincinnatus" and "A Republican" appeared in the *New York Journal* alongside "Centinel," "Old Whig," and "Timoleon." The *New York Morning Post* also published Antifederalist essays and the *Poughkeepsie Country Journal* published *Letters from the Federal Farmer* in serial form. An occasional Antifederalist article also appeared in the *Albany Gazette*. The *New York Journal* was, however, the most prolific source of Antifederalist essays, and Yates, Hugh Hughes, and Charles Tillinghast took care to insert certain pieces in its Thursday edition because of its extensive country circulation.[61] Those essays gained additional country circulation through the efforts of John Lamb whose customs office became a regional distribution point for the dissemination of Antifederalist literature. During November and December Lamb shipped packets of broadsides and pamphlets, primarily "Centinel" I and II and *Letters from the Federal Farmer*, to prominent Antifederalists in New York, New Jersey, Connecticut, Rhode Island, Massachusetts, and New Hampshire.[62]

Following Clinton's proclamation summoning the legislature, two of the state's three delegates to the Federal Convention sent him an official letter explaining why they withdrew from the convention and outlining their objections to the new Constitution. The letter closed with a request that it be forwarded to the legislature and was part of the maneuvering among Federalists and Antifederalists preparatory to the forthcoming session.[63] Once the legislature assembled it was expected that "the first object of attention" would be the "calling of a convention."[64] Instead, the Constitution was not brought to the floor of the House until January 31. In the interim there was considerable competition for delegate support and both "Cato," i.e. Clinton, and the "Rough Hewer," i.e. Abraham Yates, were reported "using their utmost abilities to create jealousies among the people."[65] Neither party was absolutely certain of its strength. Antifederalist Yates claimed a majority in both houses.[66] Federalist Richard Sill, on the other hand, was certain the lower house was Federalist, but feared that the "complexion of the senate was unfavorable." He therefore doubted if the legislature would even call a convention because of the determination of the "opposition . . . to make their stand at Poughkeepsie."[67] Samuel B. Webb, in New York, believed a convention would be called "but suppose the Antifederals will be for delaying its meeting to as distant a period as possible."[68]

Melancton Smith doubted that Antifederalists could effect such a delay. A week earlier the legislature chose Egbert Benson, Ezra L'Hommedieu, Leonard Gansevoort, and Alexander Hamilton, all "most warm advocates" for the Constitution, delegates to the Confederation Congress. Yates was also chosen, but the four-to-one split in the delegation suggested something less than the firm Antifederalist majority Yates claimed. Yates explained to Smith that the Antifederalists, although a majority, had been "outgeneralled." Smith replied: "It is still a defeat."[69] Charles Tillinghast, however, attributed the defeat to a combination of Federalist influence and the absence of Governor Clinton at the time of the election. Egbert Benson, a "strong new government man," had considerable influence in both houses, and by taking advantage of Clinton's temporary absence in New York secured the election of Hamilton as a delegate to Congress, an appointment Clinton could have prevented had he "been at Poughkeepsie at the time."[70]

Clinton was back in Poughkeepsie when the question of a state convention came to the floor of the House on January 31. In the committee of the whole Federalist Egbert Benson moved that a convention be called in conformity with the recommendation of the convention.[71] Antifederalist Cornelius Schoonmaker, a representative from Ulster County, proposed as an amendment that the preamble state that "the Convention had exceeded their powers by proposing a new instead of amending the old Constitution."[72] Benson, however, contended that the amendment was designed to cast "odium" upon both the convention and Congress. Schoonmaker and Samuel Jones of Queens denied this but insisted that the "facts" should be pointed out to the people. The delegates to the convention exceeded their powers in reporting "a new Constitution, which, if adopted, will materially

alter the Constitution and government of this state." Benson replied
that the intent of Schoonmaker's amendment was to prevent submission of the Constitution to the people. This argument was apparently
persuasive for the amendment was defeated 27 to 25. A second resolution designed to "introduce the idea of amendment" was also defeated, 28 to 23. Having failed twice, and by an increasing margin,
the Antifederalists in the House yielded. Benson's original motion,
with a provision which expanded the suffrage to include all white
males over the age of twenty-one, passed. Elections were to be held on
the last Tuesday in April, the same day as state legislative elections,
with the convention to assemble on the third Tuesday in June. [73]

The next day Federalist James Duane moved that the Senate
concur with the House measure. Abraham Yates countered with a
motion that the resolution be considered in a committee of the whole,
but this motion was defeated 12 to 7. The Senate then proceeded to
read the Assembly resolves over the objections of Yates who sought a
postponement. In reading through the resolves, two Antifederalists
raised objections. John Williams from Washington County questioned extending the right of suffrage to all white males over the age of
twenty-one while David Hopkins, also from Washington County,
criticized the timing of the elections, which coincided with state
legislative contests. No other Antifederalist followed their lead, however, and the provisions were retained. Once the resolutions were read
through Gouverneur Morris, who six months earlier was a Pennsylvania delegate to the Federal Convention, moved for concurrence;
Yates to postpone to allow time for the preparation of alternative resolutions which would "state the facts" regarding the Federal Convention's usurpation of power and explicitly provide "further powers to
the convention" respecting amendments. The unstated motive was
the small attendance in the Senate. There was barely a quorum on
February 1 and a delay might occasion either more absences or new
delegates who could swing the Senate to the Antifederalists. Yates's
objections notwithstanding the Senate rejected the motion to postpone, 10 to 9, and concurred with the House resolve, 11 to 8. [74]

On the same day that the Senate acted, Federalist Egbert Benson
reported to James Madison of their success in the House and anticipated victory in the Senate. He added that some of the foes of the
Constitution had intended "not to submit it to the people." [75] While
that may have been the private inclination of some Antifederalists in
the legislature, no such attempt was made in either house. Nor had it
been publicly suggested during the preceding months. Neither

"Cato" nor "Brutus," "Sydney" nor "Expositor" called for outright rejection of the Constitution by the legislature; while by addressing themselves to the people of the state, they implied that the people should make the ultimate decision respecting the Constitution in their election of Federalist or Antifederalist delegates.

The South Carolina legislature was the last state to approve a state convention during the winter of 1787–1788. It did so after local political issues prolonged legislative action and nearly blocked passage of a convention resolve. Governor Thomas Pinckney laid the Constitution before the legislature on January 10. The next day a committee reported a set of resolves recommending that all the inhabitants of the state who were entitled to vote for representatives to the General Assembly "choose suitable persons to serve as delegates in a state convention for the purpose of considering, and approving or rejecting the Constitution."[76] This committee report became the order of the day for the sixteenth and was the basis of extended debate in the House.

The Senate also had the message of the governor under consideration, and on January 15 a Senate committee reported out a complete set of resolves. Amended in debate, the resolutions as agreed to by the Senate on January 17 provided that the Constitution be submitted to a convention of the people for a full and free investigation and discussion. All inhabitants qualified to vote for members of the General Assembly were entitled to vote for as many delegates as they had members of the House and Senate, on February 21 and 22. The convention was to meet at Charleston on March 3.[77]

Even as these resolutions were being agreed to in the Senate, the House was involved in debate over the very merits of the Constitution. Federalists instigated this debate in an attempt to neutralize an Antifederalist propaganda campaign aimed at back-country members.[78] Under the pretext of explaining their action as delegates to the convention, Charles C. Pinckney, John Rutledge, and Pierce Butler set out to refute the objections of the "opposers of the Federal system." Rawlins Lowndes, a wealthy planter and low country aristocrat, repeated those objections in the House. Lowndes objected to the minority position of the South in the new system. He thought that a two-thirds majority to ratify treaties was not adequate to protect southern interests. He also declared that the commercial interests of the South had been sacrificed to the North while the broad powers of the president, who would always be a northerner, could be used against the South. Lowndes praised the Articles of Confederation and suggested that the states call a new constitutional convention so that "every objection could be met on fair grounds, and adequate remedies applied where necessary." Because Lowndes was the only opponent of the Constitution to speak, he repeatedly apologized for persevering in opposition to a "solid phalanx" of supporters of the Constitution. He did so, he explained, because many of the questions he raised, particularly those regarding the mode of electing both legislators and the president, were brought forth for "a number of respectable men . . . not in the habit of speaking in public."[79]

One of those gentlemen rose "with diffidence" on the last day of debate. James Lincoln of Ninety-Six District spoke for the rights of the people, as opposed to the rights of the states under the new Constitution. He objected to the change in the form of government from a democratic to an aristocratic one. The people, he declared, had fought for the power to govern themselves, and were now asked to give it up to men one thousand miles distant. He contrasted the office of the president, with its unlimited eligibility for reelection, with that of the state governor, which, while filled by a "man born and bred among you," was not eligible for reelection. He also denigrated the guarantee to the states of a republican form of government as a mere chimera, objected to the absence of a Bill of Rights, and concluded by "returning his hearty thanks to the gentleman who had so nobly opposed this Constitution: it was supporting the cause of the people."[80]

Although neither Lowndes's nor Lincoln's remarks went without rebuttal, their arguments apparently found a responsive audience. The next day the House unanimously agreed to call a convention "for the purpose of considering and ratifying or rejecting the Constitution," but on the question regarding the convention's assembling at Charleston, the resolution passed by one vote: 76 to 75.[81] Following this narrow victory, the House, with minor modifications, accepted the Senate resolves of the 15th, including the earlier date for the elections and meeting of the convention, and temporarily dropped the subject of the convention. They returned to these resolutions three weeks later when the House adopted and the Senate accepted an amendment which set the elections on April 11 and 12 with the convention to asemble on May 12.[82] The reasons for upcountry opposition to Charleston were epitomized in a related action of the Assembly on February 23 and 25. On the 23rd, a bill providing for removal of the legislature to Camden passed by a two-vote margin. Two days later, with 22 additional legislators present and voting, the measure was defeated 69 to 63.[83] Underrepresented by the malapportionment of the legislature, upcountry delegates often did not attend sessions, while on a crucial roll call vote, like that of February 25, representatives of Charleston and the surrounding areas could bring in absent delegates to ensure their dominance in the Assembly. Furthermore, upcountry legislators, when in attendance, were often induced to vote against the wishes of their constituents. As Federalist David Ramsay and Antifederalist Aedanus Burke both saw in retrospect, that pattern would apply to the state convention as well.[84]

In contrast to the other states, Rhode Island refused to approve a convention resolve until coerced into it two years later. This response reflected the dominance of the "country party," in both the Assembly and council. The country party came to power in May 1786, on the strength of its paper money program—a program designed to retire the state debt in depreciated currency.[85] When the legislature convened in October 1787, the country party refused to call a state convention. Instead it ordered the Constitution printed and distributed to the towns.[86] In February 1788, when the legislature reconvened, members of the country party, who had campaigned actively against the Constitution in the intervening months, were certain that the Constitution would be defeated if voted on by the freemen in the towns. Therefore, they provided for the freemen to vote in the towns in a statewide referendum to be held on March 24.[87]

That Antifederalists in Congress and the state legislatures (except Rhode Island) accepted the recommendation of the convention obscures the range of options initially available to them. Clearly, Antifederalists in Congress could have opposed transmitting the recommendation of the convention to the states. Antifederalists in the state legislatures could have refused to comply with the recommendation of the convention by refusing to call a convention or by altering the terms for considering the Constitution. A sizeable minority of Antifederalists in the state legislatures indeed exercised those options —in Pennsylvania, where the Antifederalists staged an abortive boycott in order to prevent passage of an election resolution, and in Rhode Island where the Antifederalist majority in the legislature rejected the proposal for a convention in favor of a popular referendum. In Massachusetts and South Carolina, too, Antifederalists were disinclined to accept proposals for state conventions, voted for alternative modes of consideration, and failing that, against the convention resolutions.

Yet, with the exception of Rhode Island, the legislatures did comply with the recommendation of the Federal Convention. That legislative compliance is in marked contrast to their earlier reluctance to relinquish or share power with a revitalized Confederation government. Several things account for the vastly different legislative responses to the proposed amendments to the Articles of Confederation and to the report of the Federal Convention. In the first place, unlike the proposed amendments, which required unanimity, the Constitution did not require nor did it obtain the unanimous consent of the thirteen states. In 1783 the Rhode Island legislature and in 1786 the New York legislature rejected impost amendments. In 1788 Rhode Island and North Carolina rejected the Constitution. Neither rejection had considerable impact. In addition, unlike the impost amendments, the Constitution was a multifaceted proposal. Therefore, though there were men in each state who objected to aspects of the Constitution, there were also aspects they favored, thus ensuring majority support for it: for example, the ban on state impost duties appealed to citizens of Connecticut and New Jersey, and the promise of federal aid along the frontier encouraged a favorable reception in Georgia. Furthermore, Federalists had legislative majorities in seven states in the fall, and the example of their approval of convention resolutions, coupled with the argument that it was undemocratic not to submit the Constitution to the people, was a factor among democratically inclined legislators. The lack of a clear alternative to approval of convention resolutions (due to a temporary breakdown in communication between New York and the state capitals) was also telling. Finally, the fact that the Antifederalist leadership, for whatever reason, accepted the proposal for conventions and the belief that they still had the power necessary to defeat ratification in a state convention induced Antifederalist legislators to acquiesce to the convention resolutions.

Once the legislatures approved elections to state conventions, the range of options available to Antifederalists was more restricted. They could, theoretically, boycott the elections on both pragmatic and constitutional grounds, arguing that the time between the passage of convention resolutions and the elections was too brief, as in Pennsylvania, and that the whole process of revision was incompatible with the provisions of the Articles of Confederation. Such a boycott, though, would be difficult to organize, counterproductive, and contrary to the previous decade's political experience. To effect a complete boycott of statewide elections was difficult. It required a high degree of coordination as well as agreement among all potential Antifederalist voters that a boycott was the best course of action. Such agreement would be particularly difficult to obtain for Antifederalists were, as I have suggested above, divided about the Constitution. Some believed it needed to be amended; others that it should be rejected altogether. Neither goal could necessarily be secured through a boycott. The problem of securing support for a boycott was compounded by the realization among voters that to fail to offer candidates to the state conventions was to yield the political arena to Federalists who were generally opposed to anything short of complete and unconditional ratification. Finally, by 1787, there existed in every state a history of bi-partisan divisions, the predecessor of modern party development.[88] In other words, the men who viewed the Constitution critically in 1787 did so with a background of active participation in the political process. They were used to organizing politically, to nominating candidates, and to appealing to the voters for popular support. That experience conditioned how Antifederalists reacted following the passage of convention elections resolutions.

Antifederalist acceptance of Article V of the Constitution was also conditioned by the realization that the only other alternative to participation was violence. In the fall and winter of 1787 Antifederalists rejected that alternative for two reasons. First, the Constitution was not so objectionable as to justify civil war. Second, civil strife was unnecessary, for Antifederalists believed the Constitution could be defeated through the state conventions.

In their attempt to block unconditional ratification of the Constitution, Antifederalists started the election campaigns considerably handicapped. At the outset, Federalists had legislative majorities in seven states. If those legislative majorities translated into convention ones, they were only two states short of their goal. Antifederalists, on the other hand, had such legislative dominance in only three states during the fall. They, therefore, needed to maintain their control in New York, Rhode Island, and Virginia, and solidify and expand their support in at least two other states. That they did just that in the elections of convention delegates is one measure of the political acumen of the Antifederalists.

NOTES TO
CHAPTER 2

1. *Hartford Connecticut Courant,* 24 December 1787, 30 March 1788. Gerry alluded to a meeting with Lee in his letter to James Warren, 18 October 1787, Sang Autograph Collection, ICarbS.

2. See my "The Impact of the Constitution on State Politics: New York as a Test Case," in James K. Martin, ed., *The Human Dimensions of Nation Making: Essays on Colonial and Revolutionary America* (Madison, 1976), p. 273.

3. To Adams, 5 October; to Shippen, 2 October; to Randolph, 16 October; and to Mason, 1 October 1787, James C. Ballagh, ed., *The Letters of Richard Henry Lee*, 2 vols. (New York, 1911), 2: 430–47, 450–58.

4. *Ibid.,* pp. 440, 447.

5. *Ibid.,* pp. 439–40.

6. New York, 1787. On Lee as the author of the *Letters* see Boyd, "Impact," p. 276, n. 14.

7. To George Washington, 11 October 1787, Ballagh, *Lee,* 2: 449.

8. To Edmund Randolph, 16 October 1787, *ibid.*, pp. 451–52.

9. Richard Henry Lee to Samuel Adams, 5 October 1787, Ballagh, *Lee,* 2: 447. Some of the more prominent Antifederalists to endorse the idea of a second convention were Mercy Warren, "A Columbian Patriot"; James Winthrop, "Agrippa"; Samuel Bryan, "Centinel"; James Hutchinson, "Old Whig"; Melancton Smith, "Plebian"; and Arthur Lee, "Cincinnatus."

10. Antifederalists' objections are summarized in Jackson Turner Main, *The Antifederalists: Critics of the Constitution, 1781–1788* (Chapel Hill, 1961), chaps. 6 and 7. The specific criticisms are taken from one or more of the essays cited immediately above. Each was raised by a far greater number of men, both in print and in the state conventions.

11. Jackson Turner Main, *Political Parties Before the Constitution* (Chapel Hill, 1975), chap. 7.

12. *Ibid.*

13. Jensen, *Ratification,* 2: 67–94.

14. *Ibid.,* pp. 95–96.

15. Tench Coxe to James Madison, 29 September 1787, *ibid.*, p. 121.

16. Samuel Hodgdon to Timothy Pickering, 29 September 1787, *ibid.*, p. 123.

17. *Ibid.*, pp. 103–10.

18. Oliver Wolcott stated that the House would have adopted the Constitution if it had been "in their power," to Mrs. Wolcott, 17 October 1787, Wolcott Papers, CtHi.

19. Allen Johnson and Dumas Malone, eds., *Dictionary of American Biography,* 20 vols. (New York, 1928–1937), 19: 309–10; Christopher Collier, *Roger Sherman's Connecticut* (Middletown, 1971), 219n; DAB, 20: 293–94.

20. Stephen Mix Mitchell to William Samuel Johnson, 18 September 1787, Burnett, *Letters,* 8: 645–46; Hughes to Charles Tillinghast, 28 November 1787, Hughes Papers, Personal Miscellany, DLC.

21. Hugh Ledlie to John Lamb, 15 January 1788, Lamb Papers, NHi.

22. Van Beck Hall, *Politics Without Parties . . .* (Pittsburgh, 1972), pp. 235–47.

23. *Ibid.*, p. 249.

24. William Lyman, a representative from Easthampton, Hampshire County, was

"surprised" by the absence of so many western legislators, to Joseph Clarke, 23 October 1787, Misc. Papers, MNF. The numbers of men in attendance are taken from the only recorded roll call vote of the session, 13 November, House Journals, M-Ar.

25. 18 October 1787, Sang Autograph Collection, ICarbS.

26. Report of debates, *Boston Gazette,* 24 October 1787.

27. *Boston Massachusetts Centinel,* 27 October 1787.

28. Kenneth Coleman, *The American Revolution in Georgia, 1763–1789* (Athens, 1958), p. 271.

29. Assembly Journal, 26 October, G-Ar. The resolves were printed in the *Georgia State Gazette*, 27 October 1787.

30. Richard McCormick, *Experiment in Independence: New Jersey in the Critical Period* (New Brunswick, 1950), p. 270. During the first federal elections it was reported that Clark, a candidate for the House of Representatives, made this and a similar offer to members of the state convention. He vigorously denied the charge. The conflicting testimony is in the *New Brunswick Gazette,* 10 February 1789, and the *Elizabethtown New Jersey Journal,* 4 February 1789.

31. Main, *Political Parties,* chap. 9 is complemented by the discussion in Gordon DenBoer, "The House of Delegates and the Evolution of Political Parties in Virginia, 1782–1792" (unpublished Ph.D. thesis, University of Wisconsin, 1972). In this and the following discussion I have relied on DenBoer's able discussion. I accept his analysis throughout, but have attempted to place Virginia's action in a broader context.

32. *Journal of the House of Delegates* (Richmond, 1828), p. 3.

33. *Petersburg Virginia Gazette,* 1 November 1787. A similar although briefer account was in the *Richmond Virginia Independent Chronicle,* 31 October.

34. *Richmond Virginia Independent Chronicle,* 31 October 1787.

35. *Journal,* p. 15. The action of the House was reported in letters from Edmund Randolph to James Madison, 28 October, Madison Papers, DLC; John Pierce to Henry Knox, 27 October, Knox Papers, MHi; and David Stuart to George Washington, 27 October 1787, quoted in George Washington to James Madison, 5 November 1787, Fitzpatrick, *Washington,* 29: 303–5.

36. Pierce to Knox, 27 October 1787, Knox Papers, MHi.

37. Stuart to Washington, 27 October, quoted in Washington to Madison, 5 November 1787, Fitzpatrick, *Washington,* 29: 304.

38. *Journal,* p. 77.

39. Archibald Stuart to Madison, 2 December 1787, Madison Papers, DLC.

40. Quoted in Washington to Madison, 7 December 1787, Fitzpatrick, *Washington,* 29: 334.

41. Mss draft of "A bill concerning the convention to be held in June next," Papers of the House of Delegates, Vi.

42. William W. Hening, ed., *The Statutes at Large of Virginia,* 13 vols. (Richmond, 1809–23), 12: 46–63.

43. Archibald Stuart used the phrase while commenting on the Hopkins motion of 30 November, to Madison, 2 December 1787, Madison Papers, DLC. It was equally applicable to the Smith resolution.

44. Edmund Randolph to Madison, 27 December 1787, Madison Papers, DLC.

45. To Nathan Dane, 21 November 1787, Dane Papers, MBevHi.

46. On Tilton as "Timoleon," see John A. Munroe, ed., *A History of Dionysius, Tyrant of Delaware* (Philadelphia, 1787/Newark, 1958), v–vi.

47. Philip A. Crowl, *Maryland During and After the Revolution*, (Baltimore, 1943), pp. 96–107; DAB, 4: 34–37.

48. *Baltimore Maryland Journal*, 28 September 1787.

49. *Baltimore Maryland Gazette*, 28 September 1787.

50. *Ibid*. For an additional attack on Chase for his antifederalism, see "A German," in the *Baltimore Maryland Journal*, 25 September 1787.

51. "A Watchman," *Baltimore Maryland Journal*, 30 October 1787.

52. *Ibid*. Three months earlier Federalists denied the "majority of individuals composing the society can rightfully control [i.e., instruct] the constitutional legislature," "Aristides" (Alexander Contee Hanson), 3 August 1787. In August, the constituents demanded paper money, a measure Hanson opposed.

53. *Votes and Proceedings of the House of Delegates* (Annapolis 1788), pp. 9–13.

54. *Votes and Proceedings of the Senate*, (Annapolis, 1788), pp. 5, 7.

55. Walter Clark, ed., *State Records of North Carolina, 1776–1790*, 16 vols., (Winston and Goldsboro, N.C., 1895–1905), 20: 196–98, 290.

56. John Sullivan to Jeremy Belknap, 4 October 1787, Belknap Papers, Massachusetts Historical Society *Collections*, 6th ser., 4: 140.

57. Journal of the House of Representatives, 13 December 1787, Nh-Ar.

58. Jere R. Daniell, *Experiment in Republicanism: New Hampshire Politics and the American Revolution, 1741–1794* (Cambridge, 1970), p. 212.

59. In *The Eleventh Pillar: New York State and the Federal Constitution* (Ithaca, 1966), Linda DePauw deemphasizes Clinton's role as an Antifederalist. As early as 1 October 1787, however, John Stevens, Jr., remarked that "the Governor, Lamb and Willet are openly opposed to it [the Constitution]"; and on 27 October reiterated that "the Governor and those who are in office are opposed to it," to John Stevens, Stevens Family Papers, NjHi. Samuel B. Webb also mentioned Clinton by name as one of four or five in New York City who opposed the Constitution, to Joseph Barrell, 13 January 1787, Worthington C. Ford., ed., *Correspondence and Journals of Samuel B. Webb*, 3 vols. (Lancaster, Pa., 1893–94), 3: 89–91. Newspapers also noted Clinton's opposition: "A letter from a member of Congress dated September 23," *Philadelphia Independent Gazetteer*, 26 September 1787; and anonymous articles in the *Lansingburgh Northern Centinel*, 8 October and 11 December; and the *Philadelphia Pennsylvania Gazette*, 29 December 1787 and 23 January 1788. Alfred Young discusses the various leaders within the Clintonian party, their political offices and family ties in *The Democratic-Republicans of New York . . .* (Chapel Hill, 1967), pp. 33–58.

60. In addition to Young, *Democratic-Republicans*, see Main, *Political Parties*, chap. 5.

61. The *New York Journal* published essays of "Cato," 27 September, 11 and 25 October, 8 and 22 November; "Brutus," 18 October, 1 and 15 November; "Countryman," 21 and 23 November; "Cincinnatus," 1, 8, 15, and 22 November; "Old Whig," 27 and 28 November; and "Timoleon," 1 November 1787. *Letters from the Federal Farmer* were published serially in the *Poughkeepsie Country Journal*, 14 November 1787 to 2 January 1788. The *Albany Gazette* published "Cato" on 4 and 25 October, 8 and 17 November, and 6 December 1787. On the country circulation of the Thursday edition, see Charles Tillinghast to Hugh Hughes, 27–28 January 1788, Hughes Papers, Personal Miscellany, DLC.

62. On Lamb's role in New England, see chap. 3. For evidence of the distribution of "Centinel" upstate see the *Albany Gazette*, 15 November, 6 and 20 December 1787, and 3 January 1788; the *Hudson Weekly Gazette*, 1 November; and the *Lansingburgh*

Northern Centinel, 25 December 1787. See also Ab Van Vechten to Jeremiah Van Rensselaer, 11 January, thanking him for a packet of *Letters from the Federal Farmer,* Mitchel Autograph Collection, PHi.

63. The letter is printed in Farrand, *Records,* 3: 244–47. The timing of the letter was such that Walter Rutherford "suspected Cl[inton] had a hand in it," to John Rutherford, 8 January 1788, Rutherford Collection, NHi.

64. Richard Sill to Jeremiah Wadsworth, 12 January 1788, Wadsworth Papers, CtHi.

65. *Lansingburgh Northern Centinel,* 15 January 1788.

66. See Smith's reply, 28 January 1788, Yates Papers, NN.

67. To Jeremiah Wadsworth, 12 January 1788, Wadsworth Papers, CtHi.

68. To Joseph Barrell, Ford, *Correspondence,* 3: 90.

69. To Abraham Yates, 28 January 1788, Yates Papers, NN.

70. To Hugh Hughes, 27–28 January 1788, Hughes Papers, Personal Miscellany, DLC.

71. *Journal of the Assembly* (New York, 1788), pp. 47–49.

72. Egbert Benson to James Madison, 1 February 1788, Fogg Autograph Collection, MeHi.

73. Report of debates, *New York Daily Advertiser,* 12 February 1788.

74. *Journal of the Senate* (New York, 1788), pp. 20–21. See also the report of the debates in the *New York Daily Advertiser,* 8 February 1788.

75. 1 February 1788, Fogg Autograph Collection, MeHi.

76. 8, 10 and 11 January 1788, Journals of the House of Representatives of the State of South Carolina, Sc-Ar. Subsequent citations will be by date only. The debates in the House have been published in *Debates Which Arose in the House . . . on the Constitution* (Charleston, 1831). This is more detailed than the journals.

77. Journals of the Senate of the State of South Carolina, Sc-Ar. Subsequent citations will be by date only.

78. David Ramsay to Benjamin Rush, 17 February 1788, Robert L. Brunhouse, ed., "David Ramsay on the Ratification of the Constitution in South Carolina, 1787–1788," *Journal of Southern History,* 9 (1943): 553.

79. *Debates,* pp. 4, 34, 31.

80. *Ibid.,* p. 54

81. *Ibid.,* pp. 56–60.

82. These were the initial House provisions dropped on 19 January following the narrow roll call victory on the place of meeting.

83. See Merrill Jensen, *The New Nation: A History of the United States During the Confederation* (New York, 1950), p. 328.

84. Aedanus Burke to John Lamb, 23 June 1788, Lamb Papers, NHi.

85. Irwin H. Polishook, *Rhode Island and the Union: 1774–1795* (Evanston, 1969), pp. 191–92; and John P. Kaminski, "Paper Politics: The Northern State Loan-Offices During The Confederation, 1783–1790" (unpublished Ph.D. Thesis, University of Wisconsin, 1972), pp. 224–25.

86. William R. Staples, *Rhode Island in the Continental Congress 1765–1790* (Providence, 1870), pp. 584–85.

87. *Ibid.,* pp. 586–87. For the Antifederalists' campaigning, see Polishook, *Rhode Island and the Union,* pp. 191–99, and Kaminski, "Paper Politics," pp. 224–28.

88. See Main, *Political Parties, passim.*

Chapter 3

FALL ELECTIONS AND WINTER CONVENTIONS IN THE NORTH

By the time twelve legislatures agreed to submit the Constitution to state conventions, seven states had met in convention and six had ratified the Constitution. Local circumstances undercut any significant opposition in four of these states. Thus, despite the limited distribution of Antifederalist pamphlets and broadsides, and campaigning by some Antifederalist candidates, Delaware, Georgia, New Jersey, and Connecticut ratified the Constitution, the first three unanimously, before the end of January 1788. These early ratifications were important to Federalists for they gave their campaign momentum. The unanimity of the Georgia and New Jersey conventions was especially encouraging because considerable numbers of delegates arrived at those state conventions with serious reservations about the Constitution. These Antifederalists, nonetheless, yielded to the superior weight of numbers and voted with the Federalist majorities to make the two states' ratifications unanimous. In Connecticut some Antifederalists proved more recalcitrant and the vote for ratification was 128 to 40. Even there, however, several prominent Antifederalists voted with the majority and those who did not acquiesced in the decision of the convention.[1]

Antifederalists were aware of the possibility of defections in the conventions well before the pattern was set in Georgia, New Jersey, and Connecticut. Initially, however, Antifederalists concentrated their efforts on the antecedent problem of mobilization. In three of the first seven states to consider the Constitution Antifederalists were well prepared to do this. In Pennsylvania, Massachusetts, and New Hampshire there was considerable hostility toward the Constitution from the outset. Antifederalists in those states had both a positive program and leaders capable of converting latent hostility into concrete political action. The initial success of that effort, particularly in Massachusetts and New Hampshire, threatened for a time to disrupt the Federalist drive for ratification. Ironically, it also ensured the ultimate success of the Constitution.

Pennsylvania Antifederalists took the lead in this effort. Even before the state legislature approved a convention resolve, the Antifederalist leadership in Philadelphia met with George Mason to agree upon common objections and to coordinate strategy.[2] Two days after the legislature called a convention, and before Federalists began their propaganda campaign, Antifederalists published the first of six broadsides released before the state election.

The *Address of the Subscribers* was a concise, well-reasoned statement of the position of Pennsylvania Antifederalists. A three-page leaflet printed in both English and German, it became one of the few Antifederalist statements widely reprinted—in all nine of the Philadelphia newspapers and in the *Pittsburgh Gazette*. In the *Address* sixteen of the Assembly seceders presented their view of the events of September 28 and 29 as well as a justification of their action. The signers acknowledged that the Articles of Confederation needed amendment and proposed that Congress be granted the power to regulate commerce and collect an impost. But, they warned, the proposed Constitution destroyed both the Articles and the state constitution. They adamantly opposed granting to the central government the power of internal taxation, noted the absence of annual elections, which were the bulwark of the rights of freemen in Pennsylvania, and argued that freedom of the press was in danger.[3]

Samuel Bryan's *Address to the People of Pennsylvania* followed the *Address of the Subscribers* by four days. As "Centinel" Bryan warned that the preservation of those liberties guaranteed by the state constitution—freedom of speech and press, trial by jury, sanctity of one's home—was "now at stake and dependent on your conduct." The members of the Federal Convention, Bryan charged, were imbued with the political theories of John Adams. As a result they departed from what Bryan viewed as the best form of government: a single legislative body elected for a short term with restrictions on the number of terms its members could serve. With control of the mode of their own appointment, and vested with the virtually unlimited power to tax "for the general welfare," Bryan added, the proposed

government "would be in practice a permanent ARISTOCRACY."
Indeed, Bryan added, some of the framers of this government intended to create a despotic government by "making no provision for
liberty of the press, that grand palladium of freedom and scourge of
tyrants," while actually abolishing trial by jury in civil cases. "Be-
sides," Bryan concluded, "the first essay [the Constitution] on the
difficult subject" of government may not be "so well digested as it
ought to be" while, if the Constitution is found to be "fraught with
dangers and inconveniences, a future general convention, being in
possession of the objections will be better enabled to plan a suitable
government."[4]

This was the major theme Antifederalists developed throughout
the campaign. In "Centinel" II Bryan stressed "that the Constitution
would necessarily annihilate the particular [state] governments" and
the liberties of the people. In "Old Whig" IV and V he, with James
Hutchinson, restated the Antifederalist alternative: a general convention called by Congress where "the plan may be reconsidered, deliber-
ately received and corrected [and] formed anew on the principles of a
confederacy of free republics."[5]

Bryan was not the sole spokesman for the Antifederalists in
Pennsylvania, nor were the objections and alternatives he proposed
original with him. Mason's objections raised similar criticisms and
many Antifederalists endorsed the idea of a second convention. The
Freeman's Journal, Independent Gazetteer, and other Philadelphia newspapers published Antifederalist essays by a "Democratic Federalist,"
"Nestor," "An Old Constitutionalist," and other unnamed correspondents. These men were not always in perfect agreement. The
"Democratic Federalist" favored the Articles of Confederation while
"An Old Constitutionalist" felt that altering or amending the new
Constitution would be sufficient. One correspondent raised only four
objections to the proposed Constitution; another thirteen. "M.C."
argued the opponents of the Constitution should be allowed to draft a
Bill of Rights which could be forwarded to the state conventions to be
considered with the Constitution itself.[6] While there was a diversity
of sentiment among the Antifederalists respecting the degree and extent of power that should be granted to the central government, there
was agreement that the Constitution allowed too great a grant. Similarly, while there was disagreement whether the basic frame of government should be the Articles of Confederation or the new Constitution, there was general agreement that either one needed amendment,
and that could be best achieved through a meeting of a second constitutional convention.

Pennsylvania Antifederalists campaigned for convention delegates on the issue of a second constitutional convention. In this campaign the Philadelphia newspapers, which published far more Federalist essays, were of less importance than broadsides. Neither the *Independent Gazetteer* nor the *Freeman's Journal,* the two major Antifederalist newspapers, circulated west of the Susquehanna River rapidly enough, or in quantities large enough to influence public opinion prior to the November 6 election. Recognizing the need for special efforts, Antifederalists worked overtime distributing copies of the *Address of the Subscribers,* "Centinel" I and II, "Old Whig" IV and V, William Findley's *An Officer of the Late Continental Army,* and John Nicholson's *A View of the Proposed Constitution.*[7]

The quantity of Antifederalist literature distributed before the election can only be surmised. Samuel Bryan later remarked that "many hundred pounds were expended" in printing and distributing his and others' essays.[8] During one four-day period in November, James Hutchinson, John Nicholson, Edward Pole, and James Boyd purchased more than one hundred copies of *Letters from the Federal Farmer* from bookseller Robert Aitken.[9] Whatever the number, Antifederalist pamphlets and broadsides did gain extensive circulation as packets of "Centinels" and "Old Whigs" were given to stage drivers and mail riders to post along their routes and to deliver to tavern and inn keepers. Also, a single "Centinel" was often read by or to a large number of men. In October Bryan, Hutchinson, and Nicholson made certain that their political allies of the previous decade received their full complement of such propaganda. John Ewing, for example, carried copies of the *Address of the Subscribers* to Joseph Hart in Bucks County, arriving in Newton on October 3.[10] Francis Murray, also in Newton, received both "Centinel" and "Old Whig" essays from John Nicholson, as well as a copy of Nicholson's *A View of the Proposed Constitution.*[11] It was reported from Easton, in Northampton County, that George Bryan's "Centinels" and "Old Whigs" served "only to light the pipes of our German farmers,"[12] indicating that both circulated there. In Luzerne County at least four men received copies of Nicholson's pamphlet, although some of the recipients were supporters of the Constitution.[13]

Among the southeastern counties there was also widespread distribution of the Antifederalist essays. The *Lancaster Zeitung* published "Centinel" I and the *Address of the Subscribers* during October. In addition, Samuel and George Bryan "constantly" sent material to a Constitutionalist supporter in Chester County. Richard Henry Lee distributed copies of his *Letters* at Chester on election day.[14] Finally,

Federalists repeatedly denied that "Centinel" and "Old Whig" were effective among the German populations in York, Lancaster, Dauphin, and Berks counties, indicating that broadside copies of both essays were circulating in the area.[15]

The *Address of the Subscribers* and other Antifederalist broadsides and pamphlets were carried farther west by the joint efforts of the city leadership and members of the Assembly and council from the western counties. News of the secession of the minority of the Assembly reached Carlisle, Cumberland County, on October 3. That evening a Federalist-dominated meeting "severely reprehended" the county's delegates for their secession.[16] In response to that attack Robert Whitehill and his followers did all they could against the Constitution; "paper against paper and almost man against man."[17] Whitehill was from East Pennsborough township, in the eastern sector of the county. In western Cumberland County Benjamin Blythe duplicated Whitehill's efforts by distributing copies of Nicholson's *A View of the Proposed Constitution* and other Antifederalist papers in Shippensburg and the surrounding area.[18]

The *Address of the Subscribers* and other Antifederalist literature also circulated in the four counties lying between the Susquehanna and the Alleghenies, i.e., in Huntingdon, Bedford, Franklin, and Northumberland counties. Representatives of Franklin, Bedford, and Northumberland signed the *Address of the Subscribers,* which was designed as a justification of their conduct to their constituents, and carried it with them on their return to their home counties. In Franklin County it and the "Centinel" essays were so widely dispersed that one Federalist, in thanking Benjamin Rush for some Federalist material, remarked that "nothing on that side of the subject had appeared for so long a time that we thought there were no Centinels in Philadelphia but the one. . . ."[19] Presumably Nicholson's pamphlet circulated in the four counties also. He had correspondents in both Franklin and Northumberland with whom he later worked in an attempt to repeal Pennsylvania's ratification, and he probably sent them essays and pamphlets in October 1787 as well.

All the members of the Assembly from the three westernmost counties—Fayette, Westmoreland, and Washington—with the exception of Hugh H. Brackenridge—voted on the morning of September 28 against calling a convention, remained away that afternoon, and signed the *Address of the Subscribers* the next day. They also distributed that and other Antifederalist literature among their constituents during October. William Findley, a representative from

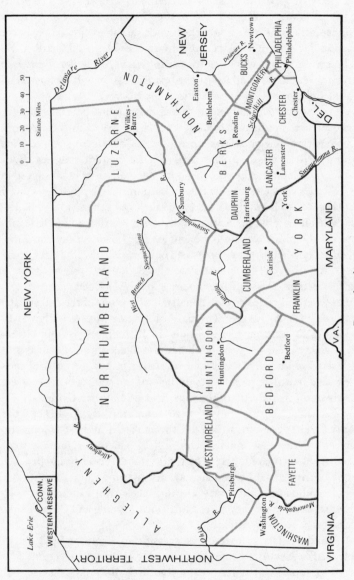

Pennsylvania.

Courtesy of the University of Wisconsin Cartographic Lab.

Westmoreland County, and his "copartners in iniquity" were reported "fraught with opposition papers" on their way westward.[20] The printing of the *Address of the Subscribers* in the *Pittsburgh Gazette* on October 20 apparently came from one of the broadside copies circulating in the area. Findley submitted a second copy to the *Gazette* on October 27. Nicholson in turn was corresponding with Alexander Fowler, a Pittsburgh merchant and Constitutionalist, and may have forwarded to him copies of *A View of the Proposed Constitution*.[21]

Having alerted the people to the dangers in the Constitution, Antifederalists nominated candidates and competed in the elections for convention delegates. Constitutionalists' strength, and therefore Antifederalists', was based primarily in the western counties. Conversely, the Republicans and therefore Federalists were strongest in the East. Nevertheless, Antifederalists nominated candidates in at least three of the Republican eastern counties and the city of Philadelphia. In Philadelphia the Antifederalist slate was headed by Benjamin Franklin. Franklin was no opponent of the Constitution but Antifederalists hoped his name at the head of their ticket would draw some votes away from the Federalist slate.[22] The four other candidates— Charles Pettit, David Rittenhouse, John Steinmetz, and James Irvine—were all state constitutionalists, as was one of the Federalists' nominees, Chief Justice Thomas McKean. McKean, however, pledged to support the Constitution "in all its parts without alteration or amendment."[23] Steinmetz was also allegedly a Federalist, and Pettit later disavowed allegiance to either party.[24] Antifederalists were forced to utilize such tactics in the city and county because of the overwhelming popularity of the Constitution in urban centers.

Elsewhere Antifederalists were more forthright. In Luzerne County, Walter Stewart attempted to "make an interest among the opposers of the new government."[25] In Chester County, Antifederalists, "stimulated thereto by their Grand Master Judge Bryan," sought to divide the Federalist majority by proposing a number of lists of candidates and thereby electing their own candidates.[26] In neither instance were they successful. Both Luzerne and Chester sent Federalists to the convention.

Antifederalists were more successful in Lancaster and Berks counties. Few details are known concerning the former election. The newspaper report of the returns for Lancaster lists only the victors, although it is evident that Antifederalists offered their own candidates and secured one seat, that of John Whitehill.[27] In Berks they fared even better. As Benjamin Rush put it after the election, the entire Berks delegation would be Antifederalist: "Men capable of believing that George Bryan is infallible and that the President of the United States will black their faces . . . [and] sell them for slaves at public vendue."[28] Dauphin County followed the lead of its eastern neighbor and sent an Antifederalist contingent of William Brown, Adam Orth, and John Hanna—Constitutionalists all. York County elected Federalists, although the published votes, ranging from a high of 916 to a low of 649, indicate that the elections were contested there as well.[29]

West of the Susquehanna Antifederalists were even more aggressive. In Cumberland County the contest was both heated and lengthy. It also intruded into the fall Assembly elections. On October 3, a Federalist-dominated meeting at Carlisle condemned the county's representatives for seceding from the Assembly, praised the Constitution, and appointed a committee to "form a ticket for a councillor and representatives for the county."[30] The men named to that ticket are not known, in part because Robert Whitehill, Thomas Kennedy, and William Mitchell were equal to the challenge. On October 13 they successfully beat back the attempt to unseat them.

Following the Assembly elections, and in preparation for the November 6 convention election, Antifederalists in the county held a convention on Robert Whitehill's farm at Stony Ridge to agree on a slate of candidates.[31] Following this Antifederalist caucus, a county-wide meeting attended by both Federalists and Antifederalists was held at Carlisle on October 25 "in order to form a ticket for members for the ensuing convention." Federalist John Armstrong was in the chair and a committee consisting of representatives of each township in the county was appointed. Antifederalists dominated that committee which proposed four candidates—John Harris, Jonathan Hoge, John Reynolds, and William Brown. The last three and Robert Whitehill were elected ten days later. All four voted against ratification.[32]

Less is known regarding the campaigns or the opposing candidates in Franklin, Bedford, Huntingdon, and Northumberland. Huntingdon and Northumberland's assemblymen signed the *Address of the Subscribers* and presumably were candidates for the convention, although there is no concrete evidence of an opposition to William Wilson, John Boyd, or Benjamin Elliot—all three Federalists—elected from the two counties. Abraham Smith and James McCalmont, both signers of the *Address of the Subscribers,* were defeated in Franklin County, although one of their two opponents, Richard Baird, voted against ratification.[33]

In the Far West Antifederalists also nominated candidates and campaigned for their election. Thus, in a speech at Greensburgh, Westmoreland County, Federalist Hugh Henry Brackenridge declared statements in the *Address of the Subscribers* were lies. In response, William Findley, writing as an "Assemblyman," asserted as one of the subscribers that "the facts in the *Address* are true."[34] Brackenridge, in turn, charged Findley with a misdemeanor for attempting to break up the Assembly, and in subsequent issues of the *Pittsburgh Gazette* continued to attack Findley, a candidate for the convention from Westmoreland County, whom he labeled the "Westmoreland Weaver."[35] Findley and two other Antifederalists were elected.

Although the record is incomplete, certain points can be established. Antifederalists mounted an aggressive propaganda campaign in Pennsylvania and circulated Antifederalist literature throughout the state before the November 6 balloting. In at least fourteen of the state's eighteen electoral units (seventeen counties and the city of Philadelphia) they nominated candidates and competed in the elections for delegates. Furthermore, while Federalists elected twice as many delegates as Antifederalists, (the division was 46 to 23) the latter did not yield. Instead they persisted in their opposition. Samuel Bryan, before the assembling of the convention, published his "Centinel" III.[36] John Nicholson sent George Latimer a copy of the *Letters from the Federal Farmer* in the hope that Latimer, a state Constitutionalist elected as a Federalist, would be persuaded by Lee's analysis of the need for previous amendments. James Hutchinson, Edward Pole, and James Boyd also apparently tried to persuade delegates and the electorate of the need for previous amendments, for all four men purchased additional copies of the *Letters* in late November.[37]

William Findley and James McLene carried their opposition to the Assembly, which met in Philadelphia on October 24. Before the meeting of the convention it was necessary for the Assembly to set the salaries and per diem expenses of the delegates. Nothing further was required. However, when a bill providing for those items was brought to the floor for its third and final reading McLene "moved to introduce a sentence into the bill which declared the number of members necessary to form a quorum should be the same . . . as for the general assembly," i.e. two-thirds. Federalists, realizing that the Antifederalist minority could again secede and thereby block ratification by the state, rejected the amendment.[38]

These efforts by Antifederalists in the legislature and out were part of an organized effort within the state. The leaders in this state campaign in turn coordinated their efforts with those of the Anti-federalist leadership in New York. During the first week in November, Richard Henry Lee, on his way from New York to Virginia, met with William Findley, James McLene, John Nicholson, Charles Pettit, James Hutchinson, Samuel or George Bryan, John Smiley, and Abraham Smith at the home of William Shippen.[39] Although no minutes of that meeting are extant, it seems likely that Lee informed the Pennsylvanians of the proposal for simultaneous meetings of the state conventions in April or May so that the conventions could jointly sponsor a list of amendments previous to ratification. Acting upon this information, the Pennsylvanians decided on their strategy for the forthcoming convention. They initiated a petition campaign calling for an adjournment of the state convention until April or May and, as William Shippen informed his son, proposed as their first step in the convention to move for that postponement.[40]

The proposal for simultaneous spring conventions was also communicated to Massachusetts Antifederalists, albeit only after the legislature had approved a January convention.[41] Indicative of this late start, the Massachusetts counterpart to Samuel Bryan's "Centinel" I, Elbridge Gerry's letter to the general court, appeared in print on November 3. In this letter Gerry outlined his objections to the new Constitution. The people were not adequately represented, nor was their right of election properly secured. The powers of the legislature were not sufficiently defined and there was an undue blending of executive and legislative functions in both the president and the Senate. Finally there was no Bill of Rights. Despite these objections, Gerry did not call for the rejection of the Constitution. Instead he proposed that it be amended before ratification.[42]

Gerry's letter circulated extensively throughout New England. It was complemented by a host of public letters, essays, and pamphlets, the most conspicuous of which included Samuel Bryan's "Centinel" I and II; the "Dissent of the Minority"; James Hutchinson's "Old Whig" essays, James Tilton's "Timoleon"; Richard Henry Lee's *Letters from the Federal Farmer,* and James Warren's "Republican Federalist" articles. The major theme in these essays, and through them the issue in the campaign for convention delegates, was the Antifederalist demand for amendments previous to adoption of the Constitution. The means to secure those amendments, implicit in Gerry's and Lee's letters, and explicit in Hutchinson's and Warren's, was a second convention called by the Confederation Congress "where the plan may be framed anew."[43]

There were two major sources of Antifederalist literature during the campaign for convention delegates in Massachusetts. One source was New York where John Lamb oversaw the distribution of a broadside "Centinel" I and II throughout western Massachusetts. Antifederalist printer John Greenleaf reprinted Richard Henry Lee's *Federal Farmer Letters* which he shipped to Edward Powars, editor of the the *American Herald,* for sale in Boston. Complementing this influx of Antifederalist literature from outside the state, James Warren oversaw the writing, publication, and distribution of essays and pamphlets from Boston. In October he arranged for the republication of essays sent to him by Gerry. He also wrote the "Republican Federalist" essays published in the *Massachusetts Centinel,* and "The Disadvantages of Federalism Upon the New Plan," an Antifederalist appeal to Boston tradesmen which he and James Winthrop distributed among members of the state legislature and throughout Boston.[44] Winthrop and Benjamin Austin, Jr., also went to neighboring counties with various Antifederalist essays, distributing them to local leaders and posting them along the road in local taverns and inns.[45] Gerry's major contribution to this effort was his letter of October 18 which prompted men like Warren, Winthrop, and Austin to act. He also coordinated the various efforts of Antifederalists; corresponded with men like John Bacon and Oliver Phelps in the West; and conferred directly with Warren, Winthrop, and Austin in the East.[46]

Statewide distribution of Antifederalist literature was only the first step in the Antifederalist campaign. Within the counties and towns local leaders disseminated this literature as part of their campaigns for election to the state convention. The records of these local electoral contests are far from complete, but enough evidence remains to illustrate the breadth as well as the limits of the Antifederalist campaign.

In Boston, the likelihood of an Antifederalist victory was slim indeed, given the overwhelming popularity of the Constitution among urban voters. Nevertheless Antifederalists were active. Edward Powars, editor of the *American Herald*, in the weeks preceding the election, published the Antifederalist "John DeWitt" essays and Warren's "Disadvantages." He also reprinted various Antifederalist articles from out of state, including George Clinton's "Cato" I.[47] Numerous lists of potential convention delegates were also printed in the *Herald* and other Boston newspapers. There was no clearly identifiable Antifederalist slate, although Samuel Adams, Benjamin Austin, and James Sullivan were all nominated. On December 5 the "Mechanicks of the North End" warned against a mixed list as a "gilded antifederal pill" but a compromise was worked out between the town's North and South End caucuses.[48] The compromise list elected on December 7, included three men suspected of harboring Antifederalist sentiments: John Hancock, Samuel Adams, and Charles Jarvis, Jr. Elsewhere in Suffolk County three or four other Antifederalists were also elected, including General William Heath from Roxbury. A member of the Massachusetts Senate and critic of the Constitution, Heath campaigned actively and defeated Judge Charles Sumner for one of the town's two seats in the convention.[49]

Antifederalists also competed in a number of elections in Plymouth, Bristol, and Barnstable counties. At Taunton, in Bristol County, at a meeting during the second week of October, it was decided to oppose the Constitution. Phanuel Bishop, who attended that meeting, was a member of the lower house. He attended the session in October, where he obtained copies of various Antifederalist essays. Upon his return to Rehoboth, he distributed them throughout Plymouth as well as Bristol and Barnstable counties. He was described as a "chief opponent" of the Constitution in that area.[50] One sign of the effect of his opposition came from the town of Sandwich which instructed its delegates to oppose ratification of the Constitution. Bishop himself was elected with two other Antifederalists from Rehoboth while Antifederalist Charles Turner won in Scituate.[51]

North of Boston the Antifederalists also campaigned aggressively. Federalists complained that Gerry's letter to the General Court did "great injury" in Middlesex and Essex counties, as did copies of "Centinel" and "Old Whig," carried there by James Winthrop.[52] Despite these efforts, Antifederalists suffered a conspicuous setback at Cambridge when the combined votes for Gerry, Nathan Dane, and James Winthrop were less than those cast for either Federalist candidate, Francis and Stephen Dana.[53] Elsewhere in Middlesex County, Antifederalists' campaigning proved more effective. More than one half of the county's delegates to the convention were Antifederalist, and, as Nathaniel Gorham complained, it was because of the campaigning of Winthrop and William Prescott that "Mr. Pitts of Dunstable" was the only man elected from "above Concord who could be depended upon. . . ."[54]

Several Middlesex towns not only elected Antifederalists, but declared themselves against the Constitution, and in at least one instance specifically instructed their delegates accordingly. Sudbury elected Captain Ashabel Wheeler "a delegate to the s[ai]d Convention" and voted "not to adopt the proposed Constitution as it now stands," but rejected a proposal to instruct Wheeler. Littleton also elected a delegate and voted instructions, but two weeks later rescinded their vote and withdrew the instructions. The town's delegate, Samuel Reed, voted nay in the convention. Sherburn also declined "positive instructions relative to your delegate [Daniel Whitney] voting for or against the proposed Constitution," but Townsend voted against the Constitution and instructed its delegate, Daniel Adams, accordingly.[55]

In Essex County Antifederalists won fewer seats than in Middlesex, but the men elected included two or three important leaders. Andover chose three delegates and then voted against adopting the Constitution by a majority of nine. One of the three men was William Symmes, described by Christopher Gore as one of the few men of "abilities elected by the Antifederalists."[56] Dr. Samuel Holten, a former member of the Confederation Congress, was elected from Danvers. Boxford elected Aaron Wood and instructed him in town meeting. Although the instructions themselves were not recorded, they were apparently to oppose, for Wood voted nay on the final roll call vote in convention. Methuen, whose delegate voted nay, explicitly declined to give instructions, and the town of Newburyport defeated an attempt by Antifederalist Daniel Kilham to instruct its elected delegates against the Constitution. A like attempt at Ipswich also failed.[57]

As a result of this effort, the Antifederalists met with limited success in the eastern counties. Several potential leaders were elected, from Roxbury, Rehoboth, Andover, and Danvers, and these men were supported by a small contingent of Antifederalist delegates. The most prominent Antifederalists—Gerry, Winthrop, and Warren—failed in their bids for convention seats, but the limited Antifederalist victories in the East took on special significance because of the acknowledged strength of the Antifederalists in the three western counties: Worcester, Hampshire, and Berkshire.

Records relating to specific elections in the West are relatively sparse; most of those extant merely record the decision of the town to send a delegate to the convention. In some instances towns refused to send a delegate. Gardner, for example, "voted not [to] send a man to Convention . . . [because] they did not like" the Constitution. Gardner was the exception. Most towns voted to send delegates, and several either voted against or instructed their delegates to vote

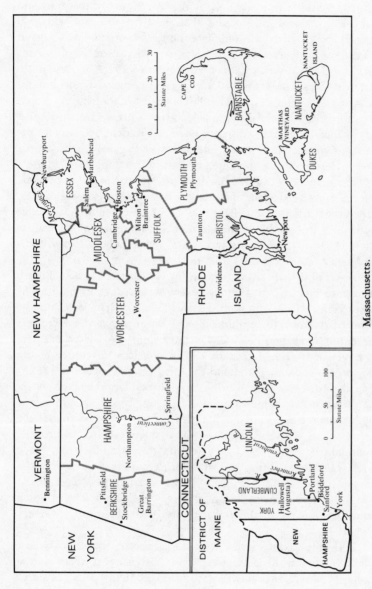

Massachusetts.

Courtesy of the University of Wisconsin Cartographic Lab.

against a Constitution which the townspeople of Harvard thought, if adopted, would "effectually destroy the sovereignty of the states and establish a national government that, in all probability will soon bring the people of the United States under despotism." Milford and Holden also instructed their delegate to vote against the Constitution, as did Charlton and Lunenburg. Northborough voted not "to accept the Constitution for the United States as it now stands" but did not instruct its delegates, and the Fitchburg town meeting appointed a committee to state the objections of the town to the Constitution. A copy of those objections was then presented to delegate Daniel Putnam. The townspeople of Lancaster also voted against the Constitution but the committee appointed to draft instructions qualified them in such a manner as to leave the delegates free to vote their personal preference. As a result one of the town's three delegates voted in favor of the Constitution.[58] But Lancaster was the exception in Worcester County. As the results of the elections became known, Federalists believed that no more than seven "good" men had been elected compared to fifty Antifederalists from the county.[59]

Fewer details are known concerning the elections in neighboring Hampshire County. Antifederalist essays were sent overland into the county from Albany through Pittsfield to Northampton, up the Connecticut River to Springfield, and reprinted in the *Hampshire Gazette* and *Hampshire Chronicle*. The impact of these newspaper essays can rarely be measured. But in a town meeting November 26 the townspeople of Bernardston and the District of Leyden voted to instruct their delegate, Agrippa Wells, "not totally to reject the above-said Constitution, being of opinion that by proper amendments it may be adopted to secure our liberties and answer the design of the general union." "With regard to those amendments," the townspeople added, "pay particular attention to those objections made against said Constitution by Mr. Elbridge Gerry and by the Minority of the Assembly of Pennsylvania as lately published in the Springfield and Northampton papers."[60] Captain Wells voted against ratification, as did the majority of the Hampshire County delegates.

Berkshire County, to the west of Hampshire, was more divided politically, and while there were fewer instructions, there were a number of heated elections. At Stockbridge, John Bacon, a "bitter enemy of the Constitution," campaigned for a convention seat, "going from house to house stating his objections" and soliciting votes. Despite his efforts Federalist Theodore Sedgwick defeated Bacon in the town meeting by tactics which a friendly observer described as "bad measures in a good cause."[61] At Great Barrington, however, Antifederalists were more successful initially. At the town meeting William Whiting was elected by a small majority which included at least one illegal voter. A committee was appointed to draft instructions and then Federalists secured a one-week adjournment. In the intervening week Sedgwick arrived at Great Barrington and aided the Federalists in regrouping their forces. At the subsequent meeting they were a small majority. They then rejected the Antifederalist instructions, voted to reconsider the election of Whiting, and replaced him with Elijah Dwight.[62] This kind of local electioneering also took place at Sheffield, Richmond, and Becket, three towns where Sedgwick attempted to organize and assist in the election of Federalist delegates to the convention.[63]

This kind of electioneering was done by both Federalists and Antifederalists. Bacon, Whiting, and Sedgwick were all active campaigners but were not always successful. Nor did Antifederalists necessarily increase their representation over what it was in the House of Representatives elected in May 1787. Stockbridge and Great Barrington, for instance, were both urban centers with close ties to the commercial interest of the East. Stockbridge had elected Sedgwick to represent it in the House the previous spring and his victory over Bacon indicated continued support for mercantile economic and political programs. However, although Sedgwick campaigned at Richmond, the delegate elected was Antifederalist. Richmond was traditionally opposed to the economic and political measures favored by towns like Stockbridge and Great Barrington. There were no unprecedented victories for either party in Berkshire County. Indeed, Nathan Dane's comment that the state "would divide [on the Constitution] as it had on all questions for several years past" was specifically applicable to Berkshire. Those towns that supported conservative fiscal programs and had favored the repression of Shays' rebellion were Federalist; those towns that favored pro-debtor legislation and were most sympathetic to the Shaysite's grievances were Antifederalist.[64]

Unlike western Massachusetts, there was little initial opposition to the Constitution in the district of Maine. Local men, however, were soon prompted to action by news from Boston and farther south. Thomas B. Wait, editor of the *Portland Cumberland Gazette,* initially "prayed that the whispers of opposition" to the Constitution "might be silent," but after reading the address of the seceders of the Pennsylvania Assembly he began to waver. Wait then proceeded to consider "every argument" on both sides before deciding against the Constitution. He objected to the absence of a Bill of Rights in particular and to the vagueness of the Constitution in general. Once convinced that the Constitution was unsatisfactory in its present form, he began to campaign against it in his newspaper and in his personal travels throughout the country.[65]

Wait's efforts were reinforced in November when the district's delegates to the General Court returned. Three of them—William Widgery, Samuel Thompson, and Samuel Nasson—were confirmed opponents of adoption. Widgery had proposed a direct vote on the Constitution by the towns instead of a convention, because many Maine towns, he knew, would be unable or unwilling to send delegates to Boston. Defeated in this measure, he, with Nasson, Thompson, and several local men, worked to secure as great a representation as possible. Widgery "waged war" with the Constitution, "the same as a new light fighting the devil," and was chosen a delegate by New Gloucester. At Sanford the town initially voted not to send a delegate, but Nasson "stirred up a second meeting" and procured his own election.[66] Topsham considered the Constitution for seven hours and then voted unanimously to oppose ratification. They chose Antifederalist Thompson as their delegate. Fryeburg, in York County, reversed the order, electing Moses Ames and then instructing him to oppose unconditional ratification.[67] Antifederalist Nathaniel Barrell was chosen at York. He reportedly behaved very indiscreetly at the town meeting and pledged "to lose his arm [rather] than put his assent to the new Constitution." There were contests elsewhere in the district. At Biddeford the town originally voted not to send a delegate. At a second meeting Federalists managed to reverse this decision. The Antifederalists then elected "A. Smith" who had stated "he would not go if he was chosen."[68]

The decision at Biddeford was apparently repeated elsewhere in the district since thirty towns did not send delegates. Still, the Maine delegation to the convention was more than twice the size of the delegation to the previous session of the General Court, and well over one half of the district's convention delegates were Antifederalist.[69] Antifederalists carried the entire state by a similar margin. Estimates varied, but both parties agreed that the Anifederalists held a minimum twenty-vote margin as the convention opened.[70]

The Massachusetts effort was duplicated in New Hampshire. Often it involved the same men, and it resulted in a similar Antifederalist victory. The Antifederalist campaign in New Hampshire began later because Federalist president John Sullivan delayed calling the legislature into session. Still, during January James Winthrop headed north from Boston with copies of Lee's *Letters from the Federal Farmer* and other Antifederalist essays. He may have carried them directly to New Hampshire or passed them on to Middlesex County Antifederalist William Prescott who campaigned in both Massachusetts and New Hampshire. These efforts were supplemented by those of Dr. Daniel Kilham of Newburyport, who made additional sorties to Exeter in February.[71]

After the legislature which called a state convention adjourned, Joshua Atherton and a few "designing men" traveled among the interior towns circulating reports that the Massachusetts convention would certainly reject the Constitution and that "general sentiment" within New Hampshire was against it as well. With these reports, and the objections of Bryan, Gerry, and Lee as reinforcement, a majority of the towns elected Antifederalists to the convention. Once an Antifederalist delegate was elected, the towns often went further. In order to prevent the conversion of delegates to federalism at the convention approximately forty towns instructed their delegates to oppose unconditional ratification.[72]

These instructions reflect, to a degree, the tone of the Antifederalist campaign. Only a few of the instructions remain, but enough to suggest the impact of Gerry's, Lee's, and Bryan's arguments. Several towns instructed their delegates "not to approve of said constitution as it now stands." Others merely "voted not to except [sic] the Constitution by the Federal Convention."[73] Some towns did not instruct their delegates at all, but of the 106 delegates in the convention, 65 or 66 of those chosen opposed the Constitution.[74] Nor would the Antifederalist majority suffer from a lack of leadership. Atherton would be in attendance representing New Ipswich, while Peabody, Kilham, and Samuel Thompson, although not delegates, would be in Exeter.[75]

In Pennsylvania, Massachusetts, and New Hampshire Antifederalists mounted extensive, coordinated campaigns. In all three states the voter turnout exceeded that in other contemporaneous elections and a greater number of towns were represented at the Massachusetts and New Hampshire conventions than in the preceding legislative sessions. In addition, and clearly a direct result of their campaign, Antifederalists won majorities in two of the state conventions. In Massachusetts Nathaniel Gorham forewarned Rufus King that it would be an uphill struggle in the state convention for the Anti-federalists had a clear majority.[76] In New Hampshire Samuel Tenney informed Federalist Nicholas Gilman of an Antifederalist edge of 3 to 2 in that state's convention.[77]

The dimensions of these electoral victories have been obscured by the eventual Federalist successes in the state conventions. Many factors contributed to the defeat of the Antifederalist majorities at Boston and Exeter, not the least of which was the issue on which they campaigned for convention seats. Most of the literature distributed from New York and Boston argued for previous amendments and a second convention, albeit in some instances implicitly. Responding to this appeal, many towns elected men who either favored or were instructed to "adopt the Constitution with amendments."[78]

If the initial suggestion of the Antifederalist leadership for the state conventions to meet simultaneously in April or May had been implemented, this action might have been sufficient. After this plan broke down James Warren pressed for an adjournment.[79] But other Massachusetts Antifederalists preferred the course suggested by Richard Henry Lee: "That the state conventions . . . direct their exertions to altering and amending the system proposed before they shall adopt it."[80] Antifederalists in the conventions in Massachusetts and New Hampshire therefore agreed to a paragraph by paragraph examination of the Constitution by the conventions before any vote for adoption, amendment, or rejection. In so doing they provided the Federalists with ample opportunity to utilize the advantages they held within the conventions and out. John Hancock had been elected president of the Massachusetts convention, but his illness placed Federalist Thomas Cushing in the chair. Cushing in turn utilized his position as presiding officer to appoint Federalist-dominated committees, which established rules and decided contested elections. The presiding officer also had the power to recognize or ignore a roll call vote detrimental to the Federalists, as John Langdon did when the New Hampshire convention voted against adoption 54 to 51.[81] Within the conventions the Federalists had other advantages as well. In both New Hampshire and Massachusetts the most prominent men were Federalists and the force of their prestige was considerable. These men also exercised a different kind of influence over particular delegates —economic pressure and social intimidation. Outside of the conventions there was manipulation of the news.[82]

All of these were important, but Antifederalists had outside support as well, at both Boston and Exeter. In the first instance, John

Lamb sent agents to Boston during the meeting of the convention to confer with Warren and other Antifederalist leaders.[83] Warren and "his emissaries" constantly engaged in attending nocturnal meetings of the "star chamber," and in "manufacturing speeches for the Antifederal junto" in the convention.[84] The Antifederalist majority in the Massachusetts convention was cohesive enough to withstand the pressures exerted by Federalists until Federalists conceded, in form at least, to a key Antifederalist demand. Federalists did not yield outright but offered, if not amendments prior to ratification, at least a pledge of amendments and adequate safeguards to ensure their adoption by the first Congress under the new Constitution.

This alternative, the first meeting of Congress in essence becoming the second convention, had been alluded to by Richard Henry Lee in his *Letters from the Federal Farmer*. The danger of recommended amendments was that once the government was in operation the vigilance of the people would decline and the people would be "inattentive to amendments."[85] General William Heath recognized this objection, but he and a few like him in the Massachusetts convention began to look to the first meeting of Congress under the Constitution as a second convention. Charles Turner of Scituate and William Symmes of Andover, for instance, had been counted part of the Antifederalist majority at the outset of the convention. But like Richard Henry Lee and Elbridge Gerry, they accepted the basic framework of the Constitution while believing amendments were needed.[86] These and others, like John K. Smith and Nathaniel Barrell, agreed to adopt the Constitution with recommended amendments, which Heath proposed be communicated to the other states for consideration by their conventions.[87] If each state considered and concurred in the recommended amendments and, like Massachusetts, instructed its delegates to Congress "to exert their utmost endeavors" to have such amendments immediately adopted, the Constitution would be secured, and the objections of men like Heath, Turner, and Symmes, as well as Gerry, would be removed.[88]

Events at Exeter, New Hampshire, followed a pattern similar to those at Boston. The Antifederalist majority in the convention was led by Joshua Atherton, and assisted from "out of doors" by Nathaniel Peabody, Daniel Kilham, and Samuel Thompson.[89] A vote on adoption with recommended amendments, however, failed by three votes. Langdon then maneuvered a vote on adjournment instead. Five Antifederalists switched and voted in favor of adjourning the convention until June. The deciding factor, according to Federalists, was Antifederalists' unwillingness to violate their instructions although personally convinced of the need to ratify in full faith of amendments.[90] To some Antifederalists in New Hampshire, adjournment was acceptable for other reasons. Three other state conventions would be in session in June, and there was the possibility of inter-convention communication and agreement on stipulated amendments. For these men, adjournment held out the promise of the amendments they and their constituents sought.

By early spring Federalists had considerable grounds for optimism. Six states had ratified the Constitution unconditionally, including Pennsylvania and Massachusetts—two states crucial to the success of any new government. The adjournment of the New Hampshire convention was both a surprise and a disappointment, but Federalists were confident of success at the next meeting in June. More alarming to Federalists was the persistence of the Antifederalists in Pennsylvania and Massachusetts. In those states, ratification notwithstanding, Antifederalists claimed that a majority of the people opposed the Constitution and they continued to work against it. In Pennsylvania this meant a statewide campaign to repeal that state's ratification and a regional campaign in which Pennsylvania Antifederalists aided their counterparts in the South in their campaigns to elect Antifederalists to the forthcoming state conventions in Maryland, Virginia, and the Carolinas.

In Massachusetts, too, considerable numbers of Antifederalists refused to accept the decision of the convention. Doubting the sincerity of the Federalist pledge to work for amendments in the first Congress, these Antifederalists vowed to continue to work against the Constitution. In the aftermath of ratification these Antifederalists looked northward to New Hampshire and worked with Antifederalists there to ensure an Antifederalist majority in the June convention. For other Massachusetts Antifederalists the forthcoming gubernatorial elections provided yet another opportunity. Thus in February the state's two most prominent Antifederalists—Elbridge Gerry and James Warren—were nominated for governor and lieutenant governor, and they campaigned on the basis of their commitment to a second convention.

By these efforts Antifederalists kept alive a spirit of opposition in their respective states and regions. Unknowingly they also contributed to their ultimate failure, for, if defeated again, in either the petition campaign or gubernatorial elections, the likelihood of a loss of support among those inclined to acquiesce to the will of the majority as expressed in the state conventions would be increased. Support could decline also among those who despaired of political action as an adequate means to secure their ultimate goal. But the Antifederalist leadership had no alternative. Neither acquiescence nor armed resistance was an acceptable alternative to a political elite who were still confident of success through the political process. Thus they once again participated within the framework of the proposed Constitution. In doing so, although their ultimate goal was potentially destructive of the new government, they functioned in form as a "loyal opposition." As such they contributed to the ultimate legitimization of the very Constitution they opposed.

NOTES TO
CHAPTER 3

1. Samuel Huntington to Samuel Johnston, 23 December 1788, Misc. Collections, Huntington Library; *Elizabethtown New Jersey Journal,* 26 December 1787; *Augusta Georgia State Gazette,* 5 January 1788.

2. George Washington to James Madison, 10 October 1787, Madison Papers, DLC.

3. Jensen, *Ratification,* 2: 112–17.

4. *Ibid.,* pp. 158–67.

5. "Centinel," No. II, "To the People of Pennsylvania," (Philadelphia, 1787); "Old Whig," "To the People of Pennsylvania," (Philadelphia, 1787).

6. *Philadelphia Pennsylvania Packet,* 23 October; *Philadelphia Independent Gazetteer,* 6, 24, and 26 October; and *Philadelphia Pennsylvania Journal,* 27 October 1787.

7. The first five were published as broadsides, the last two as pamphlets. All were in print prior to the elections on 6 November.

8. Samuel Bryan to Albert Gallatin, 18 December 1790, Gallatin Papers, NHi.

9. The precise figures are: James Hutchinson, 25; John Nicholson, 60; Edward Pole, 12; and James Boyd, 24 copies, Wastebook, Robert Aitken Papers, PHi. Aitken advertised the *Letters* for sale on 23 November 1787. Hutchinson purchased his on 27 November, the other three on 30 November. These figures are not a reflection of the total number of copies purchased or distributed in the state as Nicholson and Lee both distributed copies earlier. See George Latimer to John Nicholson, 24 November, Nicholson Papers, PHarH, and Samuel Powel to George Washington, 13 November, Washington Papers, DLC.

10. Joseph Hart to George Bryan, 3 October 1787, Bryan Papers, PHi.

11. Francis Murray to John Nicholson, 1 November 1787, Jensen, *Ratification,* 2: 207.

12. *Philadelphia Pennsylvania Gazette,* 31 October 1787.

13. Ebenezer Bowman to Timothy Pickering, 12 November; Obadiah Gore to Timothy Pickering, 12 November; Pickering to Mrs. Timothy Pickering, 17 November 1787, all in the Pickering Papers, MHi.

14. Robert Smith to George or Samuel Bryan, 26 April 1788, Bryan Papers, PHi.

15. Samuel Powel to George Washington, 13 November, Washington Papers, DLC; *Philadelphia Pennsylvania Gazette,* 21 November 1787.

16. *Philadelphia Independent Gazetteer,* 11 October 1787.

17. Richard Butler to William Irvine, 11 October 1787, Jensen, *Ratification,* 2: 177–78.

18. William Lyon to John Nicholson, 26 October 1787, Nicholson Papers, PHarH.

19. John King to Benjamin Rush, 5 November, Jensen, *Ratification,* 2: 208–9. See also a "Correspondent" in the *Carlisle Gazette,* 14 November 1787.

20. Richard Butler to William Irvine, 11 October 1787, Jensen, *Ratification,* 2: 177–78.

21. Alexander Fowler to John Nicholson, 10 November 1787, *ibid.,* pp. 287–88.

22. *Philadelphia Independent Gazetteer,* 8 November 1787.

23. *Philadelphia Pennsylvania Herald,* 7 November 1787.

24. *Philadelphia Pennsylvania Gazette,* 14 November 1787; Pettit to George Washington, 19 March 1791, Washington Papers, DLC.

25. Obadiah Gore to Timothy Pickering, 12 November 1787, Pickering Papers, MHi.

26. John Hannum to Anthony Wayne, 1 November 1787, Jensen, *Ratification*, 2: 232–33.

27. *Philadelphia Pennsylvania Packet,* 13 November 1787.

28. To John Montgomery, 9 November 1787, Jensen, *Ratification*, 2: 237.

29. *Lancaster Zeitung,* 14 November 1787.

30. *Philadelphia Independent Gazetteer,* 16 October 1787.

31. Ephraim Blaine to Benjamin Rush, 15 October 1787, Jensen, *Ratification*, 2: 228.

32. *Carlisle Gazette,* 31 October 1787.

33. John King to Benjamin Rush, 5 November, Jensen, *Ratification,* 2: 208–9; "A Correspondent," *Carlisle Gazette,* 31 October 1787. The final vote on the Constitution in the state convention is in *Ratification*, 2: 590–91.

34. *Pittsburgh Gazette,* 20 October 1787.

35. *Ibid.,* 3 November, 1 December 1787.

36. *Philadelphia Independent Gazetteer,* 8 November 1787.

37. Latimer to Nicholson, 24 November 1787, Nicholson Papers, PHarH; Wastebook, Robert Aitken Papers, PHi.

38. Report of debates, Jensen, *Ratification*, 2: 267–69.

39. William Shippen, Jr., to Thomas Lee Shippen, 7 November 1787, *ibid.*, pp. 235–36.

40. *Ibid.*

41. Richard Henry Lee to Samuel Adams, 5 October, Ballagh, *Lee,* 2: 447; Elbridge Gerry to James Warren, 18 October 1787, Sang Autograph Collection, ICarbS.

42. Elbridge Gerry to president of the Senate and Speaker of the House of Representatives of Massachusetts, 18 October, *Boston Massachusetts Centinel,* 3 November 1787.

43. "Old Whig," V (Philadelphia, 1787).

44. On Warren's authorship see Charles Warren, "Elbridge Gerry, James Warren, Mercy Warren and the Ratification of the Federal Constitution in Massachusetts," *Massachusetts Historical Society Proceedings,* 64 (1932): 143–64. The newspapers are a key source in understanding Warren's, Winthrop's, and Austin's roles. See, for example, the *Boston Massachusetts Gazette,* 30 October, 29 November, 28 December 1787; the *Boston Massachusetts Centinel,* 7 and 24 November; the *Newburyport Essex Journal,* 31 October; the *Massachusetts Gazette,* 1 January 1788; and the *Boston Independent Chronicle,* 25 October and 1 November. Several of these articles were published under the heading "Ship News" and the essays described the movements of the "Antifederal Fleet."

45. This statement is based on the newspaper attacks on Winthrop and Austin cited above. For a discussion of the broadside as a political tool see Noble E. Cunningham, "Early Political Handbills in the United States," *William and Mary Quarterly* 3rd Ser., 15 (1958): 70–73.

46. Oliver Phelps to Elbridge Gerry, 6 December 1787, Phelps and Gorham Papers, N. Gerry complained of the loss of several letters to and from John Bacon, and to his "friends in New York," to J. Harley, 15 March 1788, Sang Autograph Collection, ICarbS.

47. The "John DeWitt" essays appeared on 22 and 29 October, 5 and 19

November, and 7 December. The "Disadvantages" was printed on 19 November; "Cato I," on 8 October 1787.

48. For the different lists see "Candor," and "A Mechanick," *Boston Massachusetts Centinel,* 28 November and 1 December; two different lists in the *American Herald,* 3 December; *Independent Chronicle,* 6 December; three different lists in the *Massachusetts Gazette,* 4 December; and "Concord," *Massachusetts Gazette,* 7 December. Christopher Gore to Rufus King, 9 December 1787, King Papers, NHi.

49. Henry Jackson to Henry Knox, 16 December, Knox Papers, MHi; *Boston American Herald,* 10 December 1787.

50. "Captain McDaniel," *Boston Massachusetts Gazette,* 25 December; Christopher Gore to Rufus King, 23 December 1787, King Papers, NHi.

51. The returns are in the journal of the convention which is printed in *Debates and Proceedings in the Convention of the Commonwealth of Massachusetts* (Boston, 1856), pp. 31–43. On Sandwich's instructions see the *Boston Massachusetts Centinel,* 2 January 1788.

52. *Salem Mercury,* 5 and 20 November 1787; Nathaniel Gorham to Henry Knox, 6 January 1788, Knox Papers, MHi.

53. "A Federalist," *Boston Massachusetts Centinel,* 19 December; Christopher Gore to Rufus King, 23 December 1787, King Papers, NHi.

54. To Henry Knox, 6 January 1788, Knox Papers, MHi.

55. Sudbury Town Records, 17 December; Littleton Town Records, 17 and 31 December; Sherburn Town Records, 10 December; Townsend Town Records, 24 and 31 December 1787, M-Ar.

56. Andover Town Meeting, 31 January 1788, M-Ar; Gore to Rufus King, 16 December 1787, King Papers, NHi.

57. Boxford Town Records, 6 and 13 December; Methuen Town Records, 6 and 13 December 1787; Christopher Gore to Rufus King, 6 January, King Papers, NHi; *Newburyport Essex Journal,* 2 January 1788; Diary of Dr. Samuel Adams, 1786–1787, NN; *Springfield Hampshire Chronicle,* 21 November; *Northampton Hampshire Gazette,* 28 November 1787.

58. Gardner Town Records, 27 December; *Boston American Herald,* 21 January; Adin Ballou, *History of the Town of Milford* (Boston, 1882), p. 92; Holden Town Records, 10 December; Charlton Town Records, 10 December; Lunenburg Town Records, 24 December; Fitchburg Town Records, 20 and 28 December, Northborough Town Records, 24 December 1787, M-Ar; Abijah Marvin, *History of the Town of Lancaster* (Lancaster, 1879), p. 322.

59. Bangs to George Thacher, 1 January 1788; William F. Goodwin, ed., "The Thacher Papers," *The Historical Magazine,* 6 (1869): 260.

60. Bernardston Town Records, 26 November 1787, M-Ar.

61. Theodore Sedgwick to Henry Van Schaack, 28 November 1787, Sedgwick Papers, MHi.

62. Charles Taylor, *History of Great Barrington* (Great Barrington, 1882), pp. 316–19. The Remonstrance is in *Massachusetts Debates,* pp. 53–55.

63. Richard E. Welch, Jr., *Theodore Sedgwick, Federalist* (Middletown, 1965), pp. 59–60.

64. Dane to Henry Knox, 27 December 1787, Knox Papers, MHi. For an excellent discussion of the relationship of the commercial and cosmopolitan factors to political behavior in Massachusetts see Hall, *Politics Without Parties,* chap. 2, "Economy and Society: The Commercial Cosmopolitan Continuum."

65. *Portland Cumberland Gazette,* 18 October, 13 December 1787; Thomas B. Wait

to George Thacher, 8 January; Jeremiah Hill to Thacher, 1 January 1788, Thacher Papers, pp. 261–65.

66. Hill to Thacher, 1 January; David Sewall to Thacher, 5 January 1788, Thacher papers, pp. 260–61.

67. *Massachusetts Debates,* p. 97; J. C. Barrows, *Fryeburg, Maine: An Historical Sketch* (Fryeburg, 1932), pp. 112–13.

68. Samuel Phillips Savage to George Thacher, "Thacher Papers," p. 264; Jeremiah Hill to Thacher, *ibid.*, p. 260.

69. Seventeen delegates attended the previous session of the General Court; forty-six delegates attended the convention.

70. Nathaniel Gorham to Rufus King, 29 December 1787, King, *Life,* p. 266. Samuel Nasson believed the Antifederalists controlled the convention 192 to 144, to George Thacher, 22 January 1788, Thacher Papers, p. 266. For further details see the discussion in Main, *Antifederalists,* p. 203.

71. *Boston Massachusetts Gazette,* 1 January; *Exeter Freeman's Oracle,* 14 March; John Quincy Adams, Diary, 21 and 22 February 1788, Adams Papers, MHi.

72. John Langdon to George Washington, 28 February 1788, Washington Papers, DLC.

73. Amherst Town Records, 1 January 1788, Nh; George W. Browne, ed., "Early Records of the Town of Derryfield," Manchester Historical Association *Collections,* 9: 145.

74. Samuel Tenney to Nicholas Gilman, 12 March 1788, Gratz Collection, PHi.

75. *Exeter Freeman's Oracle,* 14 March; Silas Lee to George Thacher, 22 February, and Jeremiah Hill to Thacher, 28 February 1788, Thacher Papers, pp. 342–46.

76. Nathaniel Gorham to Rufus King, 29 December 1787, King, *Life,* 1: 266.

77. Samuel Tenney to Nicholas Gilman, 12 March 1787, Gratz Collection, PHi.

78. Jeremiah Hill to George Thacher, 9 January 1788, Thacher Papers, p. 264.

79. James Warren, "Republican Federalist," *Boston Massachusetts Centinel,* 19 January 1788.

80. Letter 5, *From the Federal Farmer.* This was one of the pamphlets Lamb, Winthrop, and Austin distributed as part of the campaign for the election of Antifederalist delegates.

81. *Massachusetts Debates,* pp. 196–97. There are no minutes for the New Hampshire Convention, but see Peter Curtenius to George Clinton, 2 March 1788, George Clinton Papers, Bancroft Transcripts, NN. On Federalist "influence" see Main, *Antifederalists,* pp. 203–5.

82. The day before Massachusetts adopted it was falsely reported that North Carolina had ratified. See the list of "many notorious falsehoods circulated by the FEDERAL party in Boston by which means a majority of 19 was obtained in the convention for the Constitution," *Philadelphia Independent Gazetteer,* 19 February 1789.

83. Bancroft, *History of the Constitution,* 2: 339. For contemporary testimony see the letter of Archibald Maclaine to James Iredell in which he states that "he was informed by a letter from that place [New York]" that New York Antifederalists did send their emissaries to the Massachusetts Convention, Griffith J. McRee, ed., *Life and Correspondence of James Iredell,* 2 vols. (New York, 1857–58), 2: 219–20.

84. *Boston Massachusetts Gazette,* 7 March 1788.

85. Letter 5, *From the Federal Farmer.*

86. *Massachusetts Debates,* pp. 224, 274, 277.

87. It is impossible to determine all the men who switched. Smith from Falmouth

and Barrell from York were initially identified as Antifederalists and switched on the final roll call as did Turner from Scituate and John Sprague from Lancaster.

88. *Massachusetts Debates*, 229.

89. John Vaughn to John Dickinson, 9 March, Dickinson Papers, PPL; *Exeter Freeman's Oracle,* 14 March; John Quncy Adams, Diary, 21 and 22 February 1788, Adams Papers, MHi.

90. John Langdon to George Washington, 28 February 1788, Washington Papers, DLC.

Chapter 4

ANTIFEDERALISTS IN NEW YORK AND NEW ENGLAND: FEBRUARY TO APRIL 1788

By mid-February 1788, Federalists were becoming more confident. Twelve states had approved conventions and six—including the Antifederalist-dominated Massachusetts convention—had ratified the Constitution. Following the Massachusetts ratification, the stream of Federalist victories abruptly ceased. On February 22 the New Hampshire convention voted to adjourn to meet again in June, and on March 24 the Rhode Island towns rejected the Constitution. No additional conventions were scheduled to meet until April. During the interim, in New England and New York, the focus of public attention and political activity shifted, first to the state legislatures, and then to the ensuing elections for convention delegates and state officers. The Constitution quite naturally dominated the elections for convention delegates. It was also a key issue in the state gubernatorial and legislative elections. Indeed the Constitution and party labels associated with it, i.e., Federalist and Antifederalist, were carried over to the spring elections, notably in New York and Massachusetts where antifederalism was strongest. This intrusion of the Constitution into state politics constituted a nationalization of the state political process like that which occurred during the Revolution. In this instance though, as the *Pennsylvania Gazette* editorialized, the labels "Whig" and "Tory" were replaced with "Federal" and "Antifederal."[1] This nationalization occurred because Antifederalists saw the state legislatures as another base from which, if unable to prevent unconditional ratification, they could continue the drive to secure their own political goals. In the process of doing just that, the Antifederalists, through their continued participation in the political process, and by their explicit acceptance of the Constitution, contributed materially to the ultimate success of the Constitution.

While aware of the long-term importance of the state legislatures, by February 1788 New York Antifederalists anticipated success in the primary arena—the state conventions. That anticipation was justified. During the fall and winter of 1787, New York Antifederalists mounted an extensive propaganda campaign designed to alert the people of New York and the surrounding states to the dangers inherent in the Constitution, and to ensure the election of Antifederalist majorities to the state conventions. Nor did John Lamb and his allies rely solely on broadsides and pamphlets. Lamb sent emissaries to Boston and Exeter where they attended the Massachusetts and New Hampshire conventions, and collaborated with Antifederalists there who were attempting to adjourn those conventions until June, when the New York and Virginia conventions would be in session. While these efforts were only partially successful, the New York Antifederalists demonstrated that they were well prepared to conduct a statewide campaign for the election of convention delegates pledged to work against unconditional ratification.[2]

This effort did not take on real direction in the state until February 1788. The state legislature, which was to call the convention, set the date for the elections of delegates, and establish requirements for voters, did not assemble in Poughkeepsie until January 11. Three weeks later both houses approved a convention resolve which made all white males over the age of twenty-one eligible to vote for convention delegates on April 29, the same day as state legislative elections. The convention was to assemble in Poughkeepsie on June 17.[3] The fact that the elections were simultaneous had a significant effect on the shape of the ensuing Antifederalist campaign. During the following months the Antifederalists' campaigns for convention delegates and state legislative seats merged into one effort as the state's political leaders set out to establish county committees, nominate convention and legislative candidates, and begin the campaign for their election.

One of the first counties in which Antifederalists organized was Albany. There Antifederalists met on February 12 and appointed a committee to coordinate their efforts in the convention election. Two weeks later the same committee called for a meeting of "two or three gentlemen from the different districts in the county" to meet in mid-March and nominate candidates for the convention. At that meeting Antifederalists agreed upon a slate of candidates for the convention, Assembly, and Senate.[4]

Even before these nominations there was extensive campaigning in the county. Federalist Leonard Gansevoort remarked that the "opposers of the New Constitution here [Albany] are indefatigable in endeavoring to excite the people against it."[5] They also, as William North bitterly complained, scattered "the 'Centinel,' *The Farmers' Letters* and every other publication against the Constitution . . . all over the county, while *The Federalist* remains at New York."[6] Following the nomination of candidates, a broadside composed of Antifederalists' objections to the Constitution and the names of the Antifederalist nominees for the convention, Assembly, and Senate also circulated throughout the county. As Jeremiah Van Rensselaer, chairman of the Albany committee, reported to John Lamb, "We are in close action from morning to night."[7] Lamb was equally active. During March 1788, he sent John Lansing, Jr., a candidate for both the convention and Assembly, three hundred copies of Mercy Warren's *Observations . . . by a Columbian Patriot* and sixty copies of the Antifederalist compilation, *Observations on the Proposed Constitution,* with a request that they "be distributed amongst the inhabitants of your county."[8]

Lamb also sent Lansing an additional two hundred copies of the Warren pamphlet with instructions to send them to men in Washington and Montgomery counties who would disseminate them "with the most expedition."[9] Even before these pamphlets arrived, "Antifederal business" had been carried on in Washington County with great spirit. State Senator John Williams was a member of the Antifederalists' county committee and a candidate for the convention. Two other members of the Washington committee, David Hopkins and Albert Baker, were also candidates for the convention, and a third, Alexander Webster, was renominated for a seat in the Assembly.[10]

In Montgomery County a meeting of the "four lower districts of the county" nominated all four members of the Antifederalists' county committee—Christopher P. Yates, Volker Veeder, John Frey, and William Harper—and John Winn and Henry Staring for the convention. That meeting also named the same six candidates for the Assembly. Antifederalists circulated copies of the nominations and various publications throughout the county.[11]

Columbia County Antifederalists met at Claverack on March 18 and nominated Peter Van Ness, Mathew Adgate, and John Bay as candidates for the convention. All three men were members of the Antifederalist county committee while the last two and John Korts were candidates for the Assembly. Van Ness was a candidate for the Senate.[12] Electioneering in Columbia County was widespread. Van Ness received one hundred and fifty copies of *Observations . . . by a*

Columbian Patriot and thirty-five copies of an Antifederalist compilation, *Observations on the Proposed Constitution,* from the New York City committee. The latter included "The Reasons of Dissent of the Minority of Pennsylvania," a piece a correspondent in the *Hudson Weekly Gazette* complained was "circulating with amazing assiduity" in the interior parts of the county.[13]

Antifederalists also conducted their business "with spirit" in Orange, Ulster, and Dutchess counties. One sign of that appeared in early February 1788, when a group of Orange and Ulster county Antifederalists met at Montgomery and, "having . . . discovered a unanimous disapprobation of the system," committed the Constitution to flames.[14] A week later a meeting of inhabitants of Kingston also "unanimously disapproved" the Constitution. Men at that meeting proposed that Alexander Addison, Johannes Snyder, and Dirck Wynkoop attend a county-wide meeting at New Paltz in late February. Leaders there also recommended that Addison and Wynkoop be the county's candidates for the convention.[15]

Despite this display of unanimity, Antifederalists within Ulster were divided. Addison and Snyder were nominated at the New Paltz meeting on February 28, but Peter Van Gaasbeek, a Kingston resident and "one of the major powers in Ulster County" politics, opposed their candidacies.[16] He maintained that Addison was not popular in his own precinct, Kingston, and that Snyder was in reality a Federalist. Van Gaasbeek, however, had another reason for opposing their nominations. He had met with county and state leaders and had drawn up a different slate of candidates which included Governor Clinton.[17] Resolution of differences did not come easily. Not until April 21, after consultation with Antifederalists in all the county's precincts and party leaders in New York, did assemblyman Cornelius Schoonmaker propose a suitable ticket which included Governor Clinton, James Clinton, Ebenezer Clark, John Cantine, Dirck Wynkoop, and himself.[18]

The dispute over the choice of convention candidates also disrupted the early selection of nominees for Assembly and agreement on a man for the Senate. In early April, Schoonmaker proposed a list to Peter Van Gaasbeek, but as late as the seventeenth no list had been agreed upon. Only on April 21 were the candidates selected, and copies of the nominations for Assembly, Senate, and convention ready for distribution throughout the county.[19]

In Dutchess County citizens from the ten precincts met at Oswego in late February and named seven candidates for the state convention. A month later the Constitutional Society of Dutchess County gathered in Amenia and nominated the same slate—Judge Zephaniah Platt, Ezra Thompson, Gilbert Livingston, John DeWitt, Jacobus Swartout, Jonathan Akins, and Melancton Smith. However, the Oswego meeting had not nominated candidates for the Assembly. The Constitutional Society did. The seven Assembly candidates included two convention nominees, John Dewitt and Jonathan Akins, and two members of the county Antifederalist committee, Lewis Dubois and Matthew Patterson.[20]

Melancton Smith's nomination to the convention provoked some local criticism. A correspondent, adopting the pseudonym "Many Antifederalists," attacked the nomination because Smith was no longer a resident of Dutchess County. Playing upon local pride, "Many Antifederalists" urged local voters to reject those men from outside the county thrust upon them by a small number of local politicians and offered an alternative list of men from the seven "most considerable precincts" in the county. In response to this charge "Cassius" declared that Smith was a property holder in Dutchess "as well as a patriot, republican and worthy citizen," i.e., an Antifederalist. "Cassius" further asserted that "Many Antifederalists" was in reality a Federalist attempting to split the Antifederalist vote in the county.[21] Smith was, as "Cassius" charged, a merchant residing in New York. But the convention resolves did not include a county residency requirement. Thus party leaders like Governor Clinton and congressional delegate Smith, although residents of New York City, where the Constitution was overwhelmingly popular, could be nominated in predominantly Antifederalist upstate counties and be fairly sure of a seat in the convention.

This is not to conclude that Antifederalists conceded the elections in the southern counties. On the contrary, Westchester, Kings, Queens, Suffolk, and New York county Antifederalists established county committees, distributed literature, nominated convention, Assembly, and Senate candidates, and worked for their elections.

In Westchester the current Assembly delegation and the Antifederalist county committee were the same, except that Philip Pell replaced Ebenezer Lockwood on the latter. Committee members received copies of *Observations . . . by a Columbian Patriot* and the compilation *Observations on the Proposed Constitution* from the New York City committee. By late February Abraham Yates thought the prospects for the county were favorable.[22]

In Kings and Queens counties the outlook was less promising.

An anonymous newspaper correspondent attacked Doughty and Wyckoff, the Kings' county assemblymen, for voting against the resolution calling for a state convention, and for being under the "absolute sway" of Queens County assemblyman, Samuel Jones.[23] Jones was a member of the city committee, leaving Stephen Carmen as the sole Queens County committeeman. Carmen, Jones, John Schenck, and Nathaniel Lawrence stood for election to the convention; Whitehead Cornell ran with Carmen, Schenck, and Jones for reelection to the Assembly.

By comparison, the Suffolk County committee was larger. It included Antifederalist publicist Thomas Treadwell and three of the county's assemblymen. Yet by early April no list of candidates for the convention had been agreed upon. David Gelston, the Antifederalist nominee for the Senate from the southern district, carried two hundred copies of the *Observations . . . by a Columbian Patriot* to the county and exhorted committeeman John Smith to "stir yourself—meet your friends somewhere—agree upon a good list—hold them up—persevere."[24] Eventually Antifederalists drew up a good list which included Treadwell, Jonathan N. Havens, John Smith, David Hedges, and Henry Scudder. All the candidates were members of the county committee and, with the exception of Treadwell, were candidates for reelection to the Assembly.

In contrast to the counties where Antifederalists nominated a single slate of candidates and actively worked for their election, New York City Antifederalists proposed several lists, which appeared most frequently in the *New York Journal* and included the names of Federalists and Antifederalists. Thus Governor Clinton, congressional delegate Melancton Smith, John Lamb, and Aaron Burr were nominated along with Alexander Hamilton, John Jay, and Isaac Roosevelt.[25] Despairing of an outright victory in the city, Antifederalists adopted such tactics in the hope that the Federalist vote might be splintered enough to allow one additional Antifederalist to obtain a seat in the convention.

Antifederalist electioneering paid handsome dividends everywhere in the state except in the city and its immediate vicinity. The final vote count showed an overwhelming Antifederalist victory as their candidates were elected in Washington, Montgomery, Albany, Ulster, Columbia, Dutchess, Orange, Queens, and Suffolk counties. Only New York, Westchester, and Kings elected Federalists. Forty-six of the sixty-five convention delegates were Antifederalists, seventeen were Federalists. The sentiments of the two delegates from Richmond were "unknown."[26]

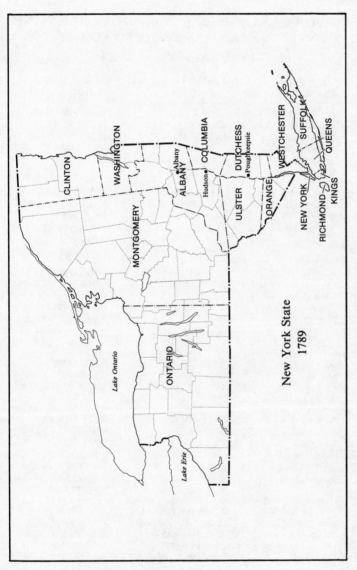

New York State, 1789.
Courtesy of the University of North Carolina Press.

NEW YORK ANTIFEDERALIST COMMITTEEMEN AND CONVENTION AND ASSEMBLY CANDIDATES*

Courtesy of the State Historical Society of Wisconsin.

COUNTY	COUNTY COMMITTEE	CONVENTION CANDIDATES	ASSEMBLY CANDIDATES
Washington	David Hopkins	DAVID HOPKINS	JOSEPH M'CRACKEN
	Ebenezer Russell	ICHABOD PARKER	PETER B. TEARSE
	John Williams	JOHN WILLIAMS	EDWARD SAVAGE
	Alexander Webster		ALEXANDER WEBSTER
	Albert Baker	ALBERT BAKER	
	Peter B. Freicel		
Montgomery	Christopher P. Yates	CHRISTOPHER P. YATES	CHRISTOPHER P. YATES
	Volkert Veeder	VOLKERT VEEDER	VOLKERT VEEDER
	John Frey	JOHN FREY	JOHN FREY
	William Harper	WILLIAM HARPER	WILLIAM HARPER
		JOHN WINN	JOHN WINN
		HENRY STARING	HENRY STARING
Albany	John Lansing, Jr.	JOHN LANSING, JR.	JOHN LANSING, JR.
	Henry Oothoudt	HENRY OOTHOUDT	JOHN YOUNGLOVE
	Jeremiah Van Rensselaer	ROBERT YATES	JEREMIAH VAN RENSSELA
	Abraham G. Lansing	PETER VROOMAN	CORNELIUS VAN DYCK
	Peter W. Yates	DIRCK SWARTOUT	JOHN THOMPSON
		ANTHONY TEN EYCK	JOHN DUNCAN
		ISRAEL THOMPSON	H. K. VAN RENSSELAER
Columbia	Peter Van Ness	PETER VAN NESS	JOHN KORTS
	John Bay	JOHN BAY	JOHN BAY
	Mathew Adgate	MATHEW ADGATE	MATHEW ADGATE
	William B. Whiting		
Ulster	Nathan Smith	GOV. GEORGE CLINTON	NATHAN SMITH
	Patrick Bailey	JOHN CANTINE	JOHN CANTINE
	Cornelius C.	CORNELIUS C.	CORNELIUS C.
	Schoonmaker	SCHOONMAKER	SCHOONMAKER
	Dirck Wynkoop	DIRCK WYNKOOP	DIRCK WYNKOOP
	Johannes Synder	EBENEZER CLARK	EBENEZER CLARK
		JAMES CLINTON	CHRISTOPHER TAPPEN
Dutchess	Peter Tappen	ZEPHANIAH PLATT	ISAAC BLOOM
	Lewis Dubois	MELANCTON SMITH	JACOB GRIFFEN
	Theodorus Bailey	JACOBUS SWARTOUT	MATTHEW PATTERSON
	Matthew Patterson	JOHN DeWITT	JOHN DeWITT
		GILBERT LIVINGSTON	GILBERT LIVINGSTON
		EZRA THOMPSON	SAMUEL A. BARKER
		JONATHAN AKINS	JONATHAN AKINS

COUNTY	COUNTY COMMITTEE	CONVENTION CANDIDATES	ASSEMBLY CANDIDATES
Orange	John Hathorn	JESSE WOODHALL	JEREMIAH CLARK
	Coe Gale	HENRY WISNER	HENRY WISNER
	Reubin Hopkins	JOHN HARING	JOHN CARPENTER
	Thomas Moffatt	JOHN WOOD	
	Peter Taulman		PETER TAULMAN
	John (———)		
Westchester	Philip Pell, Jr.	Ebenezer Lockwood	Ebenezer Lockwood
	Jonathan G. Tompkins	Jonathan G. Tompkins	Jonathan G. Tompkins
	Abijah Gilbert	Abijah Gilbert	Abijah Gilbert
	Thomas Thomas	Thomas Thomas	Thomas Thomas
	Joseph Strong	Joseph Strong	Joseph Strong
	Samuel Drake		
New York	Melancton Smith	Melancton Smith	Melancton Smith
	John Lamb	John Lamb	Nicholas Bayard
	Marinus Willett	Marinus Willett	Marinus Willett
	Samuel Jones	Samuel Jones	Aaron Burr
	James M. Hughes	John Lawrence	Henry Rutgers
		Isaac Stoutenburgh	Isaac Stoutenburgh
		Governor George Clinton	Gabriel Ludlow
		William Malcolm	Thomas Stoughton
		William Denning	William Denning
Kings	Charles Doughty	Charles Doughty	Charles Doughty
	Hendrick Wyckoff	Cornelius Wyckoff	Cornelius Wyckoff
Queens	Stephen Carmen	STEPHEN CARMEN	STEPHEN CARMEN
		SAMUEL JONES	SAMUEL JONES
		JOHN SCHENCK	JOHN SCHENCK
		NATHANIEL LAWRENCE	WHITEHEAD CORNWELL
Suffolk	Thomas Treadwell	THOMAS TREADWELL	NATHANIEL GARDNER
	David Hedges	DAVID HEDGES	DAVID HEDGES
	John Smith	JOHN SMITH	JOHN SMITH
	Jonathan Havens	JONATHAN HAVENS	JONATHAN HAVENS
	Henry Scudder	HENRY SCUDDER	HENRY SCUDDER
	Thomas Wickes		
	Caleb Cooper		
	Epenetus Smith		
Richmond			

* Those men whose names are in capitals were elected.

In addition to securing a major victory in the convention elections, the prospect of maintaining that majority in the convention was high. The Antifederalist delegation was relatively cohesive. Its members had worked together during the preceding months of the campaign, as well as in previous sessions of the legislature. Furthermore, to a greater extent than in Massachusetts, there was common agreement on the basis of opposition. The literature distributed by Lamb and the county committees, essays like Melancton Smith's "Plebeian," and the local county broadsides all stressed the same point. Antifederalists wanted previous amendments (prior to ratification) that substantially changed the structure and scope of the new Constitution.

The New York Antifederalists' position was enhanced too by the results of the Assembly elections which paralleled those for the convention. The same nine counties that elected Antifederalist convention delegates chose Antifederalist assemblymen. The three that chose Federalist convention delegates elected Federalist assemblymen. Furthermore, the counties that individually elected Antifederalists to the convention collectively chose Antifederalist senators. Those that elected Federalist convention delegates chose Federalist senators.[27]

One reason the returns were so similar was that the convention and legislative elections involved the same men. Antifederalists nominated sixty-three candidates for the convention. Of those sixty-three, thirty-five were also candidates for the assembly. Seven Antifederalist convention candidates were members of the state Senate, two of whom were seeking reelection in the spring. Thirty Antifederalist county committeemen were candidates for a seat in the legislature. In addition, the same issues dominated the convention and legislative elections. Antifederalists appealed to the voters to elect men to the Assembly because they were "men who have uniformly manifested their attachment to the liberties of America," "so that the suffrages of the county may be more united," and because their legislative candidates were "against adopting the new Constitution without previous amendments."[28]

The Constitution had a direct bearing on the outcome of the legislative elections because Antifederalists chose to make it an issue. They campaigned for seats in the legislature because they saw the state legislature as a second line of defense in the drive for revision of the proposed Constitution. As Mercy Warren explained in her *Observations . . . by a Columbian Patriot,* if the Constitution were ratified and the new government set into operation, the state legislatures would remain a source of power from which to sustain the drive for a second constitutional convention.[29]

In Massachusetts, a considerable body of Antifederalists agreed with the strategy outlined in Warren's *Observations*. Thus, following the final vote for ratification, several Antifederalists in the convention who had voted against adoption—among them Messrs. White (Bristol), Whitney (Worcester), Cooley (Hampshire), Randall (Suffolk), Swain (Middlesex), and Widgery (Cumberland)—rose to state they would, to use the words of Major Swain, "support the Constitution as cheerfully and heartily as though he [they] had voted on the other side of the question." They also pledged, as White put it, to use their "utmost exertions to induce his [their] constituents to live in peace under and to submit" to the new Constitution.[30] Federalist newspaper editors in turn praised these Antifederalists for their meritorious conduct which they contrasted to that of the Pennsylvania minority.[31] Some Antifederalists proved, however, to be less than acquiescent. Dr. John Taylor, for example, a Worcester County delegate and member of the House of Representatives from Douglas, vowed, despite his statements of acquiescence at the close of the convention, to "throw the state into confusion" rather than submit to the new Constitution.[32] Following the closing of the convention he toured the western counties "roaming about like the old dragon to devour the child now that it is born."[33] Taylor, while calling for drastic action, channeled his efforts into the political process and worked with like minded Antifederalists to maintain control of the state government as a power base from which they could continue their drive for constitutional revision prior to the operation of the new government.

Following ratification on February 6 and prior to the meeting of the General Court on February 27 Antifederalists like Taylor decided to challenge Governor John Hancock and Lieutenant Governor Thomas Cushing. In late February at a meeting at Dudley, Worcester County, a group of Antifederalists "resolved to send messengers into every town in the counties of Worcester, Berkshire, Hampshire, Bristol, and Middlesex pointing the inhabitants of these places to [Elbridge] Gerry and [James] Warren for Governor and Lieutenant Governor."[34] All of those counties had sent Antifederalist majorities to the convention in January, and state leaders hoped they would support Antifederalist candidates for governor and lieutenant governor.

The Antifederalist challenge to Governor Hancock also intruded into the meeting of the General Court which convened on February 27. Hancock, in his message to the court, praised the state convention and the proposed amendments which, "when they shall be added to the proposed plan, I shall consider as the most perfect system of government . . . known amongst mankind."[35] On the 28th a joint committee of both houses was appointed to prepare an answer to the governor's message. The report of that committee, particularly that part which related to the new Constitution, met with strong opposition in the House. Phanuel Bishop moved an amendment which expressed strong dissatisfaction with the work of the state convention because the amendments were not made a condition of ratification. As mere recommendations, Bishop maintained "they neither comport with the dignity or safety of the commonwealth."[36]

The next day the House took up Bishop's proposed amendment and, following extended debate throughout the morning and afternoon, the matter was referred to committee. The committee was weighted in favor of the Antifederalists because, as Federalist Henry Jackson complained, "the Speaker of the House [James Warren] could readily hear the nomination of an Antifederalist although the name of a Federalist rang through the whole House."[37] Federalists were able, however, to instruct the committee to report amendments so "that the said address when passed may not contain any opinion of the legislature upon the merits of the Constitution." The committee reported on March 11 when, after debate, "it was ordered that the consideration of the report subside."[38] Federalists thus blocked an Antifederalist attempt to use the legislature's reply to the governor's message as a challenge to Hancock on the issue of the previous or subsequent amendments.

Antifederalists, in turn, blocked action on an address to the people, which the convention had ordered prepared to "insure a favorable reception of the ratification."[39] The convention had voted to request the General Court to publish the address and when the convention committee presented the address to the Senate it approved a measure providing for publication.[40] In the House, however, the combined opposition of Antifederalists like Bishop and Taylor, and the prudence of Federalists doomed the measure. As Nathaniel Gorham explained: "Things were so critically situated that the publication of the papers [the address] would have been injurious" for the continuing opposition to ratification was centered in the General Court, "the people so far as applies to the federal government [being] generally quiet."[41] Publication of the address, following extended debate in the House, could have had an adverse effect and played directly into the hands of the Antifederalists who were seeking to elect a governor and lieutenant governor on the very issue of previous amendments.

The campaign for governor proved to be rather lackluster. Gerry later claimed his nomination was both "unexpected . . . and unsolicited."[42] The best that was said for Gerry was that he had been a "faithful and assiduous servant of the public" and a patriot during the war whose virtues and abilities "were at *least* equal to his Excellency's."[43] Hancock, in turn, was at the peak of his popularity. At the outset of his current term he had dealt with the aftermath of Shays' Rebellion in a manner that won him the support of many moderates and westerners.[44] As a condition of his support for subsequent amendments at the convention, Federalists agreed not to offer a candidate of their own, thereby eliminating a challenge from that sector.[45] In fact, the outcome of the election was a foregone conclusion. At the time Gerry was nominated, Antifederalists expected a three-way contest among Hancock, Gerry, and Federalist Nathaniel Gorham. Gorham had considered seeking the post, but apparently was persuaded not to with the promise of a federal post in the fall.[46] With no challenge from the Federalists, Hancock was invincible.

The real contest developed in the choice of a lieutenant governor to fill the vacancy created by the death of Thomas Cushing. Three major candidates for the post represented the three major political divisions within the state. Federalists turned to Benjamin Lincoln, the military hero who had saved the commonwealth from the anarchy of Shays. Antifederalists nominated Speaker of the House James Warren, a major leader in the opposition to unconditional ratification. Moderates, some Antifederalists, and urban artisans turned to Samuel Adams, the patriot of '74, a former ally of Hancock and an Antifederalist who voted for ratification.[47]

The rhetoric of the campaign followed in the mold set the previous spring. Federalists warned that Warren was an "inveterate Antifederal character" preparing to "mount the chariot of anarchy, to tackle in fraud and injustice as steeds, and drive like a whirlwind from east to west, distributing jealousy, dissention and treason."[48] To his supporters, of course, Warren was a "firm and honest defender of his country's rights," and the man who could avoid the "anarchy and blood-shed, which might be the consequence of introducing into office men who are for enforcing certain measures even at the point of a bayonet."[49] This was an allusion to General Benjamin Lincoln, that "virtuous, invariable and consistent patriot" whom Federalists viewed as both a "soldier and statesman," the man who during the "late rebellion had compelled the demon of chaos to fly from our [Massachusetts] borders" and for that alone merited the suffrages of the people.[50] Antifederalists saw Lincoln as the tool of a "certain aristocratic junto." Furthermore, he was a military man and should necessarily be "forever excluded from civil office in a free state."[51] Adams, both parties agreed, had been a great "patriotic character," but was "now in dotage"; a man "once possessed of firmness," but now incapable of acting "upon the busy theatre of life."[52] His supporters could only echo praise for his past achievements, while declaring that it was "the providence of God" that the lieutenant governor's chair was now vacant so that it could be bestowed upon Adams for his past service to the people.[53]

Although obscured by rhetorical cries of anarchy, aristocracy, and old age, the Constitution was an issue, particularly in the contest between Warren and Lincoln. The conspicuous role Warren played in the opposition during the preceding months inevitably made it so. But the Antifederalists seized the initiative in this electoral contest. They did so, according to Mercy Warren, because once "the present ferment" had terminated, "influential persons through the states [could] make the most prudent exertions for a new general government who [sic] may vest adequate powers in Congress for all national purposes without annihilating the individual governments."[54] To Federalists the "enemies to the federal system" were seeking "to crowd themselves into office" in order to "wreck the basis of the fabric and involve in chaos the wise plans which have been recently laid. . . ."[55] Advocates of both political persuasions agreed that the ultimate goal was a substantive restructuring of the Constitution.

The Antifederalist drive for a political power base as part of their continuing drive for fundamental constitutional revision also extended to the election of state senators on April 6. At the Dudley meeting in February Antifederalist leaders had agreed to work for the election of Gerry and Warren as governor and lieutenant governor. During the spring session of the General Court they also agreed on Antifederalist candidates for the state Senate.

The senatorial elections were not much publicized. Consequently there is little record of Antifederalist electioneering. Printed lists of Antifederalist candidates for the Senate, headed by the party's nominees for governor and lieutenant governor, were forwarded to the various counties and occasionally reprinted in the local press, but none of the broadsides has survived. The *Hampshire Gazette* reprinted a let-

ter from "D[aniel] C[ooley]," a member of the Assembly from
Amherst, which spoke of the Antifederalists' efforts to unite the
county behind one ticket, while another letter in the *Massachusetts
Centinel* warned that the "sons of anarchy" were "as busy as Beelzebub"
circulating their printed lists for governor, lieutenant governor, and
senators in Worcester County.[56] Finally, Federalists, in proposing a
statewide list of their own, warned that "the well wishers to anarchy,"
i.e. Antifederalists, were "strenuously exerting to bring into the senate persons of their own character."[57] Printed lists, like those circulated by Federalists and Antifederalists, were, however, something of
an innovation. They had been used for the first time in Senate elections the preceding spring and at least three alternative Antifederalist
and two Federalist lists were printed in one of the Worcester newspapers.[58]

Outside of Worcester, Hampshire, and Bristol counties, there
were no Antifederalist lists printed in the local press. Incomplete vote
returns printed in the *Massachusetts Centinel* did, however, identify
Middlesex and Essex candidates as on the Federalist or Antifederalist
list. In Berkshire, Barnstable, and Lincoln counties, there was an
identifiable pattern in the voting returns. In these three, as well as in
the above-mentioned counties, Antifederalist candidates polled their
greatest support from towns whose delegates in the state convention
voted against the Constitution, while Federalist candidates received
their strongest support from towns whose delegates voted for the Constitution in convention, suggesting that candidates were supported or
opposed in part at least on the basis of the constitutional issue.[59]

In Massachusetts, as in New York, national party labels were
transferred to state elections, despite the fact that the state elections
took place more than a month after the state's ratification. This use of
party labels was due, in part, to the Antifederalists' desire to control
the General Court in order to continue their drive for constitutional
revision. Furthermore, as in New York, the same men were involved
in both the campaign for convention delegates and the spring senatorial elections, and it was a natural extension of the labels "Federalist"
and "Antifederalist," as these same men again battled for political
power in the state.

Unfortunately for the Antifederalist leadership, their decision to
continue their drive for constitutional revision did not take into account the acquiescence of many Antifederalists who stood by their representatives' post ratification pledge of support for the new Constitution. Neither did the Antifederalists anticipate the widespread

alienation and subsequent abandoning of the political process among a second block of Antifederalists across the state. Gerry himself, for example, alienated by the arbitrary treatment he experienced in the state convention where he was an invited speaker rather than a delegate, disavowed any further interest in politics. Surely other Antifederalists, who had become actively involved in politics in the spring 1787 elections and again in the convention elections, felt similarly alienated. In each case their participation had little demonstrable effect on the public policy of the commonwealth. Hence the Antifederalists' bid for support in the spring legislative and gubernatorial elections, fell, in some instances, on deaf ears.

This combination of acquiescence and alienation took a heavy toll. In the gubernatorial contest Gerry, the Antifederalist candidate, polled only 19 percent of the vote against incumbent Governor Hancock, while James Warren received 29 percent of the vote in the three-way contest for lieutenant governor.[60] Final selection of the lieutenant governor was left to the General Court because no candidate received a majority of the popular vote. At the opening of its May session, the House nominated Warren and Lincoln to the Senate which chose the latter lieutenant governor by a 20 to 8 vote.[61]

In the Senate elections Antifederalists also fared poorly. In Suffolk County incumbent Antifederalist Benjamin Austin, Jr., was not even renominated, and polled only 281 votes, as opposed to 1,200-plus votes for the Federalist nominees.[62] In Essex County, incumbent Antifederalists Aaron Wood, who had been a convention delegate, Peter Coffin, and assemblyman Daniel Kilham were defeated in their bids for Senate seats, as were incumbent Walter McFarland and four other Antifederalists in Middlesex County.[63] Dr. Thomas Smith, an incumbent from Barnstable and, like Wood, an Antifederalist convention delegate, was also replaced, while Samuel Nasson failed in his bid for election from York.

Only three Massachusetts counties—Worcester, Berkshire, and Bristol—elected Antifederalists. In Worcester, Jonathan Grout, Amos Singletary, and John Fessenden were chosen. Grout and Singletary had both been members of the convention and voted against ratification. In Berkshire, Antifederalist William Whiting had been defeated in his bid for a convention seat but defeated Federalist Theodore Sedgwick in his bid for a Senate seat. Farther south in Bristol County, Phanuel Bishop, Abraham White, and Holder Slocum, all three Antifederalist delegates to the convention, were elected. White and Slocum were incumbents while Bishop had been in the Assembly the previous year. But White and the like were the minority in the Massachusetts Senate, as they and men with similar views had been the previous year.[64] More important though, with the House of Representative elections only a month away, political control of the state, which had been in the hands of the Antifederalists at the outset of the state convention, was continuing to shift to the Federalists.

Such was not the case in neighboring Rhode Island where Antifederalists maintained control of the state. The Rhode Island Assembly, which first discussed what action to take with respect to the Constitution in November 1787, reconvened for its fifth session of the political year on February 25. On the 29th, James Joslyn, seconded by Jonathan J. Hazard, proposed that the Constitution be submitted "to the freemen of the several towns in this state, in town meetings assembled, for their decision. . . ." Federalists objected to the mode, insisting that the Constitution be submitted to a state convention, but were overruled 43 to 15. The House then appointed a committee to draft appropriate legislation and adjourned for the evening. The next day that committee reported a draft bill "for submitting the Federal Constitution to the people at large. . . ." A Federalist amendment which would allow the people in town meetings to vote in favor of a state convention, instead of for or against the Constitution itself failed 36 to 16. A vote on the bill as reported from committee passed 42 to 12.[65]

One month and a day after this motion was approved the legislature was again in session. On April 2 a committee sorted and counted the returns, and reported that 2,708 freemen had voted against the Constitution, 237 for it.[66] The House then appointed a committee to draft a letter to the president of Congress explaining Rhode Island's reasons for deviating from the recommendation of the Federal Convention in its mode of considering the Constitution, and reporting the results of the voting in the towns.[67]

By the time the Rhode Island towns met to vote on the Constitution the New Hampshire Convention had adjourned and Connecticut had ratified the Constitution. Both of these states chose members of their upper and lower houses in March and April. In these contests the Constitution was not the explicit issue it was in New York and Massachusetts, but the gradual erosion of Antifederalist political strength continued nonetheless.

New Hampshire, for instance, elected state senators in March and representatives in April, but there were no competing slates of

Federalist and Antifederalist candidates. Federalists and Antifederalists were campaigning vigorously during March and April in an attempt to increase their numbers in the forthcoming June convention.[68] But this electioneering did not explicitly extend to the legislative elections. Voters cast their ballots for several candidates in each election, but none of those receiving votes was identified as Federal or Antifederal.[69]

Yet the Constitution was an underlying issue in both elections. Thus when no candidate for the Senate received a majority of the popular vote in three counties, the choice of those counties' senators was left to the House and Senate. Because of a high rate of absenteeism among the Antifederalist towns, Federalist members of the House and Senate by joint ballot were able to choose Federalists for the vacant seats and to ensure their control of that body. In the House as well, again because of absenteeism from the more traditionally Antifederalist towns, Federalists constituted a majority.[70]

Events in Connecticut followed a similar pattern. In April councillors were elected at large from among twenty men nominated the preceding October. Three prominent Antifederalists were among the twelve men composing the old council—William Williams, Erastus Wolcott, and James Wadsworth. Williams and Wolcott, however, were able to overcome their objections and voted for ratification in the January convention.[71] Only James Wadsworth was vociferous in his opposition, and had voted against ratification. In the spring balloting Wadsworth was the only incumbent on the council to fail reelection.

Wadsworth's exclusion from the council can be attributed to a variety of reasons. He had been under attack for alleged mismanagement of the state's funds as comptroller general.[72] Furthermore, he had been twelfth in the balloting the previous spring. In the spring of 1788 he declined one more place to thirteenth, hardly a precipitate drop. Still, Federalists had singled Wadsworth out for attack during and after the ratification campaign and their identification of him as "Wronghead" certainly contributed to his defeat in the spring.

The Constitution had a similar minimal effect on the election of members of the Assembly. There was no pronounced shift in the makeup of that house. The Federalists had been a majority the preceding year and they continued that dominance following the spring elections. Traditionally Antifederalist towns continued to be represented by Antifederalists, but the Federalists "were in full control."[73]

During spring 1788 the Constitution remained an issue in New York and New England. In three states—New York, Massachusetts, and Rhode Island—Antifederalists seized the initiative as they carried the issue of the Constitution to the people in state legislative and convention elections, and via a popular referendum. Furthermore, Antifederalists scored some significant victories during the spring. The New Hampshire Convention adjourned in February. Following that adjournment both parties continued their campaign for delegate support, but when the convention reassembled in June Antifederalists remained a majority. The Rhode Island towns overwhelmingly rejected the Constitution in March. And the returns from the New York convention elections indicated that Antifederalists won a resounding victory there as well.

Within these short term victories, however, lay the seeds of ultimate defeat. New Hampshire's adjournment came after a motion to adopt the Constitution failed. It was a Federalist ploy to avoid outright defeat and was indicative of the future.[74] Rhode Island's rejection had little impact outside the state. Reports of the voting were widely reprinted in the weeks immediately following the referendum, but so were the reports that Federalists had boycotted the voting. Moreover, Rhode Island's rejection had been anticipated; consequently, there was no outcry of shock or dismay similar to the one that followed New Hampshire's adjournment. Rhode Island's reputation for obstruction negated any influence her refusal to ratify the Constitution might have had on the course of ratification in the undecided states.[75]

Similarly, although the New York Antifederalists won solid majorities in the convention and Assembly, the effect of the news of those victories was minimized by their lateness. The elections themselves were held after those in every other state. Furthermore, the votes were not counted until May 3. During the interval South Carolina ratified the Constitution, and by June 5 only four states— New Hampshire, New York, Virginia, and North Carolina—were still to meet in convention.

Finally, even as these victories were being claimed, the basis for a sustained Antifederalist drive was being undercut. In New Hampshire and Connecticut the Constitution had not been an explicit issue in the popular choice of legislators. Still contemporaries recognized that the returns were "favorable" to the Federalists.[76] In Massachusetts and New York, Federalists had majorities in the Senate, while Antifederalists could claim only the New York and Massachusetts assemblies and the Rhode Island legislature. In terms of a post-ratification drive for a second constitutional convention, the absence of an institutional power base in a majority of the states was to prove as decisive as the forthcoming Federalist convention victories.

NOTES TO
CHAPTER 4

1. 13 September 1787.
2. See my "The Impact of the Constitution," pp. 275–80.
3. Broadside resolve, McKesson Papers, NHi.
4. John Lansing, Jr., et al., to anon., handwritten broadside in the Emmet Collection, NHi; *Albany Journal*, 15 March 1788.
5. To Peter Gansevoort, 13 February 1788, Gansevoort-Lansing Papers, NN.
6. To Henry Knox, 13 February 1788, Knox Papers, MHi.
7. *New York Daily Advertiser*, 10 April 1788.
8. Notation on an undated distribution list, Lamb Papers, NHi. This list includes the names of the members of each Antifederalist county committee in the state.
9. *Ibid*.
10. Abraham Yates to Abraham G. Lansing, 28 February 1788, Yates Papers, NN.
11. Christopher Yates to George Herkimer, 9 April 1788, Herkimer Papers, NUtHI.
12. *Hudson Weekly Gazette,* 20 March 1788. Van Ness's candidacy was mentioned in Henry Oothoudt and Jeremiah Van Rensselaer to Jellis Fonda, 5 April 1788, N.
13. 10 April 1788.
14. *New York Journal*, 23 February 1788.
15. "A Subscriber," *Ibid.*, 29 February 1788.
16. Michael D'Innocenzo and John Turner, "The Peter Van Gaasbeek Papers: A Resource for New York History, 1771–1797," *New York History,* 47 (April 1966): 153–59.
17. Cornelius Schoonmaker to Peter Van Gaasbeek, 4 April 1788, Van Gaasbeek Papers, NHpR.
18. A copy of the list is in Joseph Gasherie to the Citizens of Kingston, 21 April 1788, Van Gaasbeek Papers, NKiS.
19. *Ibid*.
20. *Poughkeepsie Country Journal,* 4 March, 15 April 1788.
21. *Ibid.*, 4 and 18 March 1788.
22. Abraham Yates to Abraham G. Lansing, 28 February 1788, Yates Papers, NN.
23. New York *Daily Advertiser*, 20 February 1788.
24. 9 April 1788, John Smith of Mastic Papers, NHi.
25. Nominations were printed in the *New York Daily Advertiser*, 26 April; and in the *New York Journal*, 19 February, 13 March, 4, 5, 19, and 22 April, and 1 May 1788. Melancton Smith insisted that Clinton be nominated in Ulster County arguing that it was better that he "be chosen in two places than not at all," to (?), 6 April 1788, Lamb Papers, NHi.
26. Returns for the convention, House, and Senate, with the candidates identified as "Federal" or "Antifederal" were reported in the *New York Journal*, 5 and 14 June 1788.
27. *Ibid*.

28. *New York Journal*, 1 April; Joseph Gasherie to the Citizens of Kingston, 21 April, Van Gaasbeek Papers, NKiS; and a broadside signed by Jeremiah Van Rensselaer, Chairman, Albany Antifederal Committee, 10 April 1788.

29. Mercy Warren, *Observations on the New Constitution . . . by a Columbian Patriot*, in Ford, *Pamphlets*, 1–24. Ford identifies Elbridge Gerry as the author. For a correction of that attribution see Charles Warren, "Elbridge Gerry, James Warren, Mercy Warren and the Ratification of the Federal Constitution in Massachusetts," *Proceedings*, 64 (1932): 143–64, MHi.

Federalists also nominated candidates for state legislative seats and campaigned for their election in part on the basis of their support for the Constitution. Antifederalists, however, because of their own political philosophy, placed particular emphasis on the state legislatures while Federalists generally deprecated them.

30. *Massachusetts Debates*, pp. 281–82.

31. *Boston Massachusetts Centinel*, 9 February 1788.

32. Thomas B. Wait to George Thacher, 29 February 1788, Thacher Papers, p. 343.

33. Jeremiah Hill to George Thacher, 14 February 1788, *ibid*.

34. Christopher Gore to Rufus King, 2 March 1788, King, *Life*, 1: 323.

35. House Journals, 27 February 1788.

36. *Ibid.*, 5 November; Nathaniel Gorham to Unknown, 9 March 1788, Fogg Autograph Collection, MeHi.

37. To Henry Knox, 10 March 1788, Knox Papers, MHi.

38. House Journals, 6 and 11 March 1788.

39. Samuel Harding, *The Contest Over the Ratification of the Federal Constitution . . .* (New York, 1896), p. 112.

40. *Massachusetts Debates*, p. 93.

41. Gorham to Rufus King, 6 April 1788, King, *Life*, 1: 324.

42. Elbridge Gerry to Samuel R. Gerry, 6 April 1788, Gerry Papers, MHi.

43. *Boston American Herald*, 3 April 1788.

44. See Hall, *Politics Without Parties*, p. 299.

45. Tristram Dalton to Stephen Hooper, 31 January 1788, Eben F. Stone, "Parsons and the Constitutional Convention of 1788," Essex Institute *Collections*, 35: 94; Rufus King to Henry Knox, 1 February, King, *Life*, 1: 319; and King to Knox, 3 February, Knox Papers, MHi.

46. See Christopher Gore to Rufus King, 2 March 1788, *Life*, 1: 323–24.

47. Hall, *Politics*, pp. 300–303.

48. "Federalissimo," *Boston Massachusetts Gazette*, 7 March 1788.

49. *Boston American Herald*, 3 April 1788.

50. "Junius," *Boston Massachusetts Gazette*, 28 March 1788.

51. "Republican," *Boston American Herald*, 7 April 1788.

52. "Caucus," *ibid.*, 13 March 1788.

53. *Boston Gazette*, 5 April 1788.

54. *Observations*, in Ford, *Pamphlets*, p. 19.

55. "Federalissimo," *Boston Massachusetts Gazette,* 7 March 1788.

56. "A Traveller," *Northampton Hampshire Gazette*, 2 April; *Boston Massachusetts Centinel*, 5 April 1788.

57. *Boston Massachusetts Centinel,* 2 April 1788.

58. *Thomas' Worcester Massachusetts Spy*, 26 March, 3 April 1788.

59. 9 April 1788; Hall, *Politics Without Parties*, p. 300.

60. The returns are in the Massachusetts Archives. They are summarized in *ibid*.

61. House Journal, 28 May; Senate Journal, 29 May 1788.

62. *Boston Massachusetts Centinel*, 9 April 1788.

63. *Ibid*. See also Benjamin W. Labaree, *Patriots and Partisans: The Merchants of Newburyport 1764–1815* (Cambridge, 1962), pp. 78–79.

64. The turnover in the Senate has been determined from the membership lists in *Fleet's Pocket Almanac* (Boston, 1787, 1788). The votes in convention are in *Massachusetts Debates*, pp. 87–92.

65. This account is based on the report in the *Newport Herald*, 6 March. See also the *Providence United States Chronicle* and the *Newport Mercury*, both 6 March 1788.

66. Staples, *Rhode Island*, pp. 591–606.

67. Governor John Collins to President of Congress (Cyrus Griffin), 5 April 1788, Letters from the Governor, RI-Ar.

68. See Lawrence Guy Strauss, "Reactions of Supporters of the Constitution to the Adjournment of the New Hampshire Ratification Convention, 1788," *Historical New Hampshire*, 23 (1968): 37–50.

69. See the partial returns in the *Newburyport Essex Journal,* 19 and 26 March, and the *Portsmouth New Hampshire Gazette*, 12, 19 and 26 March 1788.

70. Albert S. Batchellor, *New Hampshire State Papers* (Concord, 1892), 21: 252–53.

71. The votes in the convention and the spring ballots are in Charles J. Hoadly and Leonard W. Labaree, comps., *Public Records of the State of Connecticut* (Hartford, 1894–19—), 6: 549–52.

72. "A Parody," *New Haven Gazette*, 20 March 1788.

73. The representatives are listed in Labaree, *Connecticut Records*, 6: 54–63. The quotation is Philip Jordan's, "Connecticut Politics During the Revolution," unpublished Ph.D. Thesis, Yale University, 1962, p. 371.

74. Peter Curtenius to George Clinton, 2 March 1788, George Clinton Papers (Bancroft Transcripts), NN.

75. See Polishook, *Rhode Island and the Union*, pp. 165–70.

76. Rufus King to James Madison, 25 May 1788, King, *Life*, 1: 329–30.

Chapter 5

SPRING ELECTIONS
IN THE SOUTH

During spring 1788, Antifederalists continued their previous efforts. Pennsylvania Antifederalists mounted an extensive, two-pronged attack. In Pennsylvania and Georgia, which had previously ratified the Constitution and which did not hold legislative elections until the fall, they worked to repeal ratification. In Maryland, Virginia, and the Carolinas, Pennsylvania Antifederalists distributed literature and worked with local leaders in the campaign for the election of Antifederalist majorities to the state conventions. This led to an Antifederalist sweep of the North Carolina convention and a virtual draw in Virginia. In addition, Antifederalists were able to generate considerable support outside the conventions. That support conditioned their actions in the conventions, and induced them, following ratification, to participate in the first federal elections, in an attempt to secure their basic political goals. None foresaw the consequences of their action which at that time held out the likelihood of success.

Following ratification three options existed for Pennsylvania Antifederalists: they could accept the decision of the state convention; they could resort to armed resistance; or they could initiate political action. Varying numbers of Pennsylvania Antifederalists chose each alternative.

The extent of Antifederalist acquiescence at this time is unclear. The newspapers offer no adequate estimate, for Philadelphia's newspapers were overwhelmingly partisan in their reporting. The Federalist *Pennsylvania Journal* reported that the great majority of the people concurred in the decision of the convention and that only a handful of malcontents continued to oppose the Constitution. The Antifederalist *Independent Gazetteer* stated just the opposite—that the people did not accept the decision of the convention.[1] Private comment was also contradictory, at least about public sentiment outside of Philadelphia, which all conceded was a Federalist stronghold. Thomas Scott, a Federalist, informed Benjamin Rush that "the voice of opposition is scarcely heard," while Benjamin Blythe, an Antifederalist, claimed a majority of Pennsylvania's farmers were opposed.[2]

Some of those who did not acquiesce turned to violent protest. On December 26, members of the Union Society in Carlisle disrupted a Federalist ratification celebration, drove the Federalists from the town square, and burned a copy of the Constitution to protest Pennsylvania's ratification. The next evening Federalists returned and completed their celebration, only to be followed by Antifederalists who burned Federalists Thomas McKean and James Wilson in effigy.[3]

The Carlisle riot was a rather minor affair, but it had national repercussions. Both parties had their own versions of the event, and accounts of it were reported from New Hampshire to Georgia.[4] Federalists declared that the new government under the Constitution would be able to quell such civil disturbances and prevent their outbreak in the future. Antifederalists, on the other hand, insisted that if Federalists persevered in "pushing on the present one [Constitution]," then it would "inevitably involve this devoted country in ruin and all the horrors of civil war." For anarchy and chaos to be avoided, Federalists must "drop all proceedings in favor of the proposed Constitution and use all their endeavors to have a new federal convention called immediately."[5]

Although they used the rhetoric of anarchy, and Federalists accused them of being incendiaries bent on involving the country in civil war, most Antifederalists were chiefly concerned with mobilizing public opinion and in channeling it into concrete political programs. Late in December John Nicholson, state comptroller general and an Antifederalist pamphleteer, initiated a statewide petition campaign. Signers of the petition called on the legislature not to confirm the state's ratification because the Constitution and "the powers therein proposed to be granted to the government" were too great as well as "dangerous and inimical to liberty and equality amongst the people."[6] Nicholson, and various members of the minority sent copies of the petition to political allies in at least nine of the state's fourteen counties. Once received in a given county, the petition was copied and "sent to the several townships." Eventually over six thousand signatures were collected.[7]

Six thousand Antifederalist signatures were not, however, by themselves sufficient. Federalist legislators, a majority in the Pennsylvania House in 1788, had to be convinced of the necessity for repeal. Toward that end Antifederalists embarked on another massive propaganda campaign, one with an added dimension. Antifederalists believed that one of the most persuasive arguments for the Constitution was its promise to prevent further Shaysite actions like those that had appeared in Pennsylvania in the spring of 1787. In the winter of 1788 Antifederalists tried to turn this fear to their advantage. They argued that the Constitution, rather than promising an end to armed resistance to governmental measures, was promoting it. Samuel Bryan, in Centinel VII, for example, warned that the freemen of Pennsylvania would not submit to the new Constitution without a struggle.[8] An unidentified correspondent in the *Philadelphia Freeman's Journal* made the same point when he declared that the Federalists must "immediately drop all proceedings in favor of the proposed Constitution . . . for should they persist in attempting to force it on the people, the peace of the country must inevitably be destroyed."[9]

Such an argument was, of course, a dangerous one and invited, not Federalist conversions, but attack. Instead of being persuaded by Bryan's argument, Federalists condemned him for his refusal to accept the will of the majority as reflected in the state convention and warned that a strong central government was necessary to guard against civil strife being introduced by such anarchic and antidemocratic elements as Bryan.[10] The issue came to a head in March when the petitions calling for repeal were submitted to the state legislature. Despite the Antifederalists' best effort, no Federalist legislator was converted and the petitions were rejected.

Although Antifederalists were unable to effect a repeal of Pennsylvania's ratification (the constitutionality of such a repeal aside), the petition campaign served a useful purpose for it provided Antifederalist leaders with an outlet, a channel through which the "real majority" of Pennsylvanians could express their views. Federalist Thomas Scott correctly explained the Antifederalist leadership's purpose when he reported to Benjamin Rush that Antifederalist John Smiley had spent three hours retailing "Centinel, Old Whiganical and other Newspaper Nonsense. . . . In a word he labored to stir up the people to arms but he could not well direct them to the immediate object . . . and therefore happily thought of petitioning the assembly."[11]

In addition to the petition campaign, Antifederalists, in order to maintain and indeed extend their popular support in the state, formed local county political societies. In Centinel XIII, Samuel Bryan argued such societies "ought to be instituted [for] they would form an invincible bulwark to liberty and might better proceed to secure the blessings of a good federal government."[12] By April 1788 Bryan claimed that such societies did exist in every county and there is some evidence that members of the societies were utilized in the petition campaign, distributed pamphlets, and generally promoted the feeling of a continuing opposition throughout the state.[13]

Some sense of the influence of these societies and of Antifederalist activity is also indicated by the persistent reports of a statewide meeting of Antifederalists. As early as February 9 George Bryan informed New York Governor George Clinton of a plan for a statewide gathering of delegates "in the spring" which would decide "how far the majority of the people of this state are to abide by the decision of the violent and tyrannous minority," the Federalists.[14] William Petrikin also anticipated a "general meeting in the spring" and elections in March to choose delegates, while the *Independent Gazetteer* printed an extract of a letter from York County which reported that people there did not consider the Constitution adopted by the state and added that they were "very apt to make some experiments in the spring." A "gentleman of veracity" in Franklin County pledged that his county would elect delegates to a state-wide conference, and proposed that it be held at Reading "as early in April as possible." The idea of a spring convention was also well received in Washington and Westmoreland counties where "more solid measures" than petitions were "on the carpet."[15]

The consequences of this effort were, in one sense, anticlimactic. No "more solid measures" occurred before ratification by eleven states. The Pennsylvanians' efforts were not, however, intended to affect only Pennsylvania. Indeed, their purpose was, as Federalist John Montgomery complained, to "excite or strengthen the opposition which exists in the two neighboring southern states."[16] Montgomery was in error only in regard to the geographic extent of Antifederalist efforts.

The opposition in Maryland was in particular need of assistance from its neighbor. The Maryland legislature had served as a forum for the dissemination of Antifederalist objections to the Constitution when on November 29 Luther Martin offered his "Genuine Information" to the Assembly. That speech, considerably expanded and revised, was published during March and April 1788 in the *Baltimore Maryland Journal*. Other Antifederalist essays from Philadelphia, Richmond, and New York were also printed in Baltimore and Annapolis during the winter. Accounts of the Carlisle riot also drifted south, and at least one correspondent in the *Journal* advised the people of Maryland to "pause awhile before they proceeded to the ratification of it [the new Constitution] for a civil war with all its train of evils will probably be the consequence of such a proceeding." If ratification were delayed, alterations could be made "at a more convenient opportunity" and then the Constitution could be peaceably adopted.[17]

This call for delay was a theme common to many of the essays printed in Maryland and reflected a tactic of Antifederalist leaders. That goal had been partially achieved when the Maryland House set the date for the election of delegates for the first week in April, consistent with the initial Antifederalist plan for simultaneous spring conventions. But the Virginia legislature inexplicably approved a June convention for that state, which forced the Maryland Antifederalists to plan for an adjournment once their convention assembled if they were to cooperate with the Virginia Convention. Federalist Daniel Carroll informed James Madison that this was the plan of the state's Antifederalist leaders, while James McHenry wrote George Washington that such an adjournment would be pressed for "under the pretext of a conference with yours respecting amendments."[18] It was unlikely that they could win a majority of the seats in the state convention. Recognizing the popularity of the Constitution in the state, it became the policy of Maryland's Antifederalists to "say little in public, to work secretly as long as they can, and to burst forth all at once just before the election."[19]

Because of these delaying tactics not much is known about the Antifederalists' campaigns, particularly outside of the state's major urban centers. Antifederalists, for example, did campaign among the eight counties of the eastern shore. William Tilghman, a state judge who traveled extensively throughout the region, thought that at least two counties would elect Antifederalists. Tilghman also spoke of possible "accidents," meaning the election of Antifederalists, elsewhere in the region, but no Antifederalists were elected and, save for Tilghman's comments, no record of those Antifederalist candidates—not even their names—remains.[20]

On the western shore the record is more complete. In Baltimore, Antifederalists Samuel Sterrett and David McMechan attempted to deceive the voters by "declaring themselves in the most unequivocal manner to be Federal." On the day of the election, though, when called upon to reiterate those sentiments, the two refused. That, coupled with the fact that the two men were "supported by all the Antifederalists in the city" persuaded Baltimore Federalists to locate other candidates who overwhelmed Sterrett and McMechan in the balloting.[21]

Elsewhere on the western shore Antifederalists did not resort to such duplicity, although they did tend to delay their entry into the field. Thus in Anne Arundel County, Federalists Charles Carroll of Carrollton, James Carroll, John Hall, and Bruce Worthington campaigned for several months in favor of "ratifying the proposed national government without any amendments." On the Thursday prior to the election Jeremiah T. Chase, John Francis Mercer, and Benjamin Harrison, reportedly "at the solicitations of the people," announced their candidacy and support for previous amendments. A rider was dispatched to Charles County to ask Governor William Smallwood to serve as the fourth Antifederalist candidate. Meanwhile, Chase and Mercer "dispersed a handbill" which "alarmed the people" with dire warnings of an impending loss of civil liberties. Samuel Chase also campaigned actively for the Antifederalist ticket and on the day of the election he was put in nomination in place of Smallwood who did not arrive before the opening of the poll. Mercer, the Chases, and Harrison, because of this last-minute campaign, carried the election, reportedly by less than fifty votes.[22]

In Baltimore County, too, the Antifederalists were slow in formulating a slate of candidates. In early February, George Lux, John Cradock, Charles Ridgely of William, and Aquilla Hall were all candidates. During March, Harry Dorsey Gough also declared his candidacy, and Speaker of the Assembly Thomas Cockey and Charles Ridgely were nominated. A week before the election there was a realignment of the tickets: the two Ridgelys, Nathan Cromwell, and Edward Cockey for the Antifederalists; Gough, Cradock, Gittings, and Lux for the Federalists. When Lux objected to being pledged to vote for ratification, John Eager Howard replaced him on the ticket.[23] The Antifederalists won the election.

That success also extended to neighboring Harford County where the Antifederalist candidates were largely unopposed. William Pinckney, one of the candidates, debated a Parson Lukey prior to the election, but on the day of the election only the four Antifederalist candidates—Pinckney, Luther Martin, John Love, and William Paca—received votes.[24]

Antifederalists also nominated candidates farther west. In Montgomery three of the county's four assemblymen—Edward Burgess, Lawrence O'Neal, and William Holmes—stood for election. Burgess and O'Neal had been members of the Assembly every year but one since 1780 and apparently expected little opposition. Opposition did emerge when Benjamin Edwards, Richard Thomas, William Eakins, and Thomas Cramphin—all four representing a Georgetown mercantile interest—stood for election in support of un-conditional ratification. Both parties campaigned vigorously and the Antifederalists received aid from a nephew of George Mason who vis-ited Georgetown and "delivered his sentiments respecting the pro-posed Constitution." It was not enough, for the Federalists won re-soundingly.[25]

In Washington County five-term incumbent assemblyman Jacob Sellars and three-term incumbent Jacob Funk were reported "exerting themselves" to stir up the minds of the common people against the new Constitution. Various Antifederalist essays, includ-ing "Centinel" and Richard Henry Lee's "Publications" were also "read with attention." To counter these publications and the Anti-federalists' campaigning, Federalists called a county-wide meeting to assemble at Hagerstown on March 1. At that meeting the Constitu-tion was explained "to the general satisfaction of all present." The Antifederalist candidates were overwhelmed in the election.[26]

The outcome of the elections was a major blow to the Anti-federalists. Only twelve Antifederalists were elected to a convention composed of seventy-six delegates. Furthermore three of those—Samuel Chase, Luther Martin, and William Paca—did not meet the county residency requirement. Federalists, though, given their over-whelming majority, decided before the convention assembled to allow them their seats, for if they were excluded "it might raise discontents among the people who chose them, and the whole Antifederal party would exclaim that they were excluded lest they should show the intended form of government in its proper colours."[27]

Given the popularity of the Constitution in Maryland, and the wisdom of the Federalists in trying to avoid giving the Antifederalists any possible grounds for attacking the decision of the convention, the goal for Maryland Antifederalists became of necessity more limited. As Federalists saw, well before the convention assembled, the only hope for Maryland's Antifederalists was to press for an adjournment "until the sense of Virginia should be known."[28]

That state's Antifederalists certainly were prepared to lead.

From the outset, they had been at the forefront of the opposition, and they did not relinquish that role during 1788. From January through April the "objections" of prominent Virginia Antifederalists were distributed across the state and supplemented by propaganda emanating from Philadelphia. Indeed, the Pennsylvania literature complemented that of the Virginians. For example, Virginians cited the absence of civil liberty guarantees in the Constitution as a major flaw. Pennsylvania Antifederalists cried that civil liberties were already being destroyed in their state. Pennsylvania Antifederalists, in turn, condemned the federal government's power to tax. Virginia Antifederalists proposed a requisition system for raising needed federal revenues. In both Virginia and Pennsylvania Antifederalists demanded that the Constitution be amended before its adoption by the remaining non-ratifying states.[29]

Following legislative adjournment, many of its members, instilled with the objections of Henry, Mason, and Lee, returned to their homes to stand for election to the state convention. Factional divisions in the Assembly influenced the degree of opposition these men met in their campaigns. The Southside, for instance, was a stronghold of Patrick Henry and the "Henryite" faction in the Assembly. It was also an area largely conceded to the Antifederalists in the battle for convention delegates.[30]

Despite the absence of any extensive Federalist opposition in the Southside counties, there was considerable electioneering. Edward Carrington, in the "midst of [Henry's] influence" in Powhatan, repeatedly complained of the tactics of Henry and his supporters, as did John B. Smith who led what token opposition there was in Prince Edward County. Although Henry did not announce his candidacy until February, Federalist Smith complained that even "before the Constitution appeared, the minds of the people here were artfully prejudiced against it, so that all opposition at the election for delegates to consider it [against Mr. Henry] was in vain." Henry and Robert Lawson, who was elected with him, were both Antifederalists.[31]

In Powhatan County William Ronald and Thomas Turpin, Jr., incumbent assemblymen, also announced their candidacy and their support for amendments in early February. Ronald, however, professed a "determination to do nothing which may endanger the Union" while Turpin was explicitly allied to Henry. Because of Turpin's extremism Edward Carrington also announced his candidacy. A few days prior to the election, and in response to both Carrington's

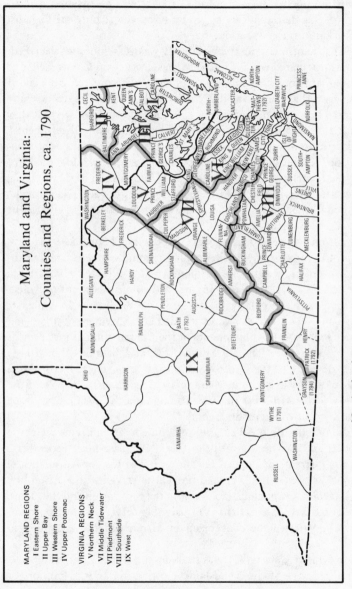

Maryland and Virginia: Counties and Regions, ca. 1790.
Courtesy of the University of Wisconsin Cartographic Lab.

candidacy and a pronounced shift in the "sentiments of the town," Turpin modified his position and "took the same ground as Carrington." He defeated Carrington by seven votes, but voted against ratification in the convention.[32]

That sentiment in the Southside was less cohesive than Federalists anticipated was indicated by the elections in Chesterfield and Buckingham counties. In both cases there were more Antifederalist candidates than seats in the convention. Federalists could have exploited this to their own advantage. Carrington proposed that they do just that in order to aid in the election of men of "discernment." But Carrington was the exception. Most of the "friends to the Constitution" in the Southside suppressed their opinions, while the Henryites "industriously propagated" theirs. And, almost as if by default, the elections "terminated in the deputation of weak and bad men who have bound themselves to vote in the negative and will in all cases be the tool of Mr. Henry."[33]

Although the Southside was the bedrock of Antifederalist support in the convention, Antifederalists throughout the state distributed pamphlets, sought out and nominated candidates, competed in the elections, and won seats in the forthcoming convention. Electioneering was particularly aggressive in the Piedmont. In Amherst, for instance, the county's two incumbent assemblymen, William and Samuel Jordon Cabell, opponents of the Constitution "in its present form," opposed Federalists Hugh Rose and Samuel Meredith (a former delegate to the Confederation Congress). The Cabells were a powerful family in the county and this was reflected at the polls. Rose and Meredith withdrew midway through the balloting when they trailed by over three hundred votes.[34]

In neighboring Albemarle, incumbent assemblyman George Nicholas and his brother Wilson Cary Nicholas, both Federalists, overcame "strenuous opposition" in their bid for convention seats. Wilson Cary Nicholas, who had previously served in the Assembly, simultaneously campaigned for a seat in the convention and the House of Delegates. Apparently that campaigning served its dual purpose. He was elected to the convention in March and the Assembly in April.[35]

In Orange County, Charles Barbour and Charles Porter opposed Federalists James Madison and James Gordon. Barbour, a "minion" of Henry, "warmly opposed" the Constitution as did Hardin Burnley, his colleague in the Assembly. Burnley, who declined to stand for the convention, distributed Antifederalist pamphlets as part of Barbour's campaign and the author of one of those pamphlets, Richard Henry Lee, publicly endorsed Barbour. Porter and Barbour solicited the support of other local leaders as well, particularly Baptists who feared that "religious liberty" was "not sufficiently secured" in the Constitution.[36] These activities alarmed Federalists who repeatedly urged Madison to return to the county from New York where he was a delegate to Congress. He did return, the "day before the election," and the next day, in a one-and-three-quarter-hour speech "at the court house door" addressed the people and secured his election.[37]

The Antifederalist setback in Orange was offset in part by the election of French Strother, another of Henry's allies, in Culpepper. Strother, an incumbent assemblyman, persuaded Joel Early, who had been "a friend to the measure [the Constitution], . . . to declare against it." Strother and Early stood for both the convention and the House of Delegates. They were elected to both, Early unseating Federalist James Pendleton in the house.[38]

The election in Spotsylvania, like that in Culpepper, ended "very unfavorably" in Federalists' eyes. James Monroe and John Dawson, both incumbent assemblymen, defeated two Federalist candidates. They were also reelected to the Assembly a month later. Monroe's views on the Constitution were not known at the time of his election, in part because he was himself undecided. Dawson, on the other hand, was recognized as a decided opponent, a member of the Henry faction and, to Federalist James Duncanson, "a worthless scoundrel" as well.[39] Campaigning in the county was extensive. In February Monroe informed Madison that the county as a whole opposed the Constitution, while Dawson reported "uncommon exertions" by both parties to elect "persons whose sentiments agree with their own." On election day Dawson, in an address at the courthouse, explained the Constitution "in so masterly a manner" as to be elected "by a large majority," the efforts of the "friends to the proposed Constitution notwithstanding."[40]

Similar electioneering characterized the southern Piedmont county of Henrico, although with opposite results. Nathaniel Wilkinson and John Marshall represented the county in the Assembly. Wilkinson, however, deferred to the candidacy of Edmund Randolph, whom most viewed as an Antifederalist.[41] Federalist Marshall and Antifederalist William Foushee, the county sheriff, sought the second seat. Outside of the city of Richmond the county was considered Antifederalist. According to Randolph, however, Foushee was "not popular enough on other scores to be elected, although he is perfectly Henryite."[42] Randolph's evaluation proved correct for he and Marshall were chosen on March 4.

Although little is known of the elections in the remaining Piedmont counties, Antifederalists did well in most of them and the Southside. Antifederalists offered candidates in nearly every county, and of the sixty-four seats at issue in the Piedmont and Southside, forty-nine went to Antifederalists.[43] Elsewhere, although Antifederalists campaigned aggressively, they did not fare as well. Of the thirty seats from the lower James and Tidewater counties and boroughs Antifederalists won only eight. Along the Rappahannock River and among the Northern Neck counties Antifederalists nominated candidates in only six counties. They won in four.

The greatest setback to Antifederalists' aspirations came in Westmoreland County when Richard Henry Lee declined to stand for election, supposedly because of the unhealthy climate at Richmond. His refusal was a particular disappointment to George Mason who looked to Lee as a potential ally in the convention and as a likely delegate to the second constitutional convention.[44] There was also a dearth of candidates in Fairfax County.

In contrast there was an excess of candidates in Stafford and Prince William counties. Arthur Lee had hoped to be elected from Stafford, but by mid-February had abandoned "the pursuit" in favor of George Mason, whom Stafford County Antifederalists had petitioned to stand for election in their district to ensure his presence in the convention, and former Stafford County assemblyman Andrew Buchanan.[45] Federalists opposed Mason and Buchanan with two strong candidates: Assemblymen Bailey Washington and William Fitzhugh. During the course of the campaign Federalist David Stuart, apparently irked at Mason's aggressive campaigning, remarked that "he [Mason] should have been satisfied with the publication of his objections, without taking the pains to lodge them at every house."[46] James Madison, informed of Mason's activity, repeated a report that Mason had "totally abandoned his moderation on this subject [the Constitution] and is pursuing his object by means which will neither add to the dignity of his character nor . . . to the success of his cause."[47] Mason and Buchanan were elected.

Arthur Lee had also hoped to be elected from Prince William, if not Stafford, but was forced to withdraw in favor of congressional delegates William Grayson and Cuthbert Bullitt. Grayson had supported Richard Henry Lee in Congress when the Constitution was reported from the Federal Convention and continued an opponent of ratification throughout the winter and spring. Grayson's views on the Constitution have often been misunderstood because Edward Carrington reported that he opposed the Constitution on the ground that it was not "national" enough.[48] In Virginia, however, Grayson was identified with the Henryites and campaigned against the Constitution on the theme of Virginia's dominant position in the Confederation, a position which would be jeopardized in the new government.[49] Grayson and Bullitt were elected without any recorded opposition.

Antifederalists were also strong in Fauquier and Loudon counties. In February Arthur Lee suggested that Richard Henry Lee "might certainly be chosen in Fauquier were you to declare yourself."[50] Lee's reluctance to declare his candidacy was not shared by Antifederalists Martin Pickett and Augustine Jennings. Both men were elected in March. In Loudon, Federalist assemblymen Leven Powell and Josiah Clapham challenged William Elezy and Stephens Thomson Mason, a nephew of George Mason. Mason was particularly active, speaking at public meetings and campaigning throughout the county. Whether because of his campaigning or his family ties, he was elected on March 10, as was Federalist Powell, making Loudon one of the few counties to elect a split delegation.[51]

West and south of Loudon, throughout the Shenandoah Valley, Antifederalists were generally in the minority. They nonetheless campaigned actively, nominated candidates, and, particularly in the farthest reaches of the valley, secured additional convention seats. One of the more spirited campaigns occurred in Frederick County where Alexander White, a Federalist candidate for the convention, vigorously attacked Richard Henry Lee and George Mason, whose comments and objections had been printed in the *Winchester Advertiser* during November. White's remarks attracted considerable adverse comment, but he and Federalist John Woodcock defeated Antifederalists John Smith and Charles Thruston.[52]

Elsewhere Antifederalist strength was spotty. There was token opposition in Rockingham and Augusta and only one Antifederalist candidate polled votes in Shenandoah.[53] In Rockbridge William Graham, rector of Liberty Hall Academy, "raised an uncommon commotion" against the Constitution. It was expected Graham would be elected, but he was defeated by the county's Federalist assemblymen, William McKee and Andrew Moore.[54]

The most ambitious effort in the West came in Washington County. There the Constitution was reported a "major topic of discussion." Copies of *The Dissent of the Minority* and *Centinel* circulated in the county, carried there by Pennsylvanian Adam Orth, himself a signer of the *Dissent*. Orth also served as an intermediary between Pennsylvania and Virginia Antifederalists, notably Arthur Campbell, former assemblyman, land speculator, and political intriguer. During March, Campbell revised the Constitution so that it was "nearer the sentiments of the great body of the yeomanry of America, especially in the Southern States" and sent the amended version to Francis Bailey, editor of the *Philadelphia Freeman's Journal*. Initially, Campbell suggested that Bailey print it on "the first page of your paper, embellished with proper capitals, and a neat type." But the next day Campbell urged instead that in the interests of a wider circulation and a more substantial impact the revised Constitution "first [be] published in a pamphlet, and speedily dispersed, especially in Pennsylvania, New York, and Virginia." Campbell was not willing to bear the expense of such a publication, but was certain that "several thousand copies could be readily sold in Virginia." Campbell, who was well known among Pennsylvania Antifederalists, also urged Orth, the bearer of his proposal, to consult with William Findley, Robert Whitehill, John Smiley, or James McLene about the proposal, and added that Dr. Ewing, whom Campbell thought the author of the "Centinel" essays, revise the piece and give his assistance.[55] Apparently some consideration was given to the proposal because Campbell's letters to Bailey and Orth ended up in the Bryan papers, suggesting that either Samuel or George Bryan was consulted on the matter. Although the proposed pamphlet was not published, Campbell's efforts illustrate both the breadth of the Antifederalists' effort and the alternative they proposed—previous amendments and a second convention.

Farther west, in the district of Kentucky, the campaign for convention delegates was a microcosm of Antifederalists' efforts throughout the state. Before the election the *Lexington Kentucky Gazette* printed several Antifederalist essays. Patrick Henry also wrote to a number of prominent Kentucky politicians warning of the danger the Constitution posed to the interests of Kentucky, particularly as it related to the navigation of the Mississippi.[56] Within the district, local leaders took steps to ensure the election of Antifederalists to the forthcoming convention. In February, Harry Innes and seven others petitioned the Mercer and Fayette county courts to read an address prepared by them "preceding the opening of the polls." In the address Innes pointed out specific faults in the Constitution, flaws which struck "immediately at the happiness and greatness of the western country." The crux of Innes's objections was sectional. Powers granted to the legislature would be wielded by a northern and eastern majority to Kentucky's disadvantage. Thus the power to regulate foreign trade signaled to Innes the closure of the Mississippi River. Congressional power to levy an impost meant the state would be unable to "encourage manufactories," while Congressional control of the militia left the state potentially helpless and vulnerable to attack. The address closed with a proposal that following the election each county send three representatives to a district-wide meeting at Danville on the first Monday in April "to consider the proposed Federal Constitution and if necessary to instruct our delegates to the state convention. . . ."[57] Such a convention was not held nor instructions issued, for in the elections there was only token opposition to the Antifederalist nominees, a majority of whom were elected.

There was more competition in the convention elections in the state as a whole. Both parties nominated candidates in at least fifty-five of the state's eighty-four counties.[58] The elections were also close. An anonymous correspondent in the April 9 *Winchester Virginia Centinel*, basing his estimate on incomplete returns, gave the Federalists a 24-delegate edge. Federalist David Henley thought the balance even closer. Thus, in a remarkable list of the members of the convention broken down by county, Henley correctly identified 85 individual Federalists and 66 Antifederalists with returns missing in only eight counties.[59] Antifederalist Arthur Lee, although not so specific as Henley, thought the Federalist majority lower, at no more than six again with incomplete returns from the "back counties," and as late as May he declared that the two parties were so evenly balanced that no man could "form a judgement [as to] what may be the determination" of the convention.[60]

Although the outcome of the convention was uncertain, the political affiliations of the majority of the delegates were known because in the campaigns Federalists and Antifederalists stated their views through the broadsides and pamphlets they distributed and in speeches at the county courthouses on election day. The voters were given a choice among clearly distinguishable Federalist and Antifederalist candidates in the bulk of the state's counties. This made the elections issue-oriented to a degree unprecedented in Virginia's history. It also stimulated the development of rudimentary party organization beyond the existing factional alignments in the Assembly and contributed to the nationalization of the state electoral process in Virginia. The development was not as formal perhaps as in New York where a vigorous party press had preserved more evidence of that state's party organization. Nonetheless in Virginia the Henryite and Nationalist factions of 1787 were, by the spring 1788 elections to the convention and state legislature, Federalists and Antifederalists. And, while the details of the legislative elections are fewer, by the end of the April legislative elections, informed Virginians could place the Antifederalist majority in the Virginia House of Burgesses at fifteen.[61]

The efforts of Virginia party leaders were not limited to their own state. Mason's and Lee's public statements circulated in North Carolina, while Henry and Campbell played a more direct role. With their aid, North Carolina Antifederalists too conducted an extensive, aggressive, and successful campaign.

The campaign for convention delegates in North Carolina continued from the adjournment of the legislature in January 1788 to the last Friday and Saturday in March. During that time there was a considerable influx of Antifederalist literature from outside the state. Arthur Campbell was presumably one of a number of "gentlemen" John Brown Cutting complained of when he remarked that "some of the gentlemen warmly opposed to an acceptance of the plan [the Constitution] in the back counties of Virginia have diffused their objections throughout those [counties] of the two Carolinas which are most remote from the Atlantic shores."[62]

Nearer the coast, the *State Gazette* printed George Mason's "Objections" in November and they were available in pamphlet form as well. Though Federalist James Iredell published a refutation of the "Objections," he was less able to counter the influence of men like Willie Jones, and his lieutenants, Timothy Bloodworth, David Caldwell, Samuel Spencer, and Joseph McDonnell who campaigned in person in their own and neighboring counties.[63]

The details of this county-level activity are spotty, but enough remains to establish the outlines. From Halifax, for instance, the home county of Willie Jones, William R. Davie reported in January that "we have nothing worth remarking here but the dissemination of Antifederal principles. Mr. Jones continues to assail the Constitution." There was apparently an abundance of candidates in the county for Davie added that Colonel Geddy "has announced himself a candidate for the convention and is a most furious zealot for what he calls W. Jones's system."[64] Despite an overabundance of candidates, five Antifederalists represented the county in the convention. Elsewhere, the voters of Granville elected Thomas Person, an outspoken opponent of ratification, and four other Antifederalists. In Northampton, five political newcomers defeated a Federalist slate headed by General Allen Jones, a former state representative. In Orange County, Antifederalists defeated William Hooper and Alfred Moore in their bid for convention seats, and in Franklin County the delegates received positive instructions to vote against ratification.[65] Four counties in the district—Chatham, Wake, Johnston, and Pitt—elected mixed delegations, and the borough town of Halifax elected Federalist Davie. Every other county chose Antifederalists.[66]

The borough towns of Newbern and Edenton elected Federalists with no recorded opposition. Elsewhere, however, both Federalists and Antifederalists campaigned for convention seats. From Tarborough, in Pitt County, James Sanders declared his willingness to serve "if I am elected. . . ."[67] Pitt was one of the four counties in the district that sent divided delegations to the convention, but Sanders was not among the delegates. Johnson and Beaufort counties also sent split delegations.

Included in the Hertford delegation was Lemuel Burkitt, a Baptist preacher and an outspoken opponent of ratification. In mid-March Burkitt convened a county-wide meeting at which he "explained" the new Constitution from an Antifederalist point of view. During the meeting, just at the point when Burkitt was "explaining" how the ten miles square would become a walled city, Federalists Major Hardy Murfree and Elkanah Watson interrupted his speech and disrupted the meeting. Two days later, during the balloting for convention delegates, Watson resorted to similar tactics, but his efforts went for naught. "B——t gained the election" to Watson's, and his fellow Federalists', "great annoyance."[68]

The campaign in Hertford was apparently indicative of Antifederalist efforts and Federalist responses throughout the district. An extract of a letter which appeared in the *New York Daily Advertiser* reported that Baptist preachers, in addition to attacking the Constitution, "even from the pulpit," had passed circular letters "from meeting to meeting, and from preacher to preacher"; circular letters which presumably provided the outlines of Burkitt's "explanation" of the Constitution.[69]

Federalists responded to this Antifederalist initiative with their own campaign and candidates. In Dobbs County, where their efforts failed, they resorted to disruptive tactics similar to those employed by Watson in Hertford. On election day, as the ballots were being counted, Federalist candidate Colonel Benjamin Sheppard and several

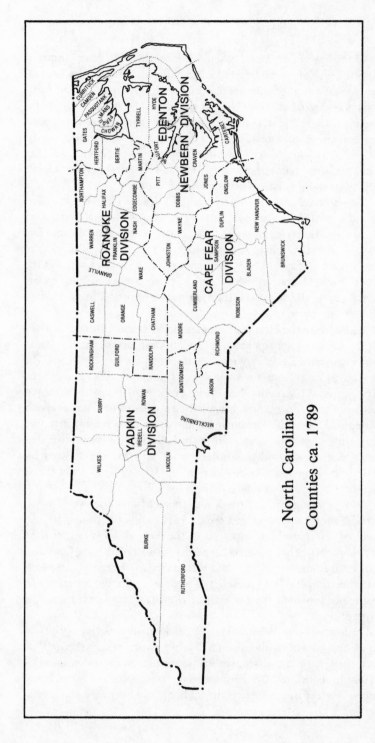

North Carolina Counties, ca. 1789.
Courtesy of the University of North Carolina Press.

others, who were losing the election, suddenly extinguished the candles, exchanged blows with the election inspectors, and absconded with the ballot box. Federalists then petitioned for a new election and were elected because Antifederalists abstained from voting, reportedly afraid to appear at the poll. The convention, because of the unusual circumstances of the election, declined to seat the delegates and the county was not represented.[70] Despite the loss of the five Dobbs delegates and lesser setbacks in Hertford, Pitt, Beaufort, and Craven, Federalists won a majority of the seats from Edenton and Newbern district.

They did not do so well in Cape Fear district. At the outset of the campaign Archibald Maclaine reported from Wilmington that "some demagogues, a few persons who are in debt and every public officer except the clerk of the county court" were opposed to the Constitution. Maclaine added that "all the low scoundrels of the county . . . by every means imaginable [were] prejudicing the common people against the Constitution."[71] His complaints about the tactics of the opposition notwithstanding, by April Maclaine was more optimistic. At that time he compiled a list of elected delegates from New Hanover, Brunswick, Bladen, Cumberland, Duplin, and Onslow counties. Maclaine identified seven of the thirty elected delegates as antifederal. Ten he considered Federalist. The remaining thirteen were "honest disinterested men"; several of whom had "positively refused to receive instruction," and men whom Maclaine believed could be induced to vote for ratification.[72] In this expectation Maclaine was to be sorely disappointed.

Maclaine's mention of elected delegates refusing instructions is particularly intriguing. There is no record of such instructions for any delegate from the Cape Fear region. Only William Lancaster, a Franklin County delegate, and William Lenoir, a Wilkes County delegate, definitely received instructions.[73] Other delegates may have been instructed, particularly from the Yadkin district and farther west, areas which, according to William Hooper, were "generally opposed."[74]

Despite the incompleteness of the data, from the details known about local elections and the final roll call in the convention, it can be reasoned that Antifederalists offered candidates for the convention in *at least* forty-three of the state's fifty-three counties and four of its six towns. Federalists offered candidates in at least twenty-five counties and five towns. Antifederalists also distributed propaganda throughout the state, campaigned aggressively and, judging from the returns, effectively. They won an overwhelming majority of the seats in the state convention which was to assemble at Hillsborough on July 21.

In contrast to their strong showings in North Carolina and to a lesser extent Virginia, Antifederalists won only a third of the seats to the South Carolina Convention. South Carolina became the eighth state to ratify the Constitution on May 24, 1788. Following ratification, and in response to letters from John Lamb, secretary of the New York Federal Republican Committee, Antifederalists Rawlins Lowndes and Aedanus Burke explained the reasons for their defeat in separate letters to Lamb. Lowndes stressed the Federalist objection in the convention that the Antifederalists were undecided and divided among themselves about which amendments were necessary. This objection could have been overcome, Lowndes added, had Lamb's plan for interconvention cooperation and agreement on specific amendments "been proposed in time."[75]

Burke's analysis of the causes of the Antifederalist defeat was more encompassing. He told Lamb that the Antifederalists "had not, previous to our meeting [of the convention] either wrote or spoke, hardly a word against it, nor took any one step in the matter." Organization was of course only one of a number of factors which "caused" the Constitution to be "carried in South Carolina, notwithstanding four-fifths of the people, do in their souls detest it." In addition, there was "not a printing press in Carolina out of the city," while those in Charleston were operated by printers "afraid to offend the great men and merchants," all of whom staunchly supported ratification. Finally, the Constitution was ratified because the convention was held in Charleston, where the "merchants and leading men kept open houses for the back and low country members the whole time the convention was sitting," and presumably induced a number of those delegates to vote in favor of ratification.[76]

Unfortunately Lowndes's and Burke's letters, written in the aftermath of defeat, distort the role of Antifederalists in South Carolina. Lowndes ignores the elections entirely and, incorrectly, states that a plan for interconvention cooperation would have carried the day for the Antifederalists. Burke, on the other hand, overlooked the role of out-of-state Antifederalists in the election campaign while including some misinformation about the efforts of local Antifederalists.

Despite Federalist control of the press, for instance, in April 1788, Arthur Bryan, a Charleston merchant and son of George Bryan of Pennsylvania, noted that "Martin's speech is now inserting in the *State Gazette* piecemeal which will have a great effect."[77] A correspondent to the *Independent Gazetteer* also reported that "Martin's information . . . is much read" and would have "great effect" on the election held on April 11 and 12.[78]

The Charleston newspapers were, of course, only one avenue of expression. Pennsylvania and Virginia Antifederalists distributed pamphlets and broadsides in South Carolina. Charles C. Pinckney, for one, complained of the Antifederalists' industry "in prejudicing the minds of our [South Carolina's] citizens against the Constitution: Pamphlets, speeches, and protests of the disaffected in Pennsylvania" being circulated "throughout the state."[79] John Brown Cutting confirmed that "some of the gentlemen warmly opposed to the acceptance of the plan [in the back counties of Virginia] diffused their objections throughout those of the two Carolinas which are most remote from the Atlantic shores."[80] Archibald Maclaine was informed that "great pains had been taken in the [South Carolina] back country to poison the minds of the people" against the Constitution, while John Vaughn attributed the opposition of that area to "a few designing men" who "in many instances" persuaded back country electors to instruct their delegates to vote against ratification.[81] In May the *Augusta Georgia State Gazette* also reported that the South Carolina electors in the back country instructed their delegates against ratification, and Jonathan Wilson remarked that in "some counties the infatuated populace made their delegates . . . [pledge] to vote against it [the Constitution] before they would vote them in."[82]

The actual extent of such instructions and of Antifederalist campaigning, for that matter, is not known. Antifederalists did nominate candidates in at least two-thirds of the state's electoral districts. They failed to win a majority of those contests or of the seats in the state convention. That defeat was less the result of a lack of candidates or an inherent weakness in their organization than the malapportionment of the South Carolina convention. In the convention the low country districts which contained 21 percent of the white population were represented by 60.8 percent of the delegates. The up country, where antifederalism was strongest, contained 79 percent of the white population but had only 39.2 percent of the delegates. Because of malapportionment, delegates representing as little as 13 percent of South Carolina's white population could have ratified the Constitution. Actually delegates representing 39 percent of the white population voted in favor of ratification, although the votes of at least five men were not consistent with the wishes of their constituents. Delegates representing 52 percent of the population voted against ratification, while those representing the remainder abstained or were absent.[83] Consequently, their best efforts notwithstanding, as long as Charleston and its environs favored ratification, the opposition in South Carolina could be only "trifling."[84]

Their defeat in the South Carolina elections aside, the Antifederalists were able to maintain a political power base throughout the South. In North Carolina, where their success was the greatest, Antifederalists had a large majority in the forthcoming convention. In Virginia the undecided back county delegates held the balance of power. The likelihood of those delegates voting with the Antifederalists seemed great in the spring for the back country throughout the South was a hotbed of Antifederalism and those same Virginia counties were represented by Antifederalists in the state legislature. To be sure, Maryland and South Carolina were overwhelmingly Federalist, and Pennsylvania and Georgia had already ratified. But in at least two of those states—Pennsylvania and South Carolina—Antifederalists claimed, with some legitimacy, that the majority of the people still opposed the Constitution, and were willing to take action to redress their political grievances.

Southern Antifederalists then approached the summer conventions with reasonable optimism. They had popular support in two of the forthcoming conventions, the threat of extralegal resistance and even civil war if the Constitution were ratified despite the wishes of the people, and the likelihood of interstate and interconvention cooperation in the call for a second constitutional convention.

NOTES TO
CHAPTER 5

1. 26 and 22 December 1787.
2. 15 March 1788, Rush Papers, PPL.
3. Jensen, *Ratification*, 2: 670.
4. The Federalist account of the riot appeared in the *Carlisle Gazette*, 2 January. It was reprinted as far north as the *Portland Cumberland Gazette*, 28 February, and the *Bennington Vermont Journal*, 10 March; and as far south as the *Savannah Gazette of the State of Georgia*, 14 February 1788.
5. "Versus Conciliator," *Philadelphia Independent Gazetteer*, 19 January; *Baltimore Maryland Journal*, 22 January 1788.
6. See "A draft of a petition in opposition to the actions of the Pennsylvania convention," Nicholson Papers, PHarH.
7. Nicholson sent petitions to political allies in Bedford, Cumberland, Lancaster, Northumberland, Westmoreland, and Washington counties. See the incoming letters of these correspondents in the Nicholson Papers, PHarH. Petitions were submitted to the Assembly from Bedford, Cumberland, Dauphin, Northampton, and Westmoreland counties.
8. *Philadelphia Independent Gazetteer*, 29 December 1787.
9. 16 January 1788.
10. *Philadelphia Pennsylvania Mercury*, 1 January; *Philadelphia Pennsylvania Herald*, 16 January 1788.
11. 3 March 1788, Rush Papers, PPL.
12. *Philadelphia Independent Gazetteer*, 30 January 1788.
13. "Centinel" 16, *Philadelphia Independent Gazetteer*, 9 April 1788. For evidence that the societies did perform these functions see John Jordon to John Nicholson, 26 January, Nicholson Papers, PHarH, and the letter from the Philadelphia Society to "A society in East Pennsboro, Cumberland County," *Carlisle Gazette*, 7 February 1788.
14. Jensen, *Ratification*, 2: 714.
15. To John Nicholson, 24 February, *ibid.*, p. 696; *Philadelphia Independent Gazetteer*, 4 March 1788; *Philadelphia Freeman's Journal*, 19 March; *Independent Gazetteer*, 4 April 1788.
16. To James Wilson, 2 March, Jensen, *Ratification*, 1: 705. For similar analyses of antifederal tactics, see Ebenezer Hazard to Mathew Carey, 14 April, Lea and Febiger Collection, PHi; *Baltimore Maryland Journal*, 21 March 1788.
17. *Baltimore Maryland Journal*, 22 January 1788.
18. 10 February, Madison Papers, DLC; 20 April 1788, *Documentary History of the Constitution*, 4: 581.
19. Alexander C. Hanson to Tench Coxe, 27 March 1788, Coxe Papers, PHi.
20. William Tilghman to Tench Coxe, 6 and 20 April 1788, Coxe Papers, PHi.
21. "A Marylander," *Baltimore Maryland Gazette*, 20 May 1788.
22. *Baltimore Maryland Journal*, 21 April; Daniel Carroll to James Madison, 28 May 1788, *Documentary History of the Constitution*, 4: 636–41.
23. *Baltimore Maryland Gazette*, 8 February; "George Lux to the Inhabitants of Baltimore County," *Baltimore Maryland Journal*, 14 and 25 March; 14 and 21 April 1788.
24. Arthur Bryan to Unknown, 28 March 1788, Lloyd Papers, MdHi.

25. *Alexandria Virginia Journal,* 18 April; *Baltimore Maryland Journal,* 4 April 1788.

26. *Carlisle Gazette,* 27 February, 19 March; *Baltimore Maryland Journal,* 4 April 1788.

27. William Tilghman to Tench Coxe, 20 April 1788, Coxe Papers, PHi.

28. *Ibid.*

29. Compare, for example, George Mason's "Objections," *Alexandria Virginia Journal,* 22 November; Edmund Randolph's "Letter to the Speaker," *Richmond Virginia Independent Chronicle,* 2 January 1788; and Richard Henry Lee's "Letter to the Governor," *Petersburg Virginia Gazette,* 6 December 1787, with *The Dissent of the Minority,* Jensen, *Ratification,* 2: 617–40, and the later, spring 1788 "Centinel" essays, printed in John D. McMaster and Frederick D. Stone, ed., *Pennsylvania and the Federal Constitution, 1787–1788* (Lancaster, Pa., 1888).

30. Throughout the ensuing discussion, I am indebted to DenBoer, "House of Delegates," chap. 5. Our accounts of the elections differ primarily in perspective. He limited his view to the state of Virginia, while I place the elections in a broader context.

31. Carrington to Henry Knox, 12 January 1788, Knox Papers, MHi; Smith to James Madison, 12 June 1788, *Documentary History of the Constitution,* 4: 702.

32. Carrington to Madison, 8 April 1788, *ibid.,* p. 566.

33. Carrington to Madison, 10 February, 8 April 1788, *ibid.,* pp. 275, 566.

34. *Richmond Virginia Independent Chronicle,* 12 March 1788.

35. "Sketch of Wilson Cary Nicholas," Carter-Smith Papers, ViU.

36. Henry Lee to James Madison, December 1787, Burnley to Madison, 17 December, James Madison, Sr., to James Madison, Jr., 30 January 1788, Madison Papers, DLC; Joseph Spencer to James Madison, 28 February 1788, *Documentary History of the Constitution,* 4: 525; Lee to James Gordon, 26 February 1788, Ballagh, *Lee,* 2: 460–63.

37. See letters to Madison from Archibald Stuart, 2 December, George Lee Turberville, 11 December, Joseph Jones, 18 December; Henry Lee, December 1787; James Madison, Sr., 9 February; and James Gordon, Jr., 17 February 1788, all in Madison Papers, DLC.

38. Duncanson to Maury, 8 May 1788, Maury Papers, ViU.

39. James Monroe to Thomas Jefferson, 12 July, Julian P. Boyd, ed., *The Papers of Thomas Jefferson* (Princeton, 1950—), 3: 353; to James Maury, 8 May 1788, Maury Papers, ViU.

40. 18 February, *Documentary History of the Constitution,* 4: 71; "Extract of a Letter, March 30," *Baltimore Maryland Journal,* 11 April 1788.

41. Archibald Stuart to James Madison, 2 November 1787, Madison Papers, DLC.

42. To James Madison, 29 February 1788, Madison Papers, DLC.

43. This is based on the list of elected delegates forwarded to David Henley and from him to his father, Samuel Henley, 28 April 1788, Personal Papers, Miscellany, David Henley, DLC.

44. Arthur Lee to Richard Henry Lee, 19 February 1788, Lee Family Papers, ViU.

45. Rutland, *Mason,* 3: 1037.

46. To George Washington, 17 February 1788, Washington Papers, DLC.

47. To George Nicholas, 8 April 1788, Durrett Micellaneous Manuscripts, ICU.

48. Arthur Lee to Richard Henry Lee, 19 February 1788, Lee Family Papers, ViU;

Edward Carrington to William Short, 25 October 1787, Burnett, *Letters*, 8: 665.

49. See a report of Grayson's election day speech in Hugh Williamson to John Gray Blount, 3 June 1788, Burnett, *Letters*, 8: 747.

50. 19 February 1788, Lee Family Papers, ViU.

51. Burr Powell, "Biographical Sketch of Colonel Leven Powell," Leven Powell Papers, ViW.

52. 16 and 23 November 1787; "Dares," and "Dion," *Winchester Virginia Gazette*, 15 and 29 February 1788.

53. Archibald Stuart to John Breckinridge, 1 March, Breckinridge Family Papers, DLC; *Winchester Virginia Gazette*, 2 April 1788.

54. Archibald Stuart to John Breckinridge, 1 March, Breckinridge Family Papers, DLC; *Winchester Virginia Gazette*, 11 April 1788.

55. "Extract of a letter from a gentleman at Washington Court House, near Holstein, Virginia, to his friend in Philadelphia," *Philadelphia Independent Gazetteer*, 5 January 1788; Campbell to Francis Baily, 8 March; to Adam Orth, 9 March 1788, Bryan Papers, PHi.

56. The letters are no longer extant, but see George Washington to Henry Knox, 30 March, and to Benjamin Lincoln, 2 April, Fitzpatrick, *Washington*, 29: 450, 452; and John B. Smith to James Madison, 12 June 1788, *Documentary History of the Constitution*, 4: 702–3.

57. 29 February 1788, Draper Papers, WHi. The signers were Samuel McDowell, Caleb Wallace, George Muter, Harry Innes, Benjamin Sebastian, Benjamin Logan, Christopher Greenup, and Thomas Allin. See also Innes to John Brown, 20 February 1788, Innes Papers, DLC. For a review of the political situation in Kentucky, see Patricia Watlington's *Partisan Spirit: Kentucky Politics, 1779–1792* (New York, 1972), chap.4.

58. These figures are derived from the data cited in the text; additional details about the county elections in DenBoer, "House of Delegates," chap. 5; and the final roll call in the convention, Elliot, *Debates*, 3: 654–55.

59. David Henley to Samuel Henley, 28 April 1788, Personal Papers, Miscellany, David Henley, DLC.

60. Quoted in Henry Knox to Jeremiah Wadsworth, 12 April, Wadsworth Papers, CtHi; to John Francis Mercer, 1 May 1788, Rutland, *Mason*, 3: 1040–41.

61. Edward Carrington to James Madison, 24 October 1788, Madison Papers, DLC.

62. John Brown Cutting to Thomas Jefferson, 11 July 1788, Boyd, *Jefferson*, 13: 331.

63. No printed copy has been found but see Louise Trenholme, *The Ratification of the Federal Constitution in North Carolina* (New York, 1952), p. 121. Archibald Maclaine complained that Martin's paper "teems with Antifederalism," to James Iredell, 29 April 1788, McRee, *Iredell*, 2: 223. Iredell's "Observations on George Mason's Objections to the Federal Constitution" is in Ford, *Pamphlets*, pp. 333–70.

For information on the North Carolina leadership, the primary sources are their respective biographies. On Jones see the DAB, 10: 210–11. Bloodworth and Caldwell are sketched in Samuel Ashe, *Biographical History of North Carolina*, 8 vols. (Goldsboro, 1905–17), 3: 15–24; 1: 206–12. The economic holdings of Spencer and McDowell, and the role they played in the convention are described in William C. Poole, "An Economic Interpretation of the Ratification of the Federal Constitution in North Carolina," *North Carolina Historical Review*, 27: 290, 291, 440.

64. To James Iredell, 22 January 1788, McRee, *Iredell,* 2: 217.

65. *Ibid*; J. Benton to Thomas Hart, 29 June 1788, Thomas J. Clay Papers, DLC; Elliott, *Debates,* 4: 202.

66. Trenholme, *Ratification in North Carolina,* p. 164.

67. To Daniel Smith, 23 December 1787, Draper Collection, WHi.

68. Elkanah Watson, *Men and Times of the Revolution* (New York, 1856), pp. 302–3.

69. 30 June 1788.

70. The documents relating to the riot have been collected in William K. Boyd, "News, Letters and Documents Concerning the Federal Constitution," Trinity College Historical Society *Historical Papers,* 14: 75–81.

71. To James Iredell, 15 January 1788, McRee *Iredell,* 2: 216.

72. To James Iredell, 2 April 1788, Iredell manuscripts, NcD.

73. Elliott, *Debates,* 4: 202, 215.

74. To Iredell, 15 April 1788, McRee, *Iredell,* 2: 222.

75. Lowndes to Lamb, 21 June 1788, Lamb Papers, NHi.

76. Burke to Lamb, 23 June 1788, Lamb Papers, NHi.

77. To George Bryan, 9 April 1788, Bryan Papers, PHi.

78. 19 April 1788.

79. To Rufus King, 24 May 1788, King, *Life,* 1: 328–29.

80. To Thomas Jefferson, 11 July 1788, Boyd, *Jefferson,* 12: 331.

81. To James Iredell, 4 June, McRee, *Iredell,* 2: 226; to Benjamin Vaughn, 4 June 1788, Copies of John Vaughn's Letters from 1789, PPAmP.

82. 10 May; to Samuel Wilson, 10 July 1788, L.C. Glen Papers, NcU.

83. Charles Roll, Jr., "We, Some of the People . . . ," *Journal of American History* 56 (1969): 22, 26, 31.

84. Edward Rutledge to John Jay, 20 June 1788, Henry P. Johnston, ed., *The Correspondence and Public Papers of John Jay,* 3 vols. (New York, 1890–93), 3: 339

Chapter 6

THE ECLIPSE OF
THE ANTIFEDERALIST
ALLIANCE

From February 16, when the Massachusetts Convention ratified the Constitution with recommended amendments, until April 21, when the Maryland Convention assembled, the focus of political activity was the electoral arena as Federalists and Antifederalists sought delegate and legislative support for their respective programs. These months of political activity came to a head when the conventions of Maryland and South Carolina, followed by those of New Hampshire, the key Virginia, New York, and finally North Carolina assembled on April 21, May 12, June 2, June 17, and July 21 respectively.

During this period the conventions were, of course, the focal point of attention. Still, political activity elsewhere affected the delegates' deliberations. In particular, the reaction of Maryland and South Carolina Antifederalists to their respective ratifications, the outcome of the spring elections to the lower house in Massachusetts, and the perceptions of Antifederalists in previously ratifying states, all shaped the actions of Antifederalists in the Virginia and New York conventions. Their collective responses were the key to both ratification by these states and the transition from the Confederation to the new government under the Constitution.

The first in that final sequence of events which led to ratification occurred in Annapolis when the Maryland Convention assembled on April 21. At the outset the Federalist majority decided to "hear the minority patiently all they had to say" but not to respond to any of their charges.[1] That strategy undercut the Antifederalists as did the initial Federalist willingness to consider amendments. Thus, after only four days, two of which were dedicated to procedural matters, the delegates voted to ratify the Constitution. Then they appointed a committee to consider a list of amendments proposed by Harford County delegate William Paca. After the committee tentatively approved thirteen amendments, Samuel Chase offered an additional fifteen, including one that reiterated George Mason's proposal for a two-thirds majority in each house of Congress to pass navigation acts and one that placed limits on the central government's power to collect impost duties. These amendments "alarmed and gave offense to many of those among the majority who suspected the motives of Mr. Chase."[2] Subsequently the committee reported that it would not recommend "any amendments whatsoever" and the convention adjourned sine die.[3]

Federalists' suspicions about Chase's motives in introducing those amendments were confirmed by post-ratification events. During May, Chase initiated a dual attack on the Constitution. In an "Address to the People of Maryland" signed by Paca and the eleven Antifederalists in the convention, they reviewed the course of the convention and presented the amendments considered by the committee. Their purpose in publishing the broadside was to lay before the public the amendments which were "calculated to preserve public liberty" so that the citizens of the state could "express their support for such alterations."[4] The channel through which they were to speak was the fall assembly elections. In June, Chase, Paca, and the other Antifederalists were already under fire because of their political views and Chase acknowledged that he expected an attempt would be made to "elect none but 'Federalists' as they falsely call themselves to our house of delegates."[5]

Antifederalists, though, also intended the broadside to circulate in Virginia to assure Virginia Antifederalists that a "very great majority of the people of this state" still supported amendments.[6] That message was also conveyed to Virginia by John Francis Mercer who wrote to the New York and Virginia conventions in order to "prevent you from forming unjust conclusions from the adoption of the Constitution in the state of Maryland . . . and the subsequent dissolution of that body without any amendments." Mercer went on to explain that while Antifederalists generally did not stand for election to the state convention, "four-fifths of the people of Maryland" were "now in favor of considerable alterations and amendments."[7] Mercer sent the letter to the Virginia convention to his brother James Mercer, a Stafford County Virginia Antifederalist, who was in Richmond during the convention. James Mercer, in turn, delivered it to George Mason, chairman of the Antifederalist committee which met with Philadelphia printer Eleazer Oswald and was in direct contact with New York Antifederalists.[8]

The argument that the people opposed what their representatives adopted was a constant theme in the Antifederalist campaign throughout the nation. The argument was given some credence during May when the Massachusetts towns chose representatives. In those elections, in contrast to the gubernatorial and senatorial ones, the party labels Federalist and Antifederalist were not transferred to candidates for the lower house.[9] This difference between the two state elections, held less than a month apart, was the result of several factors. Partially, it was simply that the House elections were less publicized than those for the governor and the Senate. Indeed, outside of Boston there was virtually no newspaper rhetoric. This reflected the smaller constituencies involved in the elections. In April, candidates appealed to an entire county or the state at large. In the elections to the House candidates appealed only to their fellow townsmen, among whom they and their political views were already known. Thus with the exception of urban centers like Boston and Newburyport, which did propose lists of nominees, there were no slates; even in Boston there was only one.[10]

The absence of party labels notwithstanding, the Constitution had considerable impact on the elections in specific contests and in the makeup of the House as a whole. That impact was most demonstrable in elections in urban centers which had been represented in the previous House by a man who became an Antifederalist. In Boston, John Winthrop, a moderate Antifederalist who ultimately voted for ratification, was not renominated. In Newburyport, incumbent Daniel Kilham, an outspoken opponent of ratification was replaced.[11] Despite these conspicuous changes, the returns as a whole reflected continued Antifederalist control of the House. Towns whose delegates voted against ratification composed over 50 percent of the membership and this did not include representatives of towns like Scituate and Falmouth, which were Antifederalist, but whose delegates voted aye on the final roll call in the convention. Antifederalist control was by no means absolute and Federalist Theodore Sedgwick from Stockbridge was chosen Speaker. Still Secretary George Minot noted that Antifederalists controlled the lower house, just as Federalists did the upper.[12] In contrast to Massachusetts, Pennsylvania Antifederalists did not have an opportunity to pursue their goal through their state legislative elections which were held annually in October. By May even the steady flow of propaganda tapered off, as first "Centinel" and then "Philadelphiensis" discontinued their efforts on April 9 and 16 respectively.

"Centinel" No. 18 illustrated the dilemma facing the Pennsylvania leadership. Committees of correspondence existed, Bryan asserted, "in every county in the state" and "are even now engaged in planning a uniform exertion to emancipate this state from the thralldom of despotism." In all probability a state-wide convention of deputies would meet when the remaining states met in convention. Pennsylvania Antifederalists could then join in a nation-wide call for a second constitutional convention. But until the state conventions assembled there was little more Pennsylvania's Antifederalists could do.[13]

As Antifederalists' efforts temporarily subsided in Pennsylvania (at least among the Philadelphia Antifederalists) they redoubled in South Carolina where the state convention assembled on May 12. At the outset of the convention Federalists were fearful that the majority for the Constitution "would be small" because of the extensive Antifederalist campaign in the back country.[14] Antifederalists, in turn, despairing of an outright victory, pressed for an adjournment. When that resolution failed, and news of ratification by Maryland arrived in Charleston, "further opposition was useless."[15] South Carolina ratified the Constitution on May 23.

Their substantial majority notwithstanding, South Carolina Federalists recognized the existence of continuing widespread discontent with the Constitution and appended a set of recommended amendments in an attempt to placate that unrest. However, according to Aedanus Burke, recommended amendments were not enough. In a letter to John Lamb, Burke stated that "⁴/₅ths of the people do, from their souls, detest it [the Constitution]." Burke also urged Lamb "should any event turn up that would require to be known to our republican friends, only make us acquainted with it." If either New York or Virginia were to reject the Constitution, Burke declared, it would "fall to pieces. . . . In such event, or any other that may give us an occasion to serve the Republic, your communications will be duly attended by me."[16]

Despite the ratification of eight states, Antifederalists were still in a position of strength. If the New Hampshire, New York, and Virginia conventions could maintain a united front, Antifederalists would, they reasoned, find broad support from across the nation. Such a stand required careful coordination within the three conventions and among them. In an effort to ensure such coordination, George Mason wrote to Richard Henry Lee in April "on the subject of the Constitution." In response Lee outlined his strategy for the forthcoming Virginia Convention. No longer an advocate of a second convention, Lee proposed that before the meeting of the convention "six or eight leading friends to amendments" meet privately in order to determine upon a course of action with regard to both their mode and extent. At any rate, Antifederalists in the convention should insist on a complete, thorough, and careful examination of the Constitution prior to any question being taken by the convention as a whole. During the paragraph by paragraph examination of the Constitution Antifederalists could form "a tolerable judgment of the sentiments" of the majority of the delegates and draft amendments which would win their support. Those amendments could then be attached to the state's ratification as a condition of ratification, stipulating that if the amendments were not adopted within two years, Virginia would "be considered as disengaged from this ratification."[17]

Mason and William Grayson, two Antifederalist leaders in the convention, agreed with Lee's recommendation for a meeting to deliberate on strategy. Two days after the opening session a "committee of opposition" was formed, with George Mason as its chairman.[18] The members of this committee included Mason and Grayson as well as Patrick Henry and Meriwether Smith, an incumbent assemblyman and a "Henryite." These men recognized the need for concerted action on the subject of amendments. They did not agree, however, with Lee's proposed conditional form of ratification. Instead, Mason and Grayson continued to favor a second constitutional convention and cooperation among the New York, Virginia, and New Hampshire conventions on previous amendments. Prior to the convention, neither the precise procedures for calling a second convention nor the steps needed to encourage interconvention cooperation on the subject of amendments was explicitly stated. Both men were uncertain if a motion for previous amendments would carry in the Virginia Convention. Therefore, they determined to work for an Antifederalist majority as their immediate goal.[19]

Tactically Mason and Grayson's insistence on an Antifederalist majority before initiating a program of interconvention cooperation was impolitic. Either a list of proposed amendments or a meeting of representatives from the three conventions would have aided the Antifederalists materially in securing and maintaining majorities in both the Virginia and New Hampshire conventions. That potential was recognized by Antifederalists in New York. In the weeks following their own convention elections they set out to implement the strategy of interconvention cooperation on previous amendments first outlined in October 1787.

In early May, Governor Clinton responded to Virginia Governor Edmund Randolph's letter of late December 1787. In that letter Randolph had enclosed the Virginia resolution of mid-December with its provisions for cooperation and communication among the conventions. In his reply Clinton wrote of the appropriateness of communications between the two states relative to the Constitution. The initiative, Clinton presumed, would come from Virginia "as the session of your convention will take place before that of this state."[20]

Ten days later John Lamb launched a broader initiative. Writing on behalf of the New York Federal Republican Committee, he supplemented Clinton's letter to Randolph with a circular letter to Antifederalists in New Hampshire, Rhode Island, Pennsylvania, Maryland, Virginia, and the Carolinas.[21] His object was the amendment of the Constitution "previous to its adoption." The means of "accomplish[ing] this desirable end" was twofold. First, Lamb suggested that Antifederalists in New Hampshire, New York, Virginia, and the Carolina conventions "open a correspondence and maintain a communication that they should understand one another on the subject and unite in the amendments they propose" to be adopted prior to ratification.[22] Once they agreed on a specific set of amendments, Lamb wanted them to "act in concert" with some "rational plan" that would ensure their adoption.[23] Although Lamb did not spell out the details of the plan for unified action, presumably the list of amendments would have been submitted to the Confederation Congress, supported by Antifederalist majorities in the New Hampshire, New York, Virginia, and the Carolina conventions, the Rhode Island legislature, and by Antifederalist minorities in Massachusetts, Pennsylvania, and Maryland. Unified action would have demonstrated widespread support for amendments prior to ratification and provided proof of agreement among Antifederalists on specific amendments.

Although Lamb's attempt to link Antifederalists across the nation in the demand for previous amendments failed, it was not because of a late start by the Federal Republican Committee or delays in the delivery of the mails.[24] Lamb's letters were a logical outgrowth of the original proposal for interconvention cooperation made in October 1787. They were intended to resurrect at least part of that plan by stimulating interconvention communication and cooperation among the New York, New Hampshire, and Virginia conventions which were to meet simultaneously in June 1788. Furthermore, Lamb's letters reached their intended recipients in New Hampshire and Virginia, and their responses arrived in New York before any of the three conventions reached a final decision.

New Hampshire Antifederalists Nathaniel Peabody and Joshua Atherton received Lamb's letter with the enclosed Antifederalist pamphlets before the opening of the second session of the New Hampshire Convention. In response Atherton informed Lamb that the majority of New Hampshire delegates were still in favor of amendments prior to ratification. He warned, however, that "no amendments" had been agreed to or even attempted by the convention delegates. If New York were to resolve "not to adopt without the necessary amendments," and forwarded that news to Exeter, then the New Hampshire Convention would almost certainly "close with your wishes and views." If New York failed to take such a positive step, then rejection by New Hampshire was in doubt.[25]

Lamb's letters to Virginia's Antifederalist convention delegates George Mason, Patrick Henry, and William Grayson reached Richmond on June 7, in ample time for interconvention correspondence on the subject of amendments.[26] In fact, a "committee of opposition" discussed amendments before Eleazer Oswald, the Antifederalist printer who served as a messenger for the New York and Virginia Antifederalists, reached Richmond. There he "closeted" himself with Mason, Grayson, Henry, and other members of the Antifederalist opposition, presumably to discuss strategy, specific amendments, and Lamb's proposal for interconvention cooperation.[27] The Virginians endorsed Lamb's proposal and forwarded a tentative list of amendments to New York through Oswald when he departed on June 11.

Even as these initial negotiations were being carried on, Lamb, encouraged by the outcome of the New York convention elections, wrote again to New Hampshire and Virginia Antifederalists, reiterating the importance of cooperation among the three conventions on specific amendments before ratification. Joshua Atherton received Lamb's letter at Exeter on June 21.[28] However, it did not contain what Atherton had previously stipulated as necessary for an Antifederalist victory: news of New York's refusal to ratify the Constitution in its present form and a list of specific amendments. Subsequently, and despite Atherton's best efforts, New Hampshire ratified by a 57 to 47 margin.

It is not clear if a similar letter was sent to Virginia. A draft exists in the Lamb papers, but there is no mention of it in any of Mason's ensuing correspondence with the New York committee. A second letter was less necessary in this instance because the Virginians were in direct contact with their New York counterparts and because the news of the New York Antifederalist election victory reached Richmond as early as June 18 independently of the Lamb committee letter.[29]

There was no breakdown in interstate communication among the Antifederalists in the three state conventions which were to meet in June and whose cooperation was to form the framework for the entire drive for previous amendments. Neither was there a disruption in the delivery of Lamb's letters to North Carolina and Rhode Island Antifederalists. In mid-May Lamb wrote to Willie Jones, Timothy Bloodworth, and Thomas Person, Antifederalist members of the North Carolina Convention. Those letters apparently reached Wilmington, North Carolina, by June 11. On that date the *Wilmington Centinel* advertised for sale a number of Antifederalist pamphlets "just arrived from New York." Among them were Mercy Warren's *Observations . . . by a Columbian Patriot*, Melancton Smith's *Address to the People of New York . . . by a Plebeian*, and Luther Martin's *Genuine Information*. Lamb enclosed these and other pamphlets in each of his letters. The notice of their availability in Wilmington serves to date the arrival of the Lamb letters in North Carolina a full six weeks before the opening of their convention.

This provided ample time for the North Carolinians to reply to Lamb. On July 1 Timothy Bloodworth, an Antifederalist from Wilmington and chairman of the North Carolina Antifederalist committee of correspondence, endorsed Lamb's proposal for previous amendments. Because the sentiments of North Carolina's convention delegates could not be collected prior to the opening of the convention, Bloodworth urged Lamb to forward the "proposed amendments" agreed upon by the three June conventions so that the North Carolina convention could act consistently with them.[30]

Willie Jones did not reply personally to Lamb's letter, presumably because he was a member of the committee of correspondence on whose behalf Bloodworth wrote. The third copy of the letter, that to Thomas Person, did not arrive until July 23. At that late date there was little Person could do. Bloodworth had already written on behalf of the Antifederalist committee. Thus Person waited another two weeks and then informed Lamb of North Carolina's refusal to ratify the Constitution by a vote of 184 to 83.[31]

According to reports in the *Newport Herald*, letters from Lamb, "accompanied by a fresh packet of pamphlets against the proposed

Constitution," were delivered to Rhode Island's Governor John Collins and several other prominent Antifederalists during May.[32] Although not extant, the anonymous letters to which the *Herald* alluded almost certainly outlined the national plan for previous amendments proposed by Lamb. The pamphlets probably included copies of Lee's *Letters from the Federal Farmer* since they stated well the New Yorker's objections to the Constitution and indirectly outlined the kind of amendments envisioned by the Federal Republican Committee.[33]

There were some delays in the delivery of Lamb's letters. Those to George Bryan in Philadelphia, Samuel Chase in Baltimore, Richard Henry Lee at Chantilly, Virginia, and Aedanus Burke, Rawlins Lowndes, and General Thomas Sumter in Charleston, were all in transit approximately a month. In none of these cases, however, did the delay significantly affect Lamb's plans. The South Carolina convention was overwhelmingly Federalist and it is doubtful that the decision of the convention would have been different had Lamb's letters been presented to it. Pennsylvania ratified the Constitution in December. George Bryan and Dr. James Hutchinson, Antifederalist leaders in Philadelphia, learned of the negotiations between New York and Virginia from Eleazer Oswald, who stopped over in the city on his way north.[34] Lee, on the other hand, was not a member of the Virginia Convention, although communication between the Virginia and New York conventions continued unabated.

During May and June, then, New York Antifederalists initiated a nation-wide correspondence on the amendment subject. The responses to their initiative were positive and included pledges of support from Antifederalists in both ratifying and nonratifying states. New York Antifederalists in the convention did not, however, immediately act upon these responses and implement the next step in their drive for previous amendments. They did not because of the discouraging news from Virginia, a state they viewed as an essential ally if the drive for previous amendments was to succeed.

Eleazer Oswald returned to New York on the evening of June 16 with letters from Mason, Grayson, and Henry to the Federal Republican Committee. Captain Tillinghast immediately carried the letters to Governor Clinton in Poughkeepsie.[35] The news in those letters was less than promising. All three Virginians believed the balance between the two parties in the convention was extremely close, although Grayson gave the Federalists a three-vote plurality, with "seven or eight dubious characters . . . on whose decision the fate of this important decision will ultimately depend."[36]

In Poughkeepsie Governor Clinton turned the letters over to

Robert Yates, chairman of an Antifederalist committee of correspondence. On June 21 Yates, in a private letter to Mason, explained that while New York Antifederalists were "willing to open a correspondence with your convention" in an official capacity, "the doubtful chance of your obtaining a majority—and the possibility that we will complete our determination before we could avail ourselves of your advice are the reasons we pursue the present mode of [unofficial] correspondence." Despite the resigned tone, Yates stressed the "fixed determination" of the New York Antifederalists not to adopt "without previous amendments"; he kept alive a hope for an unexpected Antifederalist victory in Virginia.[37] Arrival of the news of Virginia's unconditional ratification ten days later shattered these hopes.

A comparison of the final roll call with the Henley delegate count three months earlier indicates that Antifederalists were able to maintain the support they had at the close of the elections. That is in contrast to the repeated loss of support they encountered, for example, in New Hampshire, Massachusetts, and later New York. Antifederalists lost in Virginia because they were unable to persuade the undecided delegates that it was imperative that amendments precede ratification. Antifederalists' arguments could not overcome the example of the other states which recommended amendments and the prestige of Washington who, though not in the convention, was a powerful argument on behalf of unconditional ratification.[38] It is also possible that Patrick Henry hurt his own cause when he vowed on the floor of the convention that should Virginia ratify the Constitution he would continue the fight for amendments "in a constitutional way."[39] That may have been the most persuasive argument yet to that handful of undecided delegates who believed the Constitution provided solutions to problems facing the nation even as they believed it needed to be amended. Henry's pledge to continue the fight may have induced them to vote for ratification with recommended amendments, in the full expectation that Henry would ultimately succeed.

Virginia's ratification, whatever the cause, significantly altered the political situation in Poughkeepsie. There was no longer any real doubt that the new government would be put into operation, although the Confederation Congress did delay for over two months setting up the machinery for elections of a president, vice president, and members of Congress. With the certainty that the new government would become operational, with or without New York, the possibility of previous amendments on the terms initially proposed by the Federal Republican Committee and sought by the Antifederalists in convention was gone.

Apparently at this point, overwhelmed by events outside their own state, the Antifederalist majority in the New York Convention "determined they could not reject" the Constitution. Instead, the question became "which was the mode most eligible to insure a convention of the states to reconsider it, to have the essential amendments engrafted to it."[40] There were several possibilities, and the delegates debated all of them in the ensuing weeks. On July 10, following presentation of the Antifederalist amendments, John Lansing introduced a motion providing for ratification with recommended, conditional, and explanatory amendments. Federalists countered with a motion for unconditional ratification with recommended amendments. After three days of debate Melancton Smith introduced another alternative: ratification on condition only that the proposed amendments be submitted to a constitutional convention and that congressional powers over the state militia, elections, and taxation be suspended until a final determination was made by the convention. Federalists, in order to forestall adoption of Smith's proposal, proposed an adjournment of the convention to allow the delegates to consult their constituents. Instead, the convention simply recessed for the evening.[41]

The next day, July 17, Federalists proposed ratification "in full confidence" that the New York amendments would be considered by Congress. Smith, realizing that Congress could not, consistent with the provisions of Article V, call a convention on its own initiative, proposed that the convention ratify the Constitution with the condition that the state retain the right to secede if two-thirds of the states did not petition Congress to call a convention within a specified number of years. A circular letter was to be sent to the states encouraging them to do the same.[42]

Smith's motion seemingly exhausted the various alternatives. It also introduced a crucial feature in terms of Smith's own decision to acquiesce in unconditional ratification: a circular letter to the states calling upon them to petition Congress to convene a second convention. When he introduced it, however, the majority of Antifederalists opposed the idea. On July 19 John Lansing reintroduced Smith's earlier motion, which was debated for three days.[43] Finally, on July 23 the conditional clause of the motion was amended to "in full confidence" that the proposed amendments would be submitted to a general convention.[44] On July 24 Lansing made a last effort, offering his earlier motion with its reservation of the right to secede if a convention was not convened. That part of the motion was defeated, but the delegates did appoint a committee to draft a letter to the states. Written that evening, the New York Circular Letter, with its request that the states petition Congress to call a second convention, was approved by the delegates the next day.[45]

Historians have noted a number of factors which collectively induced twelve Antifederalists to vote with nineteen Federalists in favor of unconditional ratification. The threat of secession by the southern counties, the potential loss of the national capital, and the de jure ratification by ten states all took their toll.[46] All of these notwithstanding, New York Antifederalists could have refused to ratify the Constitution, just as their North Carolina counterparts did two weeks later. They chose, however, to ratify and to work for reform of the system from within. They did so, in large part because of the responses to Lamb's letters of mid-May. Article V of the proposed Constitution required Congress to convene a constitutional convention if petitioned to do so by two-thirds of the ratifying states. Letters received in Poughkeepsie during June and July from Antifederalists in other states seemed to indicate that the likelihood of Congress calling a second constitutional convention would be greater if New York ratified the Constitution. Thus Joshua Atherton, even as he encouraged the New York Antifederalists not to yield, declared that "there is a great majority in our House of Representatives unfavorable to the Constitution."[47] Certainly they could be counted on to petition Congress for a convention.

Massachusetts had been the first state to ratify in full confidence of amendments and, as in New Hampshire, its lower house, or so Antifederalists believed, favored amendments. Furthermore, Antifederalist leaders in Massachusetts were encouraging New York to ratify.[48] If New York became the third state that could be relied upon to petition Congress, then Pennsylvania would be the fourth. Although the state had ratified unconditionally, and without recommended amendments, there was a sizable and vociferous group in the state which endorsed the idea of a second convention. In addition, like Massachusetts Antifederalists, state leaders in Pennsylvania encouraged New York to ratify.[49]

Farther south the prospect of the state legislatures continuing to press for a second convention seemed equally strong. In April Maryland ratified by an overwhelming margin. Still, during June Antifederalists informed the Federal Republicans in New York that the citizens of the state supported amendments 4 to 1, and that the question of amendments was a major issue in the forthcoming state elections.[50] The logical conclusion to be drawn from that report was that the state legislature, after the October elections, would also be in favor of amendments, and receptive to a request from the state of New York that Maryland petition Congress to convene a second convention.

Virginia was an Antifederalist stronghold. The state legislature elected in April was even more Antifederalist than the convention which had just ratified the Constitution with recommended amendments.[51] Virginians were the first to propose a circular letter to the states encouraging them to petition Congress to convene another convention, although as part of a conditional ratification. Certainly they would be responsive to a similar suggestion from New York. Timothy Bloodworth was not certain what course North Carolina would follow if Virginia ratified the Constitution, but he pledged to support amendments emanating from New York. So did Aedanus Burke from South Carolina.[52] Burke maintained that despite South Carolina's ratification, the majority of the state's white population opposed unconditional ratification. And he pledged that any communication from Lamb or the Federal Republican Committee would "be duly attended to."

The exact dates these replies to Lamb's letters of May and June reached New York, and then Poughkeepsie, are not all known. Those of the Virginians reached Poughkeepsie before June 21. As for those from New Hampshire, Maryland, and the Carolinas, it can only be noted that there was ample time for the letters of Atherton (June 23), Chase (June 13), Bloodworth (July 1), and Burke (June 19) to reach the Antifederalists at Poughkeepsie while the convention was in session. There they provided testimony of the likelihood of a favorable response to an appeal by New York that the state legislatures petition Congress on the subject of a second convention.

The New York Circular Letter was instrumental in persuading Antifederalists to acquiesce in unconditional ratification. Approval of the circular letter as the "condition" of ratification, in turn, was a direct result, not of the failure of the Federal Republican Committee's efforts, but their success. The responses to the Lamb letters of May and June indicated a willingness on the part of Antifederalists throughout the union to follow the lead of New York in the quest for substantive reform of the Constitution. The rational plan for securing amendments, mentioned but never detailed by Lamb in the letters of May and June, became the New York Circular Letter of July 26, 1788.

The New York Circular Letter then marked the apex of the Antifederalists' drive for a second constitutional convention. It also signaled its eclipse because once New York ratified the Constitution, eight states were needed to obtain a second convention rather than the five sufficient to block unconditional ratification. New York Antifederalists recognized the disadvantages inherent in an unconditional ratification. Still, they believed that the necessary number of states would accede to the New York request for a second convention. That expectation proved false.

The first setback to Antifederalists' hopes came from an unexpected quarter. The North Carolina Convention, which assembled on July 21, was decidedly Antifederalist. Nor could that majority be dissuaded, as the Federalists quickly learned, from its insistence on previous amendments in the manner that the New York Antifederalists had been two weeks earlier. Thus on August 2, the delegates voted neither to ratify nor reject the Constitution and directed the president of the convention to transmit copies of the resolutions together with the proposed Bill of Rights and recommended amendments to the Confederation Congress and the executives of the states.[53]

In substance North Carolina's proposals complemented those of New York and Virginia. The difficulty was, as Federalists pointed out in debate, that by voting not to adopt the Constitution, North Carolina's call for a second convention (implicit in her resolutions and explicit in the floor debate) would have no legal standing.[54] By August, for North Carolina's support for a second convention to have real force, ratification was a necessary prerequisite.

Even more damaging to Antifederalist hopes were the responses of the state legislatures which proved the optimism of July to be false hope. During the fall, Federalist majorities in New Jersey, Connecticut, and Pennsylvania blocked positive action by those state legislatures on the circular letter.[55] Even in states where they were a majority in only one house, Federalists dominated. Thus during November the Massachusetts and New Hampshire legislatures also failed to act.[56] Equally frustrating to New York Antifederalists, the Antifederalist-dominated Rhode Island legislature insisted on submitting the circular letter to the freemen in the towns for their consideration instead of petitioning Congress.[57] Only the Virginia legislature complied with the recommendation of the New York Convention. On November 20, 1788, they approved a petition asking Congress to call a convention of "deputies from the several states, with full power to take into consideration the defects of the Constitution. . . ."[58]

Six months earlier Antifederalists realized that Melancton

Smith's faith in the circular letter was misplaced, and that the likelihood of the requisite number of states petitioning Congress to call a second convention was slight indeed. Those Antifederalists then turned to the first federal elections with the hope that the people would elect men pledged to amendments. In adopting that stance Antifederalists replicated a decision made as early as October 1787, and again in the aftermath of each state's ratification. This time some recognized the risks involved in such continued participation.

NOTES TO
CHAPTER 6

1. William Smith to Otho Holland Williams, 28 April 1788, Williams Papers, MdHi.

2. Bernard C. Steiner, "Maryland's Adoption of the Constitution," *American Historical Review* 5 (1900): 207–24.

3. John Brown Cutting to Thomas Jefferson, 11 July 1788, Boyd, *Jefferson,* 14: 336.

4. See an Antifederalist "Address to the People of Maryland," Elliot, *Debates,* 4: 547–56.

5. To John Lamb, 13 June 1788, Isaac Q. Leake, *Memoir of the Life and Times of General John Lamb* (Albany, 1857), pp. 312–13.

6. *Ibid.*

7. There are two undated manuscripts headed "To the Members of the New York and Virginia Conventions," Etting Collection, PHi.

8. The second draft is endorsed by James Mercer. He also admitted that he was in Richmond during the Virginia convention, *Annapolis Maryland Gazette,* 8 August 1788.

9. Main, *Political Parties,* p. 110.

10. *Boston Independent Chronicle,* 10 May 1788.

11. The turnover can be determined by a comparison of the lists of members in *Fleets' Pocket Almanac* (Boston, 1787, 1788).

12. George R. Minot, Journal, January 1789, Sedgwick Minot Papers, MHi.

13. *Philadelphia Independent Gazetteer,* 9 April 1788.

14. Archibald Maclaine to James Iredell, 4 June 1788, Iredell Papers, Nc-Ar.

15. Rawlins Lowndes to John Lamb, 21 June 1788, Leake, *Lamb,* p. 308.

16. Aedanus Burke to John Lamb, 23 June 1788, Lamb Papers, NHi.

17. To George Mason, *Mason,* 3: 1041–44.

18. William Grayson to Nathan Dane, 4 June 1788, Dane Papers, DLC.

19. William Grayson to John Lamb, 9 June, Leake, *Lamb,* pp. 311–312; Mason to John Lamb, 9 June 1788, Rutland, *Mason,* 3: 1057–58.

20. Randolph's letter and Clinton's reply are in Moncure D. Conway, *Omitted Chapters in the Life and Papers of Edmund Randolph* (New York, 1889), pp. 110–11.

21. Lamb wrote to New Hampshire Antifederalists Joshua Atherton and Nathaniel Peabody. The letter to Peabody, 18 May, is in Personal Miscellany, Library of Congress. Atherton's reply, 11 and 14 June is in Leake, *Lamb,* pp. 312–13. On 19 May the *Newport Herald* identified Lamb as the source of anonymous letters and pamphlets sent from New York to Rhode Island Antifederalists. Lamb sent his letter to Pennsylvania Antifederalist George Bryan under cover of Philadelphia broker Edward Pole. Pole's reply, 20 June, is in the Lamb Papers. In his reply Samuel Chase of Maryland mentioned letters from Lamb to Chase and Maryland Governor William Smallwood. Chase to Lamb, 13 June, Leake, *Lamb,* pp. 310–11. Lamb wrote to Virginia Antifederalists Patrick Henry, George Mason, William Grayson, and Richard Henry Lee. The letter to Lee is in the Lee Family Papers, ViU. Mason's reply of 9 June is in Rutland, *Mason,* 3: 1057–58; that of Lee, 27 June, in Ballagh, *Lee,* 2: 474–75; and those of Henry and Grayson, both 9 June, in Leake, *Lamb,* pp. 307–8, 311–12. Willie Jones, Thomas Person, and Timothy Bloodworth, all of North Carolina, also received copies of the circular letter from Lamb. The one to Jones is in

North Carolina Manuscripts, NcD. Bloodworth's reply, 1 July, and Person's, 6 August, are in William K. Boyd, comp., "News, Letters, and Documents," pp. 77–81. The only other known recipients of the letters were South Carolinians Rawlins Lowndes, Aedanus Burke, and Thomas Sumter. Lowndes's reply, 21 June, is in Leake, *Lamb*, p. 308; Burke's, 3 June 1788, the Lamb Papers, NHi.

22. See letters to Peabody and Jones cited in note 21. Nowhere did Lamb stipulate the previous amendments he and the members of the "Republican Committee" desired. However, judging from Melancton Smith's *Address to the People of the State of New York . . . By a Plebian* (Ford, *Pamphlets*, pp. 102–4) which Lamb forwarded with the mid-May letters, it seems clear that the New Yorkers wanted at least a stipulation that all powers not expressly granted to the central government were reserved to the states; an increase in the number of representatives in the House; some limitations on the central government's power to tax; a restriction on the jurisdiction of the federal courts; and guarantees regarding the right to time and place of national elections.

23. See the draft of Lamb's letter to members of the Virginia and New Hampshire conventions, 6 June 1788, Lamb Papers, NHi.

24. Cf. Main, *Antifederalists*, p. 236; Robert Rutland, *Ordeal of the Constitution: The Antifederalists and the Ratification Struggle of 1787–1788* (Norman, 1966), p. 210; Young, *Democratic-Republicans*, p. 111; and DePauw, *Eleventh Pillar*, p. 211.

25. 11 and 14 June 1788, Leake, *Lamb*, pp. 312–13.

26. William Grayson to John Lamb, 9 June, *ibid.*, pp. 311–12. The same day James Madison informed Alexander Hamilton that Oswald arrived on Saturday, which was 7 June 1788, Syrett, *Hamilton*, 5: 4.

27. Madison to Hamilton, 9 June, *ibid.* For additional comments on Oswald's role see Madison to Washington, 13 June, Washington Papers, DLC; Henry Lee to Hamilton, n.d., Syrett, *Hamilton*, 5: 10; and Washington to Henry Knox, 17 June, Fitzpatrick, *Washington*, 24: 518.

Oswald irked Federalists because of his efforts. Henry Chapman, a New York merchant, complained to a friend in Philadelphia, "That restless firebrand the printer in your city is running about as if driven by the devil, seemingly determined to do all the mischief he can. Indeed in my opinion he is an actual incendiary and ought to be the object of legal restraint," to Stephen Collins, 20 June 1788, Papers of Stephen Collins, DLC.

28. A draft of letters to members of the New Hampshire and Virginia conventions, 6 June 1788, is in the Lamb Papers, NHi.

29. *Richmond Virginia Independent Chronicle.*

30. To John Lamb, 1 July 1788, in Boyd, "News, Letters and Documents," pp. 77–79.

31. To John Lamb, 6 August 1788, *ibid.*

32. 29 May; "A Rhode Islander," 12 June 1788.

33. See Lamb's letters of 18 May 1788, cited in note 21.

34. Thomas Willing to William Bingham, 29 June 1788, Gratz Collection, PHi.

35. John Lamb to George Clinton, 17 June, Lamb Papers, NHi; George Clinton to John Lamb, 21 June 1788, Leake, *Lamb*, pp. 315–16.

36. To John Lamb, 9 June 1788, Leake, *Lamb*, p. 311.

37. See his covering letter to Lamb, 21 June 1788, *ibid.*, pp. 315–16.

38. Main, *Antifederalists*, p. 227.

39. Elliot, *Debates*, 3: 652.

40. See the report of the debates in the *Poughkeepsie Country Journal*, 29 July 1788.

41. Portions of the debates are printed in Elliot, *Debates,* 2: 205–414. More complete are Gilbert Livingston's "Notes on Debates in the New York Convention, 1788," Yates Papers, NN. For an analysis of the notes taken by Livingston, Francis Childs, John McKesson, and Melancton Smith, see the editorial note in Syrett, *Hamilton,* 5: 11–13.

42. Livingston Notes, Yates Papers, NN.

43. Elliot, *Debates,* 2: 411–12.

44. *Ibid,* p. 412.

45. *New York Independent Journal, Supplement Extraordinary,* 28 July 1788.

46. The best account is in Young, *Democratic-Republicans,* pp. 110–14, which expands Main, *Antifederalists,* pp. 238–39.

47. To John Lamb, 23 June 1788, NHi

48. De Witt Clinton Notes, 16–19 July 1788, DeWitt Clinton Papers, NNC. Clinton does not identify the Massachusetts Antifederalists by name.

49. *Ibid.*

50. Samuel Chase to John Lamb, 13 June 1788, Leake, *Lamb,* p. 310.

51. James Madison to Alexander Hamilton, 22 June 1788, Syrett, *Hamilton,* 5: 61–62.

52. Bloodworth to John Lamb, 1 July, Boyd, "News, Letters, and Documents," pp. 77–79; Burke to John Lamb, 23 June 1788, Lamb Papers, NHi.

53. Elliot, *Debates,* 4: 244–47.

54. *Ibid.* The Letter was first printed in the *Poughkeepsie Country Journal,* 5 August. It was reprinted as far north as Portland, Maine, on 21 August, and as far south as Savannah, Georgia, the same day. No printing has been located in any Delaware newspaper.

55. 30 October 1788. *Votes and Proceedings of the Thirteenth General Assembly . . . New Jersey . . .* (Trenton, 1788), pp. 7–9. Connecticut's action is described by Jonathan Trumbull: "The Circular Letter for the Convention of the State of New York being among the letters which the Governor laid before the assembly, [it] had of course a reading. . . . This was all that passed respecting it for although we had in our assembly the champion of the Antis [James Wadsworth], with some of his principal aids, yet no one had hardiness enough to call up the consideration of that letter . . . ," to George Washington, 20 October 1788, Washington Papers, DLC. The Pennsylvania Assembly acted on 8 September and 4 October. *Minutes of the Twelfth General Assembly . . . Pennsylvania . . .* (Philadelphia, 1788), pp. 219–21, 276.

56. In Massachusetts the Letter was referred to committee, but no report was made during the session, House Journals, 31 October 1788, M-Ar. New Hampshire Antifederalist Joshua Atherton complained all opposition had ceased in that state, the language of former opponents being, "It is adopted, let us try it," to John Lamb, 23 February 1789, Lamb Papers, NHi.

57. 1 November 1788, Rhode Island Acts and Resolves, RI-Ar.

58. 20 November 1788, *Journal of the House of Delegates* (Richmond, 1828), p. 66.

Chapter 7

THE CAPSTONE OF LEGITIMACY: THE FIRST FEDERAL ELECTIONS

Federalists and Antifederalists believed that the latter could win through the first federal elections what they had lost in the state conventions. This view had been a major consideration in inducing New York Antifederalists to acquiesce in unconditional ratification. In July 1788 George Washington expected that "a considerable effort will be made to procure the election of Antifederalists to the first Congress; in order . . . to undo all that has been done."[1] Federalists were concerned because they realized there was widespread dissatisfaction with the Constitution even in states like New York and Virginia which had earlier ratified it. Furthermore, by the fall Antifederalists had hammered out a national slate of amendments. During the course of ratification eight state conventions and the minority of two others recommended more than 200 amendments. Since there was considerable duplication, the number of different amendments was only 100. Even then there was considerable overlap as many of these amendments sought the same goal by slightly different means. From the amendments they proposed, it was clear, by fall 1788, that Antifederalists in the various conventions agreed on the need to materially restrict the powers of the new government by curtailing the judicial power, by limiting executive authority, and by holding the new government to those powers expressly delegated to it. In essence Antifederalists hoped to preserve the sovereignty of the states within the general framework of the new government. Because the Antifederalists intertwined the call for such substantive amendments with that for procedural guarantees of the right to freedom of speech, press, and the like, they could, Federalists feared, repeat their earlier successes in the convention elections and shipwreck the new government "in sight of the port."[2]

Federalist fears proved unwarranted. During the fall and winter Antifederalists were unable to recoup their earlier losses. Several factors limited the Antifederalists in the first federal elections. Most important, ratification altered the mode by which Antifederalists could effectively work to obtain amendments. By the fall of 1788 it was necessary for states which were dominated by Antifederalists to ratify the Constitution if they wished to have a voice in congressional deliberations concerning amendments. North Carolina and Rhode Island Antifederalists refused to recognize that changed political reality, stayed out of the Union, and therefore deprived Antifederalists of needed seats in the House of Representatives.

Antifederalists were further weakened by a resurgence of federalism among the state legislatures which drafted the first federal election laws. This Federalist predominance directly affected the outcome of the elections in several states by providing for at large or district elections and strict or lenient residence requirements.

The greatest threat to Antifederalist hopes, however, came from within their own ranks. Antifederalists had the support of a majority of the voters through the winter and spring of 1788. By fall the situation was changing. A majority of the voters still supported amendments —both substantive and procedural—but some now looked to Federalists to implement the Constitution and obtain the promised amendments. A second body of Antifederalists doubted that Federalists, once elected, would fulfill their convention pledges, or feared that they would introduce only minor procedural amendments which did little to correct the major faults they saw in the Constitution. These Antifederalists therefore advocated varying degrees of noncooperation including violence which could compel Federalists to rectify the new Constitution and non-participation until the same ends were achieved. Most Antifederalists rejected both options as they sought to draw their followers to a third: the election of Antifederalists to the first Congress.

In that effort, Antifederalists faced nearly insurmountable obstacles. In eight states—New Hampshire, Massachusetts, New York, Pennsylvania, New Jersey, Maryland, Virginia, and South Carolina —they nonetheless sought some seats in the House of Representatives as a base from which to sustain the drive for substantive amendment of the Constitution. In doing so, Antifederalists, albeit not always consciously, ensured the smooth transition from the Confederation government to that under the new Constitution. When the federal elections ended in July 1789 (North Carolina and Rhode Island excluded), and the transfer of power was completed, the same people who initially opposed the new Constitution accepted it.

During the ratification campaign Federalists had quickly secured ratifications in Delaware, Pennsylvania, New Jersey, Georgia, and Connecticut. In all five states they also dominated the legislatures which drafted the first federal election laws. Those laws, in turn, ensured the exclusion of any Antifederalist from these states' delegations. Antifederalists within each of those states nonetheless accepted the Constitution.

In Connecticut, for example, given the geographic distribution of the final roll call vote in the state convention, one could surmise that some Antifederalists would be elected to the House of Representatives. However, Connecticut Antifederalists did not oppose the adoption of a state-wide election law and made no demonstrable effort to send one of their own to the House. As Simeon Baldwin observed in March 1788, "This state is at present very quiet in its politics. The federal party have evidently obtained the superiority, and both sides seem quietly disposed to lay down their arms."[3] Connecticut was solidly in the Federalist column.

Somewhat surprisingly, an Antifederalist candidate did emerge in New Jersey, a state that earlier ratified the Constitution unanimously. Abraham Clark, a prominent East Jersey politician, sought one of the state's four seats in the House of Representatives. Although Clark had not opposed the Constitution during the campaign for ratification, he did favor amending its "exceptionable parts."[4] In response to Clark's candidacy, Federalists adopted a state election law and then interpreted it in such a way as to ensure Clark's exclusion from the state's delegation.

First, the Federalist-dominated legislature adopted an at-large election law which provided the more numerous West Jersey Federalists with the opportunity to outvote East Jersey residents who, in a district election, could have marshaled enough votes to send Clark, a favorite son, to Congress. Then those same West Jersey Federalists turned that opportunity into reality in February and March 1789. The New Jersey election law stipulated that the polls open on February 11, 1789, and remain open until "legally closed." By February 23, seven East Jersey counties' polls were complete and the returns submitted to the state council. Once the vote totals for these seven counties became known, West Jersey Federalists continued the balloting until they were certain sufficient votes had been cast to defeat Clark. Clark's allies in Essex County, the one East Jersey county that had not submitted its ballots, attempted to do the same thing, but on March 18, the state council declared the West Jersey Federalist candidates elected on the basis of the ballots returned. A later appeal to the House of Representatives proved ineffective and New Jersey sent a Federalist delegation to the House.[5]

New Jersey and Connecticut were among the first states to ratify the Constitution. Only in Connecticut had there been considerable opposition to ratification, but by the time of the first federal elections, Antifederalists accepted the Constitution and looked to Federalists to implement it. In Delaware and Georgia, too, the few who had criticized the Constitution were acquiescent. Only in New Jersey did Antifederalist Abraham Clark persist in the drive to secure amendments. At the same time, Clark accepted the Constitution while he sought to amend it in a constitutional manner. The eligible voters of East Jersey who supported Clark in his bid for public office did the same.

Initially, Pennsylvania Antifederalists were less acquiescent. During the course of ratification in the other states, however, an increasing number of Pennsylvania Antifederalists reluctantly accepted the Constitution. The first federal election in Pennsylvania expanded that acceptance to include, ultimately, the entire electorate.

Antifederalists had worked against such acquiescence throughout the spring. One measure frequently suggested as a means to sustain Antifederalist opposition was a meeting of delegates from throughout the state to outline a set of amendments and work with Antifederalists in other states to secure their adoption prior to ratification. The Cumberland County Circular Letter, which called for such a convention to meet at Harrisburg, did so only after ten states had ratified the Constitution and the way had been prepared for the full organization of the new government. The purpose of the Harrisburg Convention was therefore expanded to include more than "amendments and such mode of obtaining them as . . . shall be judged most expedient and satisfactory." The Cumberland County Circular Letter also suggested that since the Pennsylvania Assembly would probably enact an election law before the Harrisburg Convention assembled in September, it would be "expedient to have proper persons put in nomination by the delegates in conference, being the most likely method of directing the views of the electors to the same object, and of obtaining the desired end."[6]

During July and August, township and county meetings throughout the state appointed delegates to the forthcoming convention and passed resolutions supporting amendments. But as soon as the delegates assembled, at Harrisburg, differences among Antifederalists surfaced. Albert Gallatin, a Fayette County delegate, prepared a set of resolutions which stressed continued opposition to the unamended Constitution. Gallatin reiterated Antifederalist aversion to confusion and bloodshed, in the process using them as a threat, and he called for prompt revision of the Constitution. In order to expedite such revision, Gallatin proposed a "general conference" of delegates from the several states to consider which amendments "may seem most necessary" and "the most likely way to carry them into effect."[7] Gallatin's proposal was, in effect, an adaptation of the Lamb proposal of May 1788. But other delegates argued that the time for such extralegal action was past. As early as June, Charles Pettit, a Philadelphia delegate to the convention, had warned that the ratification of the Constitution, at that time by eight states, had legitimized it in the eyes of the "large proportion of the people of every state." Pettit then urged that the only way to regain the support of those voters was for the party to accommodate itself to the changed mood of the people while making one final effort to secure amendments. Hence Pettit recommended that the state's Antifederalists explicitly declare their support of the new government, and work to be included among those who would implement it.[8]

A majority of the delegates, even as they agreed with Gallatin's goals, favored Pettit's means. Thus the report of the Harrisburg Convention recommended that the people of the state "acquiesce" in the organization of the new government, called for a speedy "revision of the said constitution" by a general convention, and proposed that a petition be presented to the state legislature calling upon that body to petition Congress to call a second constitutional convention in conformity with Article V of the new Constitution.[9] Although not part of their formal report, the delegates to the convention also agreed on a slate of Antifederalist candidates for the United States House of Representatives. That "Harrisburg ticket" included nominees from each of the state's geographic regions: Charles Pettit and Blair M'Clenachan from Philadelphia in the east; William Irvine and Robert Whitehill from the central portion of the state; and William Montgomery and William Findley from the west. The ticket also included two representatives of the state's German population, Daniel Hiester and Peter Muhlenberg. Finally, the ticket included spokesmen from the various ideological wings of the party.[10]

The ticket itself was simply the first step in an intensive effort to secure the support of all Antifederalists in the first federal election. It was followed by a series of broadly based appeals to the electorate. Thus, in November "A Friend to Liberty and Union," for example, assured the freemen of Pennsylvania that the Antifederalist nominees were committed to "effectuating the great object of the late Continental Convention" even as they favored "carrying into execution the new government and at the same time amending it." "A Friend" also called upon the more radical wing of the party to support the ticket. "It has become the duty of good citizens," he argued, "to make a beginning with the Constitution as it is, confiding in the hope of obtaining all essential amendments in a constitutional mode [which] is certainly more eligible to reform the Constitution than any violent or irregular opposition to attempt to overthrow it."[11]

As if these divisions were not enough, Antifederalists were also undermined by a block of German Americans who protested the absence of sufficient "German representation" on the Harrisburg and Lancaster [Federalist] tickets. To remedy this, they proposed to remove Antifederalist Robert Whitehill from the Harrisburg ticket and to replace him with a Federalist nominee for the House, Frederick Augustus Muhlenburg. Likewise they altered the Lancaster ticket by deleting two Federalist nominees and replacing them with two Germans, Peter Muhlenburg and Daniel Hiester.[12]

The outcome of the elections saw the choice of six Federalists and the two German candidates. A key to this victory was the relatively low voter turnout in the western and previously Antifederalist counties. James Madison commented on the "indifference" among the Antifederalists.[13] The impact of that "indifference" and of the German nominations is particularly noticeable in the areas where comparable electoral returns are available. In Berks County, for example, which elected Antifederalist convention delegates in November 1787, one-third fewer voted Antifederalist in the first federal election. By contrast, Federalists in neighboring York County increased their voter turnout by approximately one-third. Antifederalists still had sufficient support, had the elections been by district, to send a representative or two to the House of Representatives. As it was they sent none.[14]

In the aftermath of the House elections, few options remained available to Pennsylvania's Antifederalists. In January the state's voters went to the polls again, this time to choose presidential electors, but in many instances Antifederalists simply "left it to the others

[Federalists] and did not vote."[15] There was still interest in amendments among Pennsylvania's electorate, but former Antifederalists now looked to Federalists to obtain them while the party's leaders, in the aftermath of their overwhelming defeat, moved to exculpate themselves from their Antifederalist past and, with an eye to their own political future, to declare their support for the new government.[16]

The Federalist victory in the Pennsylvania House elections was a major one, for that state contributed eight members to a House which consisted of only fifty-nine men. Federalists were a consistent majority in Pennsylvania. Furthermore, the state ratified the Constitution in December 1787, which made it more difficult for Antifederalists to retain their support in the face of repeated Federalist victories across the nation. The crucial test for Federalists would not come in Pennsylvania but in states where ratification occurred later, and where Federalist political control was not so great—states like Massachusetts, Maryland, and South Carolina.

The Massachusetts legislature enacted an election law which provided for eight representative districts. Each candidate had to be a resident of the district in which he ran and had to receive a majority of the votes cast. Each district consisted of either one, two, or three contiguous counties, with no counties divided. The makeup of the districts led to a considerable bias in favor of the eastern and predominantly Federalist counties, for the four eastern districts (excluding the district of Maine), which had voted in favor of ratification in the state convention had only 35 percent of the population, but they were to have 50 percent of the state's representatives in Congress. Maine, and the three western districts which had voted against ratification of the Constitution, had 65 percent of the population but would elect only 50 percent of Massachusetts's congressmen.[17]

The importance of this districting became clear following the December 18 balloting. Four districts chose a representative without a run-off election. In Plymouth-Barnstable Federalist George Partridge, a Plymouth County sheriff, won without opposition. In Bristol-Dukes-Nantucket Federalist George Leonard defeated Federalist David Cobb and Antifederalist Phanuel Bishop. Bishop, elected to the state Senate the preceding spring, was an outspoken critic of the Constitution, but found little support outside of his home county in the December balloting.[18]

The most significant of the December 18 choices came in Suffolk County where Samuel Adams, an Antifederalist who "stumbled at the threshold" of the new Constitution, but nonetheless voted for ratification with recommended amendments, sought a seat in the House of Representatives. In the campaign Adams's supporters stressed his years of service to the state and union, his personal integrity, and his consistent republicanism. In response to the charge that Adams would, if elected, help southern Antifederalists "pull down the pillars of the [new] government," Adams's defenders insisted he was a "decided Federalist" who put the highest priority on reestablishing the commerce and manufacturing of the nation, not on obtaining amendments.[19] Adams was unable, however, to escape his previous antifederalism and lost to Federalist Fisher Ames. Ames, who had represented Dedham in convention, narrowly defeated Adams in Boston and handily carried the remainder of the county. The final total was Ames, 818, Adams, 521, with 274 votes scattered among thirteen others.[20]

Adams's defeat, although disappointing to Antifederalists, was consistent with the federalism of Suffolk County. More surprising was the election of George Thacher from the district of Maine. Thacher was a delegate to the Confederation Congress and a Federalist, while the Maine delegation to the state convention was decidedly Antifederalist. Thacher implied that he favored some amendments, and won the support of the district's leading Antifederalists: William Widgery, Samuel Nasson, and Daniel Cony. Nasson even campaigned aggressively for Thacher's election. Thacher's Antifederalist support was so solid that the only opposition to him came from Federalists. Thacher won easily.[21]

In the four remaining districts no candidate received a majority of the votes cast and a second election became necessary. The failure of any candidate to obtain a majority in the first election in Essex district came as no surprise to a "Correspondent" in the *Salem Mercury* who observed two days before the election that "from present appearances it is probable the voters of this district will be very unequally divided" between four candidates—Samuel Holten, Benjamin Goodhue, Jonathan Jackson, and Nathan Dane.[22] Holten and Dane were both prominent Massachusetts politicians and Antifederalists; Goodhue and Jackson were Federalists. Little is known about the first election although the two Antifederalists ran third and fourth in the balloting. Following that poor showing, both men apparently withdrew from the contest. Given the choice between Goodhue and Jackson, the latter the author of an outspokenly antidemocratic pamphlet, *Thoughts Upon The Political Situation of the United States,* the voters of Essex chose Benjamin Goodhue on January 29, 1789.[23]

Before the first election in Middlesex district, newspapers in Boston "nominated" Elbridge Gerry, Nathaniel Gorham, Joseph B. Varnum, and John Brooks. Gorham received the highest vote count in the December 18 balloting but withdrew before the second election.[24] Much to the chagrin of his supporters, Elbridge Gerry did likewise. In a letter to the electors of Middlesex district, published less than a week before the second election, Gerry urged the voters of the district to "turn your attention to some other candidate [for] circumstanced as I am, to me an election would by no means be agreeable." Gerry went on to declare that he was not an "enemy" to the new Constitution, as had been charged. He acknowledged he still favored amendments, but distinguished between support for amendments and opposition to the regular operation of the new government, which Gerry thought would be "highly criminal."[25] With the two front runners out of the race, the logical choice seemed to be Joseph B. Varnum. Elected to the state convention as an Antifederalist, Varnum had voted for ratification. That apparently alienated Antifederalists in the district, while Federalists, who viewed him as unreliable, proposed General William Hull, a Middlesex judge with no previous political experience. During the final week of the campaign, Gerry's supporters insisted, despite his denials, that he would serve if elected, but Federalists reiterated that since Gerry was not a candidate, the voters should choose Hull. In an age when electioneering still seemed inappropriate to many voters, Gerry's declaration of noncandidacy proved decisive. He carried the run-off election by a better than three to one margin and after considerable reflection reluctantly agreed to serve.[26]

The second election completed the choice of representatives in six of Massachusetts's eight districts. The voters of Worcester district finally made a choice on March 2. In the first election the predominantly Antifederalist district divided with Timothy Paine, Jonathan Grout, Artemus Ward, and Moses Gill the top vote getters. Of the four, only Grout was an Antifederalist, although all four men had endorsed amendments for, as "An Observer" stated in the *Boston Independent Chronicle,* "To have any votes [in Worcester] a man must be known to be in favor of the amendments."[27] In the second election Paine, a representative from Worcester, received a plurality of the votes cast but not the necessary majority. The third election saw a marked increase in voter turnout, when 3,484 ballots were cast— 1,500 more than in each of the preceding elections. Although there is not a clear explanation for the increase, the fact that Grout, who was the front runner in the first election, slipped to second in the first run-off election, may have stimulated the voters to act in order to ensure that their representative would be an Antifederalist. Grout was the beneficiary of most of the additional votes cast in the second run-off and was elected on March 2.[28]

The most protracted election took place in the Hampshire-Berkshire district which required four run-off elections before Federalist Theodore Sedgwick was elected in May 1789. Surprisingly, while the district had voted against the Constitution in the state convention, and supported the Gerry-Warren ticket in the gubernatorial election, only one Antifederalist, William Whiting, a former county court justice suspected of Shaysite sympathies, announced in the first election. The other major candidates—Sedgwick, Samuel Lyman, William Williams, and John Worthington—were all Federalists. All five men, as in Worcester, claimed to support amendments, although Sedgwick, privately, did not. During the first two elections, voter turnout was relatively low with Sedgwick and Lyman, both incumbents in the state house, alternating as the top vote getter. Whiting remained a distant third. Extensive campaigning during February stimulated voter interest and the turnout doubled in the second run-off election on March 2. Still no candidate received a majority and a fourth election proved necessary. That election was also indecisive, although Whiting finally withdrew. That withdrawal and "damned Sedgwickian tricks" (including holding back the votes of pro-Lyman towns), gave Sedgwick a seven vote majority in the May 30 balloting.[29]

Although their victory was not as complete as in Pennsylvania, Federalists were still pleased by the outcome of the Massachusetts elections. Six of the eight men elected were Federalist, and one of the two Antifederalists, Gerry, was acceptable to Federalists who had encouraged him not to resign after his initial election.[30] The Massachusetts elections were important, too, because they fostered the growth of complex party organizations which encouraged participation in the electoral process. This was particularly true of the protracted elections in Middlesex, Worcester, and Hampshire-Berkshire. That participation drew Antifederalists into the framework of the government and electoral process established by the Constitution. In some instances it also rewarded them with the election of an Antifederalist, while in every district it held out hope for future elections. That, coupled with the example of men like Elbridge Gerry, who insisted they were "duty bound" to support a government ratified by the majority until it could be amended, even before the close of the first federal elections, disposed the majority of Massachusetts Anti-federalists to "live quietly" under the new government in expectation of Congress paying "proper attention to the amendments proposed to the general Constitution."[31]

In contrast to Massachusetts, where Antifederalists elected a majority of the delegates to the state convention, Maryland Anti-federalists were overwhelmed in the convention elections and ineffective in the convention. Even so, Federalists were still wary in the fall because they feared that Antifederalist Governor William Smallwood would call the existing legislature, "who are less federal than their successors are likely to be," into special session to draft a federal election law. While such a strategy was "much wished for by the opponents" of the new government, Smallwood did not act to call such a session because of delays by the Confederation Congress in the passage of an election resolution until September 13, too close to the state legislative elections to permit a special session.[32]

The legislature elected in Maryland in October 1788 demonstrated the validity of Madison's observation, and the dubiousness of Antifederalists' claims that a majority of the people in that state still opposed the Constitution. Across the state the Federalist victories were as decisive as in the state convention elections. Only voters in Baltimore, Harford, and Anne Arundel counties (the same counties that elected Antifederalists to the state convention) chose Anti-federalist legislators in the fall.[33] With a majority in the state legislature, Federalists enacted an election law designed to ensure an exclusively Federalist delegation in Congress. The law divided the state into six districts and required that candidates be residents of the district in which they ran. District elections, though, held out the possibility that an Antifederalist could be elected from the Harford, Baltimore, Anne Arundel counties region. Consequently, Maryland Federalists added a provision which allowed voters to vote for one candidate from each district, making the election, in effect, at large. Thus, even if a district returned an Antifederalist majority, Federalist voters across the state could still ensure the election of a Federalist from that district.[34]

The legislature passed the election law on December 22. Three weeks later the election occurred. During the interval, both parties nominated slates of candidates, and because of the general election feature of the law, distributed their ticket throughout the state. Of all the candidates, only two—Samuel Sterrett, an unsuccessful candidate for the state convention, and John Francis Mercer, a convention dele-

FIRST FEDERAL ELECTION DISTRICTS

Massachusetts		County of
		Suffolk
		Essex
		Worcester
		Middlesex
		Counties of
		Hampshire & Berkshire
		Plymouth & Barnstable
		York, Cumberland, & Lincoln (Maine)
		Bristol, Duke's & Nantucket

Maryland	District	Counties of
	1	St. Mary's, Charles, & Calvert
	2	Kent, Cecil, Talbot, & Queen Anne's
	3	Anne Arundel & Prince George
	4	Harford & Baltimore, & the City of Baltimore
	5	Worcester, Somerset, Dorchester, & Caroline
	6	Montgomery, Frederick, & Washington

New York	District	County of
	1	Westchester (lower) & New York City
		Counties of
	2	Kings, Queens, Suffolk, & Richmond
	3	Dutchess & Westchester (upper)
	4	Ulster & Orange
	5	Columbia, Washington, Clinton, & Albany (east)
	6	Albany (west) & Montgomery

Virginia	District	Counties of
	1	Hampshire, Berkeley, Hardy, Shenandoah, Monongalia, Ohio, Randolph, Harrison, & Frederick
	2	Mercer, Bourbon, Madison, Fayette, Lincoln, Jefferson, Nelson (Kentucky)
	3	Botetourt, Rockbridge, Montgomery, Greenbrier, Washington, Augusta, Russell, Rockingham, & Pendleton
	4	Prince William, Stafford, King George, Loudoun, Fairfax, & Fauquier
	5	Albemarle, Amherst, Fluvanna, Goochland, Louisa, Orange, Spotsylvania, & Culpeper

Virginia (*cont.*)	District	Counties of
	6	Campbell, Charlotte, Bedford, Buckingham, Prince Edward, Franklin, Henry, Pittsylvania, & Halifax
	7	Essex, Richmond, Lancaster, Westmoreland, Northumberland, Gloucester, Middlesex, King & Queen, King William, & Caroline
	8	Norfolk, Accomac, Northampton, Princess Anne, Nansemond, Isle of Wight, Surry, & Southampton
	9	Brunswick, Sussex, Greensville, Prince George, Dinwiddie, Amelia, Mecklenburg, Lunenburg, Powhatan, & Cumberland
	10	New Kent, Elizabeth City, York, Warwick, Charles City, Henrico, Chesterfield, Hanover, & James City

South Carolina	Judicial Districts of
	Beaufort & Orangeburgh
	Georgetown & Cheraw
	Judicial District of
	Charleston
	Camden
	Ninety-Six

gate from Anne Arundel County—were Antifederalists. Their four companion candidates were Federalists in national politics. In the first federal election national issues were a major factor in only the third and fourth districts. In the fourth Sterrett came out in favor of amendments and attacked his opponent, William Smith, whom he characterized as an inhumane aristocrat. Although Sterrett sought to avoid the Antifederalist label (the ticket was labeled "The Watchful Guardians of the Rights of the People"), Federalists linked Sterrett to Virginia's Patrick Henry and to alleged Antifederalist plans to destroy the new Constitution. The persistent antifederalism of Baltimore County showed through as Smith carried the city but Sterrett the county and the district. Had Maryland adopted a strict district election law, Samuel Sterrett would have served in the first Congress. As it was, votes from the four predominantly Federalist districts gave Smith a victory. Likewise, third-district voters preferred John Francis Mercer, but the state-wide returns made Federalist Benjamin Contee the representative.[35]

Federalist strategy of a modified district election worked well in

Maryland. Because of it the entire Maryland delegation was Federalist. The election law was only one reason the Antifederalists lost. Maryland was simply Federalist, like its neighbors to the north and east. Antifederalists finally accepted that in the fall when they ran only two candidates. More important, during the fall and winter of 1788, Maryland Antifederalists retreated from their earlier aggressive stand against the Constitution. During the state legislative elections Chase and Mercer denied they were enemies to the Constitution, as did the latter in the first federal election.[36] By the close of the first federal election in Maryland, Antifederalism existed only in the vocabulary of Federalist politicians who, as in New Jersey, used it to attack their opponents.

On the surface the situation in South Carolina was similar to that in Maryland. The reality was far different. Both states ratified the Constitution by large margins, but South Carolina's ratification occurred to a great extent because of malapportionment in the state convention. That malapportionment gave the Federalist-dominated low country a majority of the seats even though they constituted a minority of the white population. Federalist control of the state legislature was similarly based. In the fall of 1788 Federalists used that control to adopt an election law that, by dividing the state into five districts, ensured some Federalist representation in the House even as it placated the Antifederalist majority.

Little is known about the actual elections. In Charleston district Federalists divided among themselves. William Smith, a prominent lawyer, was elected. Daniel Huger won uncontested in Georgetown, the second low country district, while Antifederalists carried the three back country districts. In Beaufort-Orangeburgh, Aedanus Burke, a member of the state House and an Antifederalist who voted against ratification, defeated Federalist Richard Barnwell. The voters of Camden district chose Antifederalist Thomas Sumter, a state representative and convention delegate who, like Burke, voted against ratification. In the far west, in Ninety-six district, Thomas Tudor Tucker, an Antifederalist delegate to the Confederation Congress, was chosen.[37] A "blacklist" indeed to South Carolina Federalists, but one that served to placate back country voters by giving them majority representation in the state's delegation.[38]

Had Antifederalists been able to send similar delegations to Congress from states like Massachusetts and Pennsylvania they could have worked together to secure the amendments pledged at Charleston and Boston. As it was Burke, Tucker, and Sumter were part of a small, powerless minority. Burke, who had earlier offered his support to New York Antifederalists in order to prevent the success of the new government, was reduced to collecting data for a proposed history of the adoption of the Constitution. Burke's effort was not an objective searching out of the facts. Instead, he was determined to prove that the "late great Revolution," as he characterized it, was accomplished through unscrupulous means.[39] The importance of Burke's literary effort is that it was history, and that the "late great Revolution" was an accomplished fact accepted by Burke and the voters who elected him to the House of Representatives.

The first federal elections in Maryland, Massachusetts, and South Carolina fostered acceptance of the Constitution by the electorate. In Maryland that acceptance came because of the overwhelming federalism of the state. Political leaders like Samuel Chase and John Francis Mercer finally accepted that political reality, denied their former antifederalism, and attempted to move into the camp of the Federalists. In Massachusetts and South Carolina, in contrast, the first federal elections offered those dissatisfied with the Constitution hope that the Constitution would be amended if they channeled their efforts into the political process. As the people responded to that opportunity, as in the back country South Carolina elections and the later Massachusetts run-off elections, those disaffected found their efforts rewarded sufficiently to accept the new Constitution.

The greatest threat to Federalist dominance in the House potentially came from the three last states to ratify the Constitution. In New Hampshire, Virginia, and New York Antifederalists nearly prevented unconditional ratification. More important, in the fall of 1788 they retained control of the lower house in New Hampshire and New York, and of both houses in Virginia. Despite this strength, Antifederalists elected only six representatives from the three states, and by the close of the elections, the people in all three states accepted the new Constitution.

In New Hampshire, Antifederalists failed to elect a single candidate to the House of Representatives. This came about in part because of the New Hampshire election law which directed that the voters cast their ballots for any three men. In the event no candidate received a majority in the balloting, a run-off election was to be held among the top six vote getters. In the first balloting in December 1788, Nathaniel Peabody, an Antifederalist who had been defeated in his bid for a seat in the Senate, and Joshua Atherton, who sought a seat in the House of Representatives in order to "stop the operation of the

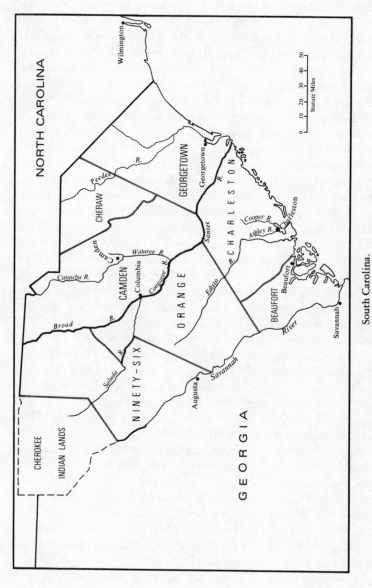

South Carolina.

Courtesy of the University of Wisconsin Cartographic Lab.

new system until amendments are incorporated," ran seventh and eighth.[40] With only Federalists to choose from, voter turnout declined markedly. Antifederalists, nonetheless, at that point, and indeed at the time of the December balloting, were reconciled to the new government, for as Atherton explained to John Lamb, despite the fact that "in our general Assembly [for a] long time [there was] a decided majority against the new Constitution, opposition has ceased and the language is 'it is adopted, let us try it.'"[41]

Some Virginia Antifederalists shared that sentiment. On June 27, Antifederalists met to "prepare an address to reconcile their [the delegates'] constituents to the new plan of government." To the surprise of many at the meeting, a draft address to the public, introduced by George Mason, was similar to *The Dissent of the Minority of the Pennsylvania Convention* in that it "tend[ed] to irritate rather than quiet the public mind." When a number of delegates present objected, Mason withdrew it and the meeting adjourned.[42]

Mason and Virginia Antifederalists did not, however, forsake all political action. During the fall session of the legislature Virginia Antifederalists elected two Antifederalist senators, Richard Henry Lee and William Grayson; passed legislation prohibiting federal office holders from simultaneously holding state office; petitioned Congress to "immediately" call another constitutional convention; adopted a district election law that divided the state into ten districts; required that candidates be residents of the districts in which they ran; and agreed upon a slate of Antifederalist candidates for the House of Representatives.[43]

Despite this strong showing, Antifederalists were unable to maintain the degree of cooperation they demonstrated at Richmond and antifederalism proved unattractive to the voters in the first federal elections. In three of Virginia's ten districts, for example, despite early agreement on candidates among Antifederalist legislators, no nominee challenged the Federalist candidate. In the first, second, and third districts Federalists Alexander White, a convention delegate who voted in favor of unconditional ratification, John Brown, a Confederation Congress delegate, and Andrew Moore, another convention delegate who voted for unconditional ratification, won with no recorded opposition. This was offset in part by the absence of Federalist candidates in the sixth and ninth districts where Antifederalist Isaac Coles and Theodorick Bland ran unopposed.[44] But of the five districts the choice of a representative reflected the position of the majority of the district's delegates to the state convention in only four. In Kentucky the voters, like their counterparts in the district of Maine, chose Antifederalist convention delegates, but turned to a Federalist delegate to the Confederation Congress to represent them in the House of Representatives.

The problems created by the unwillingness of previously agreed upon nominees to run was further compounded in other districts where several men expressed a willingness to fill that void. In the fourth district, for example, at least four Antifederalists desired the nomination. Thomas Lee and Cuthbert Bullitt, the latter an unsuccessful candidate for a convention seat a year earlier, as well as Stevens Thomson Mason—a nephew of George Mason—and John Pope were all rumored to be candidates. George Mason finally persuaded the district's Antifederalists to unite behind Pope, a state senator, but to no avail as he lost to Federalist Richard Bland Lee.[45]

Similar problems plagued Antifederalists in the seventh district where Spencer Roane, a son-in-law of Patrick Henry and later a prominent state judge, Meriwether Smith, a "Henryite" legislator, and Arthur Lee all sought the nomination.[46] Although Lee later withdrew, he issued a broadside that offers considerable insight into the Virginia elections. Lee acknowledged in his "Address of the People" that he had favored previous amendments, but declared that now that the Constitution was adopted, he would *support* (m.e.) it even as he continued the fight for amendments.[47] Lee apparently mirrored sentiment in the district, for Federalist Francis Corbin also declared his support for "those amendments which have been sanctioned by so great a majority of the convention."[48] Corbin's and Lee's declarations, taken together, suggest relatively widespread support for amendments among Virginia's electorate, Federalist and Antifederalist. The declaration itself did little good for either candidate because Lee withdrew in the interests of party unity while Federalists rallied behind John Page. Neither Corbin nor Smith withdrew formally, but they did not find substantial support. Federalist John Page, a state legislator, won handily.[49]

The excess of candidates did not alter the outcome of the election in the seventh district, but a split in the Federalist vote in the eighth allowed Antifederalist John Parker to be elected. One of the two Federalist candidates, Isaac Avery, actually withdrew before the election in favor of Thomas Mathews, a delegate to the state convention who had voted for ratification. Avery nonetheless received two hundred votes, drawing enough support away from Mathews to give Parker a slender plurality.[50] This setback was offset by a similar split in the Antifederalist vote in the tenth district where former Governor Benjamin Harrison and Miles Selden both sought a seat in the House of Representatives. Federalists agreed on Samuel Griffin, a member of the state house, who won with "rather more than one third of the votes."[51]

The election in nine of Virginia's ten districts paled in comparison to the attention paid to and significance of the election in the fifth district where James Madison and James Monroe both sought to represent the state in the House of Representatives. Given the importance Antifederalists in the state house attached to the exclusion of James Madison from a seat in the Senate, their choice of James Monroe as their candidate for the fifth district is somewhat surprising. There were certainly more experienced men available in the district and more consistent Antifederalists than Monroe who many had believed would vote for ratification in the state convention. In addition, Monroe was a personal friend of Madison.

Perhaps Henry and the Antifederalists in the legislature who persuaded Monroe to run believed the district would not support a more extreme Antifederalist. Furthermore, Monroe's personal friendship with Madison did not check Monroe's vigorous campaign effort. Indeed Madison and Monroe both campaigned throughout the district, frequently travelling together. Both men solicited the endorsement of prominent political and religious leaders in the district, wrote private letters in which they clarified their position on various issues, and encouraged the recipients of those letters to circulate them along with other campaign literature.[52]

The major issue in the campaign was that of amendments. Support for Monroe, who voted against ratification in the state convention, was urged on the grounds that he was "uniformly in favor of amendments" and during the campaign Monroe pledged to work for all the Virginia convention's recommended amendments and the call for a second constitutional convention.[53] Madison, on the other hand, had opposed amendments, and Antifederalists exploited that by reporting that he was "dogmatically attached to the Constitution in every clause, and syllable and letter" and that he would not promote any amendments "either from conviction or a spirit of accommodation."[54] During the campaign Madison worked to dispel this now false rumor, for by February 1789, with ratification secured, Madison accepted the need for some amendments. He did not endorse all of the amendments recommended by the Virginia Convention and he remained opposed to a second constitutional convention. But during the campaign for a seat in the House of Representatives, Madison pledged to work for prompt congressional amendment of the Constitution.[55]

Aside from the question of amendments, the other major issue in the campaign was the concern of many Baptists that the Constitution posed a threat to religious liberty. Antifederalists, although not Monroe personally, exploited this fear by spreading a false rumor that Madison no longer supported religious freedom. To counter this Federalists pointed to Madison's record in support of religious liberty in the Virginia legislature, while Madison himself assured various religious leaders of his continued support for their rights.[56] His well-deserved reputation as a champion of religious and civil liberty, his shift on the issue of amendments, and aggressive campaigning by Madison and his political allies paid off as Madison defeated Monroe 1308 to 972.[57]

The first federal elections in Virginia demonstrated, even as they fostered its further development, the high degree of acceptance of the Constitution among the state's voters. At the outset of the campaign Antifederalists recognized the strong inclination on the part of the electorate to accept the new government. Thus they acquiesced in the nomination of John Brown in Kentucky, and turned to moderate Antifederalists like Josiah Parker, Arthur Lee, and James Monroe. And Madison's defeat of Monroe demonstrated that voters not only accepted the Constitution, but were willing to place the responsibility for securing amendments in the hands of those who promised in their campaigns to fulfill their own earlier convention pledges. The first federal elections in Virginia demonstrated that the people accepted the document when they chose seven Federalists, including one of its primary architects, to represent them in the House of Representatives.

Initially Federalists were sanguine about their prospects in New York. They had secured ratification in July only by endorsing the New York Circular Letter which stated that the Constitution was "exceptionable" to a majority of the delegates and that its revision, "at a period not far remote," was imperative if it were to gain, "the confidence and goodwill," i.e., acceptance, "of the great body of the people."[58] Antifederalists faced even greater difficulties, the foremost of which was divisions in their own ranks. Abraham Yates spoke for one block of "non-adopting" Antifederalists when he declared that "Our only safety now is in getting amendments confirmed. I mean to try for it and I believe the first thing necessary will be to pass a law to inhibit the state officers, the legislature, the executive and the judicial from taking the oath to support the new government until our amendments have been confirmed in due form."[59] In December 1788, Yates introduced such a bill in a special session of the legislature, but it found little support, even in the Antifederalist-dominated lower house. Most Antifederalists in New York, while they agreed with Yates's goals, preferred the course suggested by Abraham G. Lansing: the election of Antifederalists to the first Congress "in order to bring about the reformation we desire."[60] During November and December Antifederalists in New York City met at Fraunces Tavern to take preliminary steps toward that end. In a circular letter to "The Counties within the State" the Federal Republicans warned against divisions among Antifederalists based on differences arising from the state convention, and stressed the need for cooperation in the forthcoming legislative session to ensure the adoption of an election law favorable to the Antifederalists.[61]

The legislature that assembled in Albany in December "superseded" the work of the Federal Republican Committee, which held no further formal meetings. Once the legislature passed an election law, though, the members of the committee—John Lamb, Marinus Willett, Samuel Jones, Charles Tillinghast, and William Malcolm, among others—renewed their efforts which paralleled in form the massive campaign of the previous spring. The first federal elections paralleled the state convention election in substance, too, for the same men were involved in a continuing political battle over the same issue—the nature and scope of the new government. Antifederalists wanted amendments to limit and curtail that new government; Federalists did not. The parallel between the two was apparent in district one where the Antifederalists had no real hope of electing their own candidate. Given the overwhelming federalism of the city, local Antifederalists opted to exploit a potential split among Federalists who were divided over the respective merits of John Laurance, a city lawyer, and Jacob Broome, a merchant. William Malcolm, a member of the Federal Republican Committee, chaired the meeting that nominated Broome after several Federalists expressed publicly their discontent over the nomination of a lawyer to represent the greatest commercial center in the new nation. In theory a Federalist split opened the way for an Antifederalist candidate, and Philip Pell, an Antifederalist lawyer, did receive nominal support. Still, Pell had no real chance of being elected and it seems likely that Antifederalists encouraged the Laurance-Broome split less with the hope of electing

Pell than in the belief that such divisions could be useful to Clinton during the April gubernatorial campaign. Laurance won by an eight to one margin.[62]

Outside of the city and its environs, Antifederalists were considerably stronger. In district two Federalists and Antifederalists both nominated William Floyd. A signer of the Declaration of Independence and a state senator in 1789, Floyd initially opposed the Constitution. He nonetheless had the support of his brother-in-law Ezra L'Hommedieu, who declined nomination in favor of Floyd. Floyd won with no opposition.[63]

The fourth district was a major Antifederalist stronghold. On February 24, a meeting occurred at Montgomery to decide on a candidate. Delegates at that meeting divided with a "party from Orange [County] . . . obstinate for the nomination of General Hathorn." A delegate to the Confederation Congress, Hathorn had been speaker of the state house, and a member of the Orange County Antifederalist committee the year before. Peter Van Gaasbeek and other Ulster County Antifederalists favored Cornelius Schoonmaker, a delegate to the convention who voted against unconditional ratification. In order to avoid an "open rupture," and because both men supported amendments, the meeting "unanimously agreed to hold up both . . ." as candidates. Hathorn defeated Schoonmaker, his only recorded opponent.[64]

In district six Antifederalists nominated Jeremiah Van Rensselaer, an Albany Antifederalist, who voted against ratification. Van Rensselaer had been chairman of the Albany Antifederalist Committee the year before and utilized that campaign organization again in the first federal election. In nominating Van Rensselaer, the district's Antifederalists called for amendments, and the election of "persons as were for obtaining them." That theme was reiterated by anonymous essayists in the Albany and Poughkeepsie newspapers and proved to be the central issue in the campaign. Van Rensselaer defeated Federalist Abraham Ten Broeck by 241 votes, out of a total of 2,671 cast.[65]

Elsewhere Antifederalists did not fare so well. In district five, Matthew Adgate, an Antifederalist who voted against ratification in the state convention, lost to Federalist Peter Silvester.[66] In district three, Antifederalists nominated Theodorus Bailey, an Antifederalist who was "decidedly" in favor of amendments, and a person "who from principle and inclination will exert himself to obtain them." As in district six, Antifederalists campaigned throughout the district, making their commitment to amendments, "on which the liberties of

America depend," their primary issue. Despite this effort Bailey lost to Federalist Egbert Benson.[67]

In the aftermath of the elections, which saw the choice of three Federalists and three Antifederalists, Abraham G. Lansing attributed the Antifederalists' modest showing to a lack of campaigning. It is clear though that Antifederalists lost in the third and fifth districts because their appeal was too narrow. In district three, for example, Federalists stressed that if two-thirds of the states petitioned Congress to call a general convention, Congress was required to act. "The Congress *shall* call one. In that case they are obliged to call one whether it is or is not agreeable to their wishes." Likewise, if the states did not petition Congress, Congress could not act. "It would be a violation if they should do it." Since, Federalists argued, the end would be the same, it was better to elect Federalists, for their candidates were possessed of a "superior knowledge" in the other important and more discretionary areas of Congressional concern—"finance, commerce, manufactures, and husbandry."[68] Throughout the state Federalist candidates received votes from men who had previously voted Antifederalist, and still wanted amendments, but accepted the Federalist pledge made at Poughkeepsie to work for amendments, and in the first federal elections campaign to work for other interests of the state.[69]

Following their setback in the first federal elections, New York Antifederalists, too, modified their public positions on the Constitution. In his gubernatorial campaign Governor Clinton attempted to downplay his antifederalism while in the May legislative elections, which saw Federalists win a majority of the seats in both houses of the legislature, former Antifederalists abandoned that party label. Dissatisfaction with the Constitution still existed, but once the new government began operation even the most obstreperous of the "non-adopting" Antifederalists became reconciled to the new government, and were concerned chiefly with the policies it pursued.[70]

The first federal elections proved a resounding Federalist success. Only eleven of the fifty-nine members of the first House of Representatives—Gerry and Grout from Massachusetts; Van Rensselaer, Floyd, and Hathorn from New York; Bland, Coles, and Parker from Virginia; and Burke, Sumter, and Tucker from South Carolina —were Antifederalists. More important than the precise number of Antifederalists was the virtual elimination of antifederalism as an organized opposition party and the acceptance of the Constitution by the majority of the electorate.

That the voters, a majority of whom had opposed the Constitution in 1787 and 1788, now accepted it, was due in large part to the willingness of Antifederalists to operate within the parameters of the new Constitution. Political participation does not in itself guarantee that the participants accept the constitutional system within which they operate. In Pennsylvania, for example, following the adoption of the "democratic" constitution of 1776, Republicans operated within the framework of the constitution even as they sought to replace it. Antifederalists, too, operated within the parameters of the proposed Constitution even as they sought to overthrow it. But Pennsylvania Republicans, for the fourteen years of their campaign (the Constitution was replaced in 1790), consistently challenged the legitimacy of the Constitution which was declared adopted by the convention that drafted it. By participating in the convention system, Antifederalist arguments that the Constitution did not have the support of the majority of the people were less persuasive, particularly after Federalists won ratification in eleven states. Further Federalist victories in state legislative elections, in defeating Antifederalist repeal efforts, and in the first federal elections confirmed the legitimacy of the new government.

Antifederalists also accepted the Constitution because their leaders encouraged them to do so. From the outset of the ratification conventions, Antifederalist delegates deferred to Federalist majorities, as in Georgia and New Jersey where Antifederalists voted with the majority for unanimous ratification, and in Connecticut where a number of prominent Antifederalists also voted with the Federalist majority. In Massachusetts, even Antifederalists who voted against ratification nonetheless vowed to return home supporters of the new Constitution and to work among their constituents to ensure a proper submission by the voters that sent them to Boston. Not all Antifederalists followed this lead in the spring of 1788, but enough did to debilitate a post-ratification Antifederalist drive in the state legislative and gubernatorial elections, and in the ensuing first federal elections. In the South Carolina, New Hampshire, Virginia, and New York conventions, some Antifederalist convention delegates, after they voted against ratification, declared their support for the Constitution and pledged to work for its acceptance among their constituents. The acquiescence of these middle-range political elites and their supporters at home was duplicated at the highest level at the close of the first federal elections when men like Elbridge Gerry, Charles Pettit, Samuel Chase, and Richard Henry Lee encouraged

Antifederalist acceptance of the outcome of the ratification elections process. Overwhelmed at the polls, deprived of effective leadership, and facing further defections among their own ranks, Antifederalists acquiesced.

Finally, Antifederalists reluctantly accepted the Constitution because continued opposition seemed both futile and destructive. Such opposition was futile in that the majority did now accept the new Constitution; it was destructive in that further resistance could lead only to political oblivion or anarchy and civil war.

While a handful were willing to run that risk, the majority were not, for to them the Constitution was the legitimate frame of government for the states. Not all of these former Antifederalists were enthusiastic about the Constitution, but they acquiesced and looked to the Federalists to fulfill their earlier convention and federal election pledges. Antifederalists of course had warned that would not happen. Since October 1787, and through his last "Centinel" in December 1788, Samuel Bryan insisted that the new government would "enslave" the people. Had the government acted early to deprive people of their rights—of speech, press, or representation—it might have destroyed the achievement of the preceding eighteen months. But the government took no such action. Indeed the long arm of the federal government touched few of the people directly in 1789, even as it acted to guarantee to all, by recommending amendments, the very rights that Antifederalists had warned were in jeopardy.

In retrospect William Petrikin, a Carlisle, Pennsylvania, Antifederalist, criticized the delegates to the Harrisburg Convention who persuaded that convention to turn to the first federal elections as the best means of continuing the drive for substantive restructuring of the Constitution. Petrikin complained that such political participation, (and his criticism could be extended to Antifederalist participation in the convention elections as well), drew Antifederalists away from "decisive" and presumably more successful measures.[71] The decisive measures Petrikin outlined—committees of correspondence, a statewide meeting, and channels of communication throughout the United States—were all measures implemented by the Antifederalists in the preceding months. They had not produced the desired effect. Neither did the Antifederalists' decision to channel their activity into the electoral process in 1788–1789. But that certainly held out a greater promise of success than an undirected show of force against a yet to be established government. Had Antifederalists held the majorities they won in the state conventions or won more seats in the first federal elections, they could have debilitated the new government even before it was set in operation. With this increased likelihood of success though came the risk of total defeat. The Antifederalists' decision to accept that risk is the key to understanding the initial acceptance of the Constitution by the American people.

NOTES TO
CHAPTER 7

1. To James McHenry, 31 July 1788, Jensen, *Elections,* 1: 55.

2. George Washington to James Madison, 23 September 1788, *ibid.,* p. 141; Kenneth R. Bowling, "James Madison's Tub to the Whale: The Adoption of the Bill of Rights and the Capture of the Antifederal Leviathan," unpublished manuscript in the possession of the author.

3. To James Kent, 8 March 1788, Baldwin Collection, CtY.

4. To Thomas Sinnickson, 23 July 1788, Burnett, *Letters,* 8: 764.

5. See Richard P. McCormick, "New Jersey's First Congressional Election, 1789: A Case Study of Political Skullduggery," *William and Mary Quarterly,* Third Series, 6 (1949):237–50; and Kenneth R. Bowling, "Federalists and Antifederalists After Ratification: The First Congressional Elections, 1788–1789" (unpublished M.A. Thesis, University of Wisconsin, 1964), pp. 25–36. The latter is the definitive study of the congressional elections pending the completion of *The Documentary History of The First Federal Elections.* I have relied on Bowling throughout this chapter.

6. 3 July 1788, Jensen, *Elections,* 1: 240.

7. Albert Gallatin, Draft Resolution, Proceedings of the Harrisburg Convention, 3–6 September 1788, *ibid.,* pp. 259–60.

8. To Robert Whitehill, 5 June 1788, Whitehill Papers, Cumberland County Historical Society.

9. Report of the Proceedings, Proceedings of the Harrisburg Convention, 3–6 September 1788, Jensen, *Elections,* 1: 260–64.

10. The ticket was not part of the formal report, but was communicated in a "clandestine manner . . . to the inhabitants of the interior." It was not printed in Philadelphia until November. See "A Friend to Truth and Freedom," *Philadelphia Federal Gazette,* 7 November 1788, *ibid.,* pp. 331–35.

11. *Ibid.*

12. To the German Inhabitants of the State of Pennsylvania, 13 November 1788, *ibid.,* pp. 339–40.

13. To Henry Lee, 30 November 1788, *ibid.,* p. 370.

14. Cf. the convention election returns in Jensen, *Ratification,* 2: 235 and Jensen, *Elections,* 1: 378–79.

15. Alexander McKeehan and George Logue to John Nicholson, 8 January 1789, Jensen, *Elections,* 1: 382.

16. Charles Pettit to George Washington, 5 August 1788, 19 March 1791, Washington Papers, DLC.

17. Jensen, *Elections,* 1: 476–77.

18. *Ibid.,* pp. 575–76, 583–85.

19. *Boston Gazette,* 8 December; "Prudence," "To the Freemen of the County of Suffolk," *Boston Independent Chronicle,* 11 December; "Belisaurius," *Boston Gazette,* 15 December; "Common Sense," *Boston Independent Chronicle,* 18 December 1788; Jensen, *Elections,* 1: 550, 552–53, 559–60, 567–68.

20. *Ibid.* p. 609.

21. See Silas Lee to George Thacher, 14 February 1788, "Thacher Papers," pp. 338–39.

22. 16 December 1788, Jensen, *Elections,* 1: 599.

23. The Second Election in Essex District, *ibid.,* pp. 627–35.

24. Henry Jackson to Henry Knox, 21 December 1788, *ibid.*, pp. 600–601.

25. *Boston Independent Chronicle*, 22 January 1789, *ibid.*, pp. 647–48.

26. Elbridge Gerry to Samuel Dexter, 14 February, and Gerry to James Warren, 15 February 1789, *ibid.*, pp. 655–56.

27. 22 January 1789, *ibid.*, p. 662.

28. The Third Election in Worcester District, 2 March 1789, *ibid.*, pp. 676–84.

29. The documents are printed in *ibid.*, pp. 684–742. The quote is from Thomas Dwight to Theodore Sedgwick, 9 July 1789, p. 742. A convenient summary is in Bowling, "Congressional Elections."

30. Henry Jackson to Henry Knox, 15 February 1789, Knox Papers, MHi.

31. Elbridge Gerry to the Electors of Middlesex, *Boston Independent Chronicle*, 22 January; James Sullivan to Richard Henry Lee, 11 April 1789; Jensen, *Elections*, 1: 647–48, 574–75.

32. James Madison to George Washington, 21 July 1788, *ibid.*, pp. 42–43.

33. Dorothy M. Brown, "Politics of Crisis: The Maryland Elections of 1788–1789," *Maryland Historical Magazine* 57 (1962): 201–2.

34. *Laws of Maryland. Made and Passed at a Session of Assembly Began . . . November . . . 1788* (Annapolis, n.d.), chap. 10.

35. Bowling, "Congressional Elections," pp. 81–91; Brown, "Politics of Crisis," pp. 204–8.

36. Chase's moderation is indicated by his attempt to avoid the Antifederalist label as in his 3 October 1788 appeal "To the voters of Baltimore-Town." For Mercer, in addition to the discussion in the text, see Edmund Randolph to James Madison, 26 July 1788, Madison Papers, DLC.

37. Jensen, *Elections*, 1: 171–200.

38. John F. Grimke to Henry William Harrington, 16 January; John Brown Cutting to John Rutledge, Jr., 21 February 1789, *ibid.*, pp. 205, 214.

39. See Samuel Bryan to John Nicholson, 21 November 1789, Nicholson Papers, PHarH; and Answer to Burke's Questionnaire, post 21 November 1789, George Bryan Papers, PHi.

40. Joshua Atherton to John Lamb, 23 June 1788, Lamb Papers, NHi.

41. 23 February 1789, Jensen, *Elections*, 1: 839–40.

42. "A Spectator of the Meeting," *Richmond Virginia Independent Chronicle*, 9 July 1788.

43. The best analysis is in DenBoer, "House of Delegates," chap. 8. The Antifederalist slate is no longer extant, but for evidence that there was agreement among legislators on the candidates, see James Duncanson to James Maury, 17 February 1789, Maury Papers, ViU.

44. DenBoer, "House of Delegates," pp. 254–56; Bowling, "Congressional Elections," pp. 101–5.

45. DenBoer, "House of Delegates," pp. 256–57.

46. *Ibid.*, pp. 257–59.

47. *To the Freeholders of the Counties . . . Arthur Lee* (Fredricksburg, 1788).

48. *Richmond Virginia Independent Chronicle*, 21 January 1789.

49. DenBoer, "House of Delegates," pp. 257–59.

50. *Ibid.*, pp. 260–61.

51. *Ibid.*, pp. 259–60.

52. *Ibid.*, pp. 261–67.

53. Anonymous manuscript, Amherst County Records, Vi.

54. Madison to George Washington, 14 January 1789, Washington Papers, DLC.

55. Madison to George Lee Turberville, 2 November 1788. Madison Papers, DLC.

56. "To the Several Religious Denominations of the Fifth District," *Virginia Herald and Fredricksburg Advertiser,* 15 January 1789; Madison to George Eve, 2 January 1789; Madison Papers, DLC.

57. *Virginia Herald and Fredricksburg Advertiser,* 12 February 1789.

58. Jensen, *Elections,* 1: 44–45.

59. To William Smith, 22 September 1788, Museum, Manor of St. George, Long Island, New York. See also Yates's "To the Members of the Legislature of New York, 8 December 1788, Yates Papers, NN.

60. To Abraham Yates, 3 August 1788, Yates Papers, NN.

61. Young, *Democratic-Republican,* pp. 134–35.

62. Lamb Papers, NHi., Bowling, "Congressional Elections."

63. *Ibid.,* p. 133.

64. Peter Van Gaasbeek to Abraham Bancker, 26 February 1789, Bancker Family Papers, NHi.

65. *New York Daily Advertiser,* 27 February, 11 April 1789.

66. Young, *Democratic-Republicans,* p. 133.

67. *Poughkeepsie Country Journal,* 24 February 1789; "Cassius," 3 March 1789; *New York Journal,* 19 April 1789.

68. "An Impartial Citizen," *Poughkeepsie Country Journal,* 24 February; "An Elector," *Hudson Weekly Gazette,* 24 February 1789.

69. Peter Van Schaak to Henry Van Schaack, 22 February 1789, Van Schaack Collection, NNC.

70. Young, *Democratic-Republicans,* chap. 7.

71. William Petrikin to John Nicholson, 23 March 1789, Jensen, *Elections,* 1: 406–7; Albert Gallatin to Alexander Addison, 7 October 1789, Gallatin Papers, NHi.

BIBLIOGRAPHICAL ESSAY

The primary sources for this study are identified in the notes. Less frequently cited are the wide variety of secondary sources that also shaped my thinking. The most important of these are Jackson Turner Main's, *The Antifederalists: Critics of the Constitution, 1781–1788* (Chapel Hill, 1961), which is supplemented by his "The Antifederal Party," in Arthur M. Schlesinger, Jr., ed., *History of the United States Political Parties I: 1780–1860 From Factions to Parties* (New York, 1973), and Robert Rutland's, *Ordeal of the Constitution: The Antifederalists and the Ratification Struggle of 1787–1788* (Norman, 1966). Readers familiar with Main's and Rutland's work will readily discern our different conclusions. Those differences are attributable to two things. First, many of the primary sources that I relied on in reevaluating the Antifederalists were not available at the time Main wrote. Notable among these are the John Nicholson and Tench Coxe papers, both of which weighed heavily in my reinterpretation of the extent of Antifederalist political organization. Second, Main and Rutland come to their conclusions in part because they concentrate on the state conventions that ratified the Constitution. From that perspective their generalizations about an inept, ineffectual opposition seem valid. But if one focuses instead on the electoral maneuvering that both preceded and followed the state conventions, then a different conception—that of a viable, organized opposition—seems more accurate.

A number of works on the Confederation also shaped my thinking. The seminal work on the Confederation remains Merrill Jensen's *The Articles of Confederation: An Interpretation of the Socio-Constitutional History of the American Revolution, 1774–1781,* (Madison, 1940), *The New Nation . . .* (New York, 1950), and *The American Revolution Within America* (New York, 1974). Jensen's work is supplemented by a wealth of studies of politics in the individual states. Jere R. Daniell's *Experiment in Republicanism . . .* (Cambridge, 1970) only partially replaces Richard F. Upton, *Revolutionary New Hampshire,* (Hanover, 1936). Van Beck Hall's *Politics Without Parties: Massachusetts, 1780–1791* (Pittsburgh, 1972) is excellent. Irwin Polishook's *Rhode Island and the Union, 1774–1795* (Evanston, 1969) focuses on Rhode Island's response to national issues. John Paul Kaminski, "Paper Politics: The Northern State Loan-Offices During the Confederation, 1783–1790" (unpublished Ph.D. Thesis, University of Wisconsin, 1972) concentrates on domestic issues, particularly paper money. As such the two studies complement one another nicely. The definitive study of Connecticut remains Philip H. Jordan, "Connecticut Politics During the Revolution," (unpublished Ph.D. Thesis, Yale University, 1962).

Of the many studies dealing with New York State, I found E. Wilder Spaulding's *New York in the Critical Period* (New York, 1932) and Alfred E. Young, *The Democratic-Republicans of New York, The Origins, 1763–1797* (Chapel Hill, 1967), the most useful. Robert Brunhouse's *The Counter-Revolution in Pennsylvania, 1776–1790* (Harrisburg, 1942), an able account, is complemented by Owen S. Ireland's "The Ratification of the Federal Constitution in Pennsylvania" (unpublished Ph.D. Thesis, University of Pittsburgh, 1966). For Delaware John Monroe's excellent *Federalist Delaware, 1775–1815* (New Brunswick, 1950) is supplemented by his introduction to *Dionysius, Tyrant of Delaware* (Newark, 1958). Richard P. McCormick, *Experiment in Independence: New Jersey in the Critical Period* (New Brunswick, 1950) is still the best for that state. The best account of Maryland politics during the Confederation is Philip Crowl's *Maryland During and After the American Revolution* (Baltimore, 1943).

The southern states, until recently, have been neglected. That void is partially filled by Gordon DenBoer's "The House of Delegates and the Evolution of Political Parties in Virginia, 1782–1792" (unpublished Ph.D. Thesis, University of Wisconsin, 1972), a complete study of Virginia during the Confederation. His study is excellent because it does not arbitrarily end with ratification, but continues to investigate the state's politics through the first federal election. What DenBoer has done for Virginia, Richard Leffler is doing for North Carolina. His dissertation will expand his "Political Factionalism in North Carolina, 1783–1788" (unpublished M.A. Thesis, University of Wisconsin, 1969), to cover the period from the end of the war in 1783 through the reorganization of state parties in the mid-1790s. Jerome Nadelhaft's "Revolutionary Era in South Carolina, 1777–1788" (unpublished Ph.D. Thesis, University of Wisconsin, 1965) served as a major source for my analysis of South Carolina's politics. The best work on Georgia is Kenneth Coleman's *The American Revolution in Georgia, 1763–1789* (Athens, 1958).

There are a number of able studies of the formation and adoption of the Constitution. George Bancroft's *History of the Formation of the Constitution . . .*, 2 vols. (New York, 1882) is still the best general account. Max Farrand provides an able summary of the convention in *The Framing of the Constitution of the United States* (New Haven, 1913) as does Merrill Jensen in *The Making of the American Constitution* (Princeton, 1964). Ratification is dealt with by Main and Rutland, as well as by several of the state studies cited above. I found several additional studies useful. Lawrence G. Strauss's "Reactions of Supporters of the Constitution to the Adjournment of the New Hampshire Ratification Convention, 1788," *Historical New Hampshire,* 23 (Autumn 1968): 37–50, provides some insight. Samuel Harding's *The Contest Over the Ratification of the Federal Constitution in the State of Massachusetts* (New York, 1896) is still sound. A convenient summary of Rhode Island is Patrick Conley, "Rhode Island in Disunion, 1787–1790," *Rhode Island History* 31 (1972): 99–115. Linda G. DePauw, *The Eleventh Pillar: New York State and the Federal Constitution* (Ithaca, 1966) is a major study, although she discounts the antifederalism of the Clintonians and ignores entirely their post-ratification effort to obtain in the first federal elections the substantive reform of the Constitution they called for at Poughkeepsie.

Philip Crowl's analysis of "Antifederalism in Maryland, 1787–1788," *William and Mary Quarterly* 3rd. ser., 4 (October 1947): 446–69 is outdated because of the availability of new manuscript sources. The major studies of North Carolina ratification are Louise I. Trenholme, *The Ratification of the Federal Constitution in North Carolina* (New York, 1952) and William C. Pool, "An Economic Interpretation of the Ratification of the Federal Constitution in North Carolina," *North Carolina Historical Review* 27 (April–October 1950): 119–41, 289–313. George C. Rogers relies too heavily on the Aedanus Burke letter to John Lamb in his "South Carolina Ratification of the Federal Constitution," South Carolina Historical *Proceedings,* 31 (1961): 41–61. Finally, on Georgia, see John P. Kaminski, "Controversy amid Consensus: The Adoption of the Federal Constitution in Georgia," *Georgia Historical Quarterly*, 58 (August 1974): 244–61.

On related matters, the impact of apportionment on the state conventions is considered in Charles Roll, Jr., "We, Some of the People, Apportionment in the Thirteen State Conventions Ratifying the Constitution," *Journal of American History* 56 (June 1969): 21–40. The second convention theme has been discussed in Edward P. Smith, "The Movement Toward a Second Constitutional Convention in 1788," in J. Franklin Jameson, ed., *Essays in the Constitutional History of the United States . . .* (Boston, 1889), and more recently in Linda Grant DePauw's "The Anti-Climax of Antifederalism: The Abortive Second Convention Movement, 1788–1789" *Prologue* (Fall 1970): 98–114.

Kenneth R. Bowling discusses the congressional elections in "Federalists and Antifederalists After Ratification, The First Congressional Elections, 1788–1789" (unpublished M.A. Thesis, University of Wisconsin, 1964), as does Dorothy M. Brown, "Politics of Crisis: The Maryland Elections of 1788–1789," *Maryland Historical Magazine,* 57 (1962): 195–209, and Richard P. McCormick, "New Jersey's First Congressional Elections, 1789: A Case Study of Political Skullduggery," *William and Mary Quarterly,* 3rd. ser., 6 (1949): 237–50. Bowling also summarizes the elections in his outstanding "Politics in the First Congress" (unpublished Ph.D. Thesis, University of Wisconsin, 1968). His analysis of the Bill of Rights has been developed in "James Madison's Tub to the Whale: The Adoption of the Bill of Rights and the Capture of the Antifederal Leviathan," (unpublished manuscript in the possession of the author).

Thus, my explanation of the acceptance of the Constitution adds an additional perspective to Lance Banning's "Republican Ideology and the Triumph of the Constitution, 1789–1793," *William and Mary Quarterly,* 3rd ser., 31 (1974): 167–88 and to Richard Buel's, *Securing the Revolution: Ideology in American Politics, 1789 to 1815* (Ithaca, 1972).

Similarly, my analysis of the Antifederalists fills a gap in the literature on political party development. Thus my conclusions concerning Antifederalist party organization follow logically from Jackson Turner Main's *Political Parties Before the Constitution* (Chapel Hill, 1975) even as they suggest that parties, as defined by William Nesbit Chambers in his *Political Parties in a New Nation: The American Experience, 1776–1809* (New York, 1963) existed, at least from 1787–1789. Finally, my findings on the impact of Antifederalist participation are compatible with Gabriel Almond and Sidney Verba, *The Civic Culture, Political Attiudes and Democracy in Five Nations* (Boston, 1963), chap. 8.

INDEX